Photography Rules

Photography Rules

Essential Dos and Don'ts from Great Photographers

Paul Lowe

FRANCES
LINCOLN

Contents

Introduction

'I didn't write the rules – why should I follow them?'
W. Eugene Smith

It's a truism that rules are made to be broken, so compiling an entire book of them might seem at first glance to be an act of folly. Indeed, many of the photographers approached to contribute to the project responded with a variation on 'I don't believe in rules,' or 'I don't follow any rules; there are no rules in photography.' However, when pressed, they usually relented to give a nugget of advice or a principle that they followed, so the enterprise of collating a volume of the collective wisdom of the profession seemed to be validated. What follows in this book is therefore an eclectic mix of rules, advice, guidelines and knowledge based on hard won experience from a wide range of viewpoints. Much of the book was crowdsourced directly from photographers, editors, curators, educators and industry professionals who responded with their own personal rule, or in some cases list of rules, and I want to thank them all for their time and effort in contributing their thoughts and their photographs. Most of the rest came from surveying what photographers have said about their practice and how they go about navigating the world of image-making, from interviews, writings and public statements about their craft. Finally, a few rules that are demonstrably widely accepted across all areas of photography have been included. The intention was to cast the net wide, and to cover contemporary practitioners as well as icons from the past. Of course, as with any endeavour of this kind, there has to be a selection process, so the book makes no claim to cover every possible rule that can be applied to photography, and equally makes no claim to have covered every photographer who could potentially have made a contribution. Equally, some of the rules are contradictory; one person's essential principle is anathema to another, but we celebrate this diversity and debate as one rule that can perhaps be applied is there is no one size that fits all. However, the book does offer a wide-ranging, insightful and hopefully entertaining exploration about what photographers and the people that work with photography think are the important issues to consider in developing a successful practice. The reader can take whatever advice they find useful and applicable to their approach, but hopefully they will find valuable insights and stimulation from all of the entries.

The book is not a systematic 'how to' guide to photography but it does have a reasonably logical progression of entries, organized into three main categories of rules: 'Making Photographs', 'Being a Photographer' and 'Professional Practice'. These follow the journey of the photographic process from even before the image is made through to building a long-term corpus of work to its distribution to the world. Individual genres and approaches to photography are interspersed throughout, covering fields such as portraiture, documentary and photojournalism, landscape and commercial photography.

'Making Photographs' broadly reflects on the process of actually producing images in the field, including the technical and aesthetic considerations of taking photographs. 'Being a Photographer' deals with the bigger picture of how a photographer relates to the world and to the projects they work on, including researching and producing stories or bodies of work, and the ethical concerns of representing the lives of others. Finally, 'Professional Practice' covers the practicalities of making a sustainable living and getting your work seen by an audience. Taken together, they provide a rich source of advice about all aspects of the photographic process, from the moment of taking the image to sharing it with an audience, and offer valuable guidance for aspiring professionals making their way into the industry as well as amateurs who want to further develop their eye for a compelling photograph.

The process of culling down hundreds of potential entries into just 177 did reveal some common themes across a significant number of photographers, however, with the principles of simplicity, consistency, patience, creativity, serendipity and sheer hard graft appearing with predictable regularity. Along with these attributes, photographers also spoke frequently about the need to develop control of the basic functions of the camera – exposure, composition and framing, focus and so on – to the point where they become second nature, allowing you to work intuitively, so that the technology is no longer a barrier to seeing. Indeed, there was a common theme that although each format and type of camera has its own distinctive voice, the most important element – to paraphrase Cartier-Bresson – is the connection between the photographer's mind and their subject. Taken as a whole, then, the rules in this book offer a road map to developing your photographic vision, guided by the expertise of the world's leading image-makers. The camera is your passport to the world, and the photograph is the record of your direct experience and interpretation of it.

Making Photographs

Be open to chance

Brassaï *Rue de Lappe*, 1932

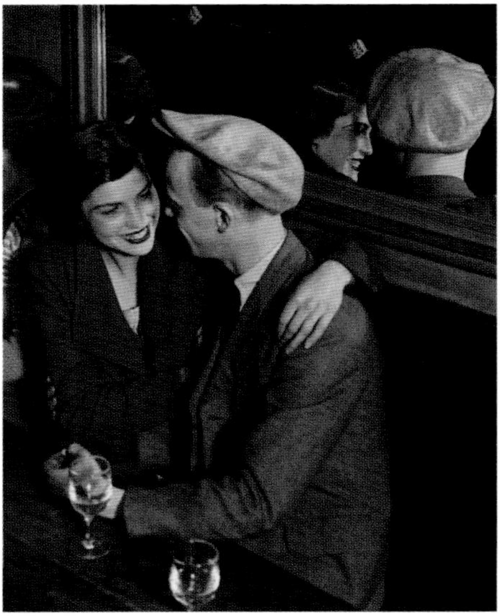

'Chance is always there. We all use it. The difference is a poor photographer meets chance one out of a hundred times and a good photographer meets chance all the time.'

The Hungarian-French photographer Brassaï was known as the 'eye of Paris' for his intimate documentation of the life of the city in the 1930s, and his images are full of wonderful moments of intimacy and symmetry. His motto was to always be open to the possibility that a situation could change in the blink of an eye, shifting suddenly from being devoid of visual or emotional interest to having the potential for a great photograph. The question is what the photographer does with that moment, how alert they are to its possibilities; as Brassaï described, 'chance is always there. We all use it. The difference is a poor photographer meets chance one out of a hundred times and a good photographer meets chance all the time.' He noted that 'surreality lies within ourselves, in objects that have become banal because we no longer see them, in the normality of the normal'. Stay tuned into the ever-changing world around you, and open to the opportunities it offers.

Take control of the situation

Tom Hunter *Death of Coltelli*, 2009

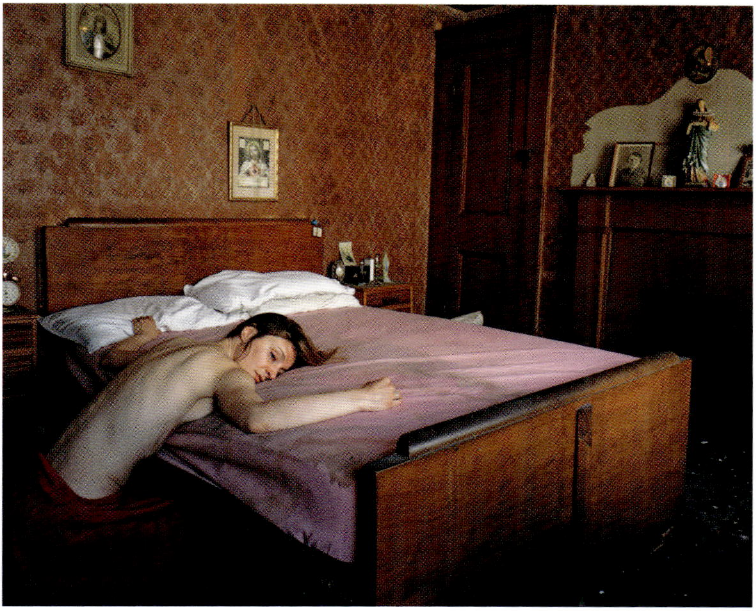

Tom Hunter's carefully staged portrait tableaux take their inspiration from stories from everyday life of the London borough of Hackney, where he was lived for the last three decades, and from the paintings of the Old Masters, with their complex layers of metaphor and symbolism. He works with a large-format camera, in a collaborative way with his subjects, saying that the photographer should 'always engage with your subject, make sure you are really aware of everything they are doing, it's the slightest of differences that separates a great portrait and a so-so image.' His images look documentary but are full of hidden meanings. To achieve this the photographer must be a director, not a passive observer. He advises that if you see a 'way they look or move that you think is interesting, don't be afraid to get them to re-enact that moment for the camera. Take control of the situation and the subject: don't be a passive observer, you are the director of your photography'.

Get close

Bruce Gilden *USA. New York City. Woman Walking on Fifth Avenue*, 1992

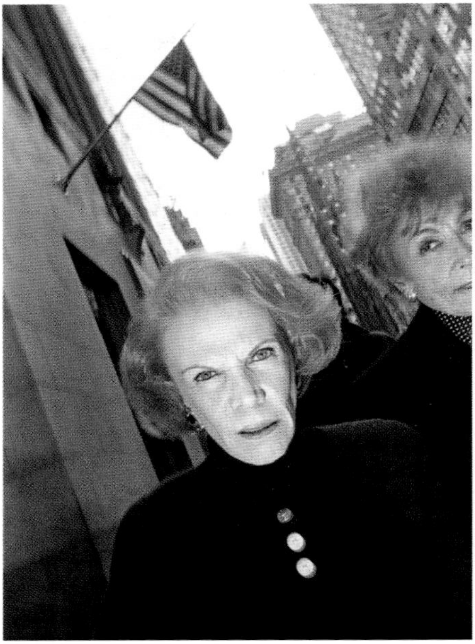

'That's the combination that I'm striving for – a strong emotional punch in the gut, yet the picture is beautifully composed.'

Magnum photographer Bruce Gilden is renowned for his edgy, dynamic and in-your-face street photography. Working mostly with a wide-angle 28mm lens, Gilden works in very close proximity to his subjects, saying that 'I'm known for taking pictures very close, and the older I get, the closer I get.' Gilden frequently works with flash, and his images have a powerful sense of the character of the people who pass by his lens, often for a fleeting moment as he moves like an athlete along the street.

He has an uncanny ability to combine aesthetics with content, claiming that 'that's the combination that I'm striving for – a strong emotional punch in the gut, yet the picture is beautifully composed.' He has been drawn to those on the edges of society, stating that 'I like intensity. I like to see their soul. I show my soul – I'm blunt.'

Turn the photo upside down

Marc Riboud *Painter of the Eiffel Tower*, 1953

'Turning a photograph upside down is the best way to judge a photo. That way you see how it's really composed.'

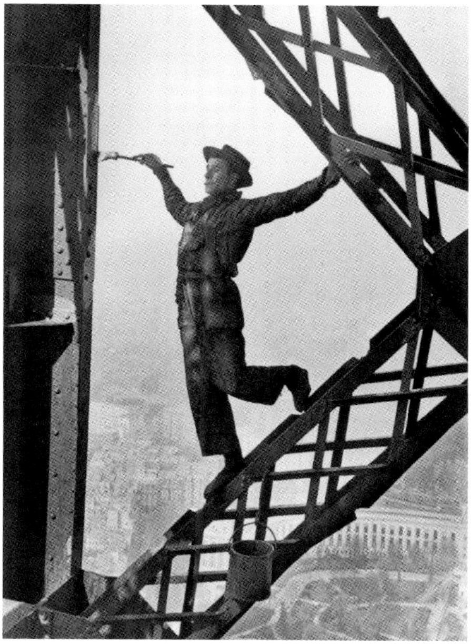

Looking at the edited contact sheets of great photographers is a very rewarding experience, as it shows how they develop an image sequentially as they explore the subject visually. It is also a great guide to editing and selecting the best shot. The French Magnum photographer Marc Riboud had a useful trick to help judge the quality of an image, recommending that 'turning a photograph upside down is the best way to judge a photo. That way you see how it's really composed.' This technique was also used by Henri Cartier-Bresson, and it works to shift attention away from the content of the image towards its pure aesthetics and form. If it still looks good and works visually then it is worth keeping in the selection. With a digital camera, you can also try flipping the image from left to right to see how that affects the balance of the frame.

Know your lenses

Bill Brandt *A View of Hadrian's Wall near Hexham in Northumberland*, 1943

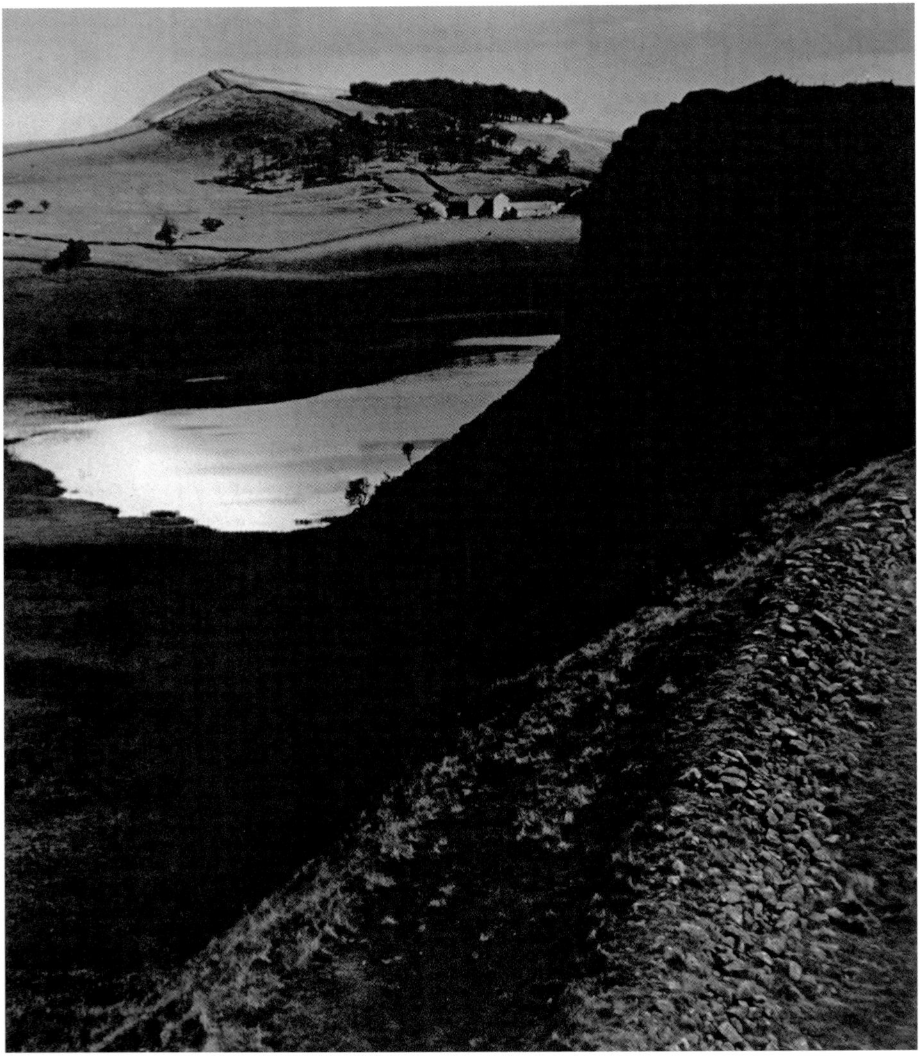

'See the subject first. Do not try to force it to be a picture of this, that or the other thing. Stand apart from it. Then something will happen. The subject will reveal itself.'

You should be so familiar with the characteristics of each lens that you instinctively know its field of view and how different apertures will affect the final image. A 300mm telephoto will give a shallow depth of field compared to a 24mm, and the subtle difference between a 35mm and a 28mm can make or break a photograph. As demonstrated by this image, one of a series he made of Hadrian's Wall, the great British photographer Bill Brandt was a master of perspective and setting foreground against background, and advised that 'it is essential for the photographer to know the effect of his lenses. The lens is his eye, and it makes or ruins his pictures.' Go out with just one lens for a day and really explore how that particular focal length works, how it translates the three-dimensional world into a two-dimensional space. Long lenses will flatten perspective, wide angles will exaggerate it. Brandt also commented that you should 'see the subject first. Do not try to force it to be a picture of this, that or the other thing. Stand apart from it. Then something will happen. The subject will reveal itself.' Follow his rule and let the subject dictate the image, not the lens dominate it.

Make a lot of pictures

Harry Callahan *Sunlight on Water*, 1943

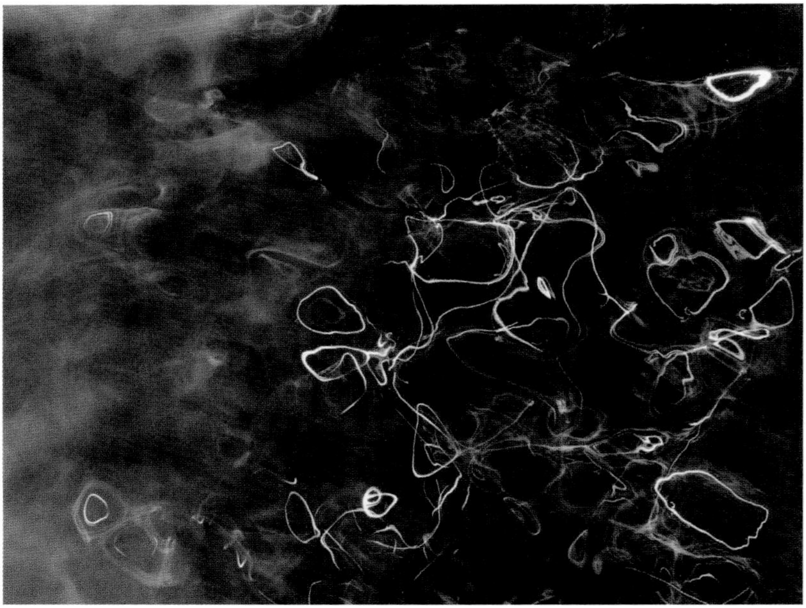

Harry Callahan was a prolific image-maker, going out almost every morning to shoot, and then spending his afternoons working in the darkroom. However, he was highly selective about his work, remarking that 'I guess I've shot about 40,000 negatives and of these I have about 800 pictures I like.' His guiding principle was simple: you have to shoot a lot; as he argued, 'to be a photographer, one must photograph. No amount of book-learning, no checklist of seminars attended, can substitute for the simple act of making pictures.' He felt that image-making was very much a process of learning and experimentation, relating that he photographed 'continuously, often without a good idea or strong feelings. During this time the photos are nearly all poor, but I believe they develop my seeing and help later on in other photos.' Follow Callahan's advice and embrace the journey.

Watch the background

Lee Friedlander *Knoxville, Tennessee*, 1971

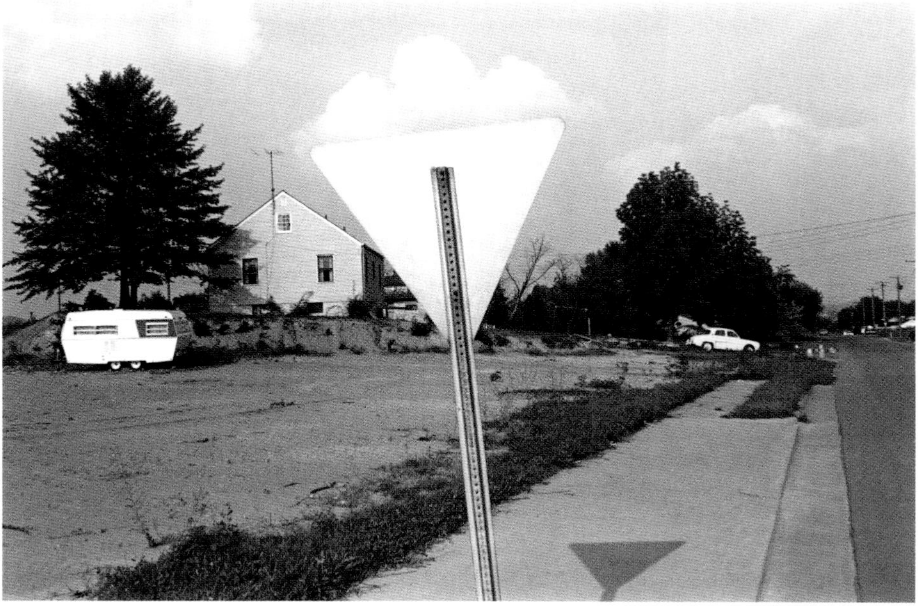

The classic mistake in outdoor portrait photography is not noticing how elements in the background of your shot can distract from the main subject, with lamp posts growing out of a person's head being a prime example. This can happen for a variety of reasons, most of which are preventable by paying a little more care and attention to composition, framing and depth of field. Make sure you really look at the scene through your viewfinder, and pay special attention to any background elements that might distract from the main subject. This is exacerbated by the fact that usually when we are looking through the lens, it is wide open, so that the background is thrown out of focus. Using your depth of field preview button – if you have one – can really help with this as it will show everything that will be sharp in the final image. Conversely, you can use a shallow depth of field to throw the background out of focus and really concentrate the attention on the subject.

Use natural light

Alfred Eisenstaedt *Actress Sophia Loren Playing Cards with Photographer Pierluigi*, 1961

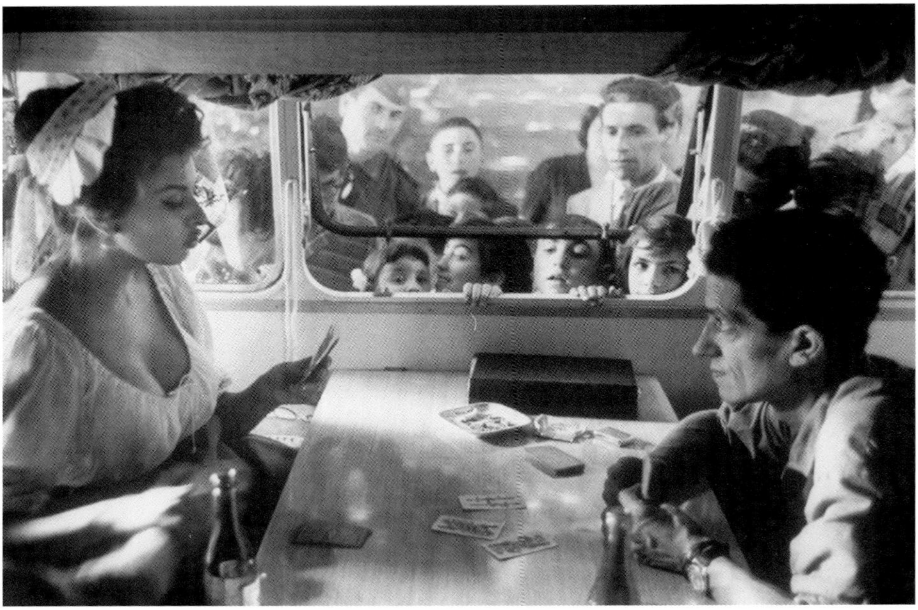

Like his contemporary, Henri Cartier-Bresson, Alfred Eisenstaedt shunned using flash, preferring to rely on the ability of the Leica cameras to shoot hand-held with fast lenses and film. He explained his reasoning for shooting in available light, which he called 'Rembrandt light' because it showed the 'natural modulations of the face' and made for a 'more alive, real, and flattering portrait'. He felt that flash ruined the natural atmosphere of the situation, arguing that 'If you have the eyes to see it, the nuances of light are already there on the subject's face. If your thinking is confined to strobe light sources, your palette becomes very mean.' With modern digital sensors, almost any scene can now be recorded without needing extra illumination.

Limit your tools

Anton Corbijn *Mick Jagger*, 1996

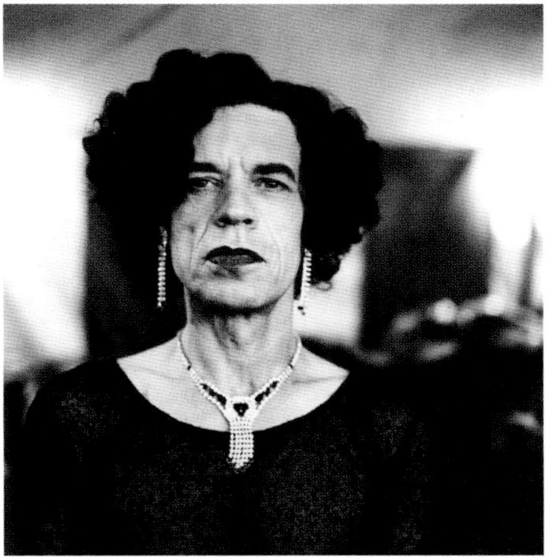

'Limit your tools, focus on one thing and just make it work.'

The concept of KISS – Keep It Simple Stupid – can be a valuable one in photography. It's far too easy to get caught up in a myriad of technical choices of camera gear to the extent that you lose sight of the purity of the scene in front of you and your relationship to it. The Dutch photographer Anton Corbijn is known for his powerful and raw portraits of musicians and celebrities, and his philosophy is simple – 'limit your tools, focus on one thing and just make it work'. He usually shoots hand-held, with a shutter speed fixed at a 30th or 60th of a second, and finds that this consistency of technique liberates his vision, saying that 'you become very inventive with the restrictions you give yourself'. Go out and shoot with the minimum of equipment, and let the subject speak for itself, don't become obsessed with gear.

The negative is just the start

Ansel Adams *The Tetons – Snake River, Grand Teton National Park, Wyoming*, 1941

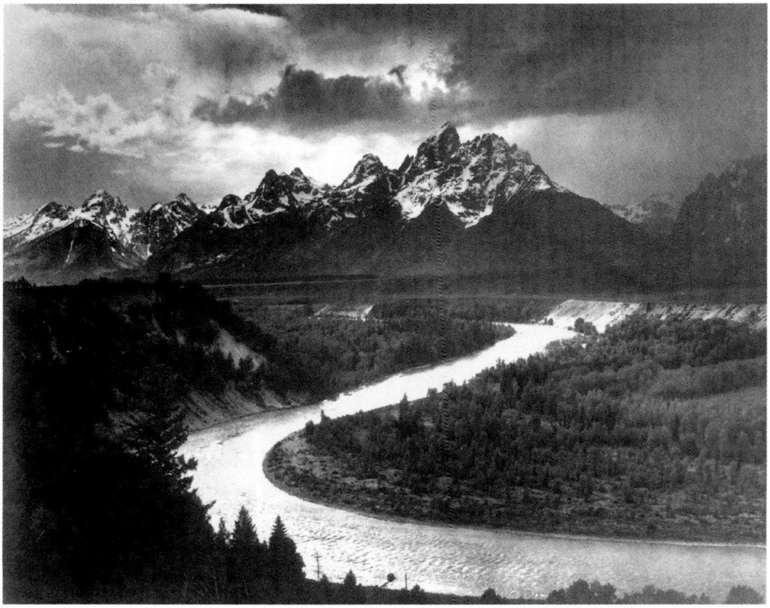

Known for his obsessively detailed control of the technical aspects of the medium, Ansel Adams produced exquisite black-and-white large-format landscapes of the American West, full of detail and drama. He developed the zone system of exposure and printing, which used ten zones from pure white to pure black to help him previsualize the final print from the scene in front of him. This approach gave a negative with a full range of tones that could be manipulated in the darkroom to produce exactly the effect the photographer wanted. As Adams declared, the initial exposure is just the start of the journey to a final image: 'the negative is comparable to the composer's score and the print to its performance. Each performance differs in subtle ways.' This observation is just as true of a digital RAW file as it is of a black-and-white negative.

If your pictures aren't good enough, you're not close enough

Robert Capa *Farewell Ceremony for the International Brigades, Les Masies. Spain. October 25th*, 1938

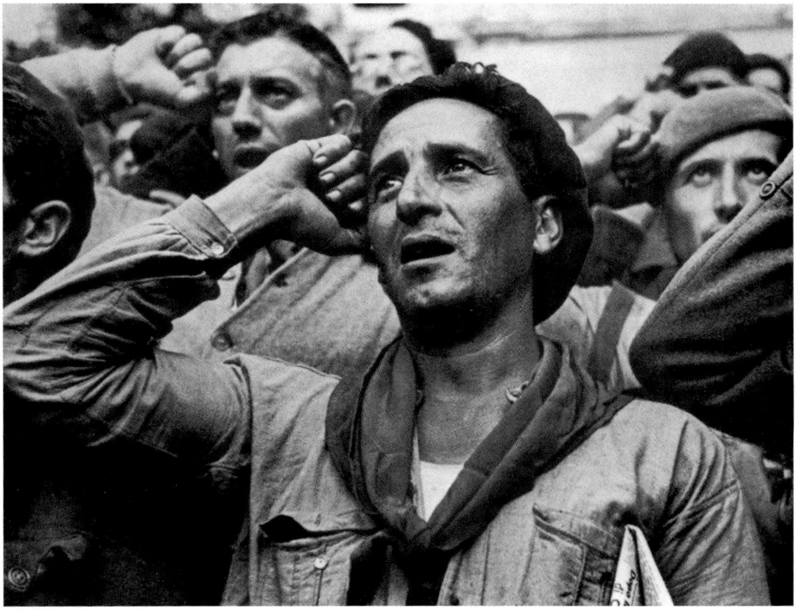

'If your pictures aren't good enough, you're not close enough.' This quote from Hungarian photojournalist Robert Capa is arguably one of the most famous rules of photography, and is usually interpreted as a command to get as physically proximate to the subject as possible, using a wide-angle lens to fill the frame. However, Capa was a partisan, passionate photographer who invariably took sides in his work, and was committed to the anti-fascist struggle from the early 1930s onwards after his exile from his homeland. Capa was a supporter of the French Communist party, and worked regularly for its publications, especially during the Spanish Civil War, where he made this powerful study of the demobilization of the International Brigade. Shot from a low angle to emphasize the heroic pose of the soldier, the photograph shows Capa's emotional and political affinity with the subject. Follow his imperative and try to identify with your subject as much as you can.

Manage the verticals

Charles Sheeler *Exterior of the Ford Automobile Factory in Detroit, Michigan*, 1927

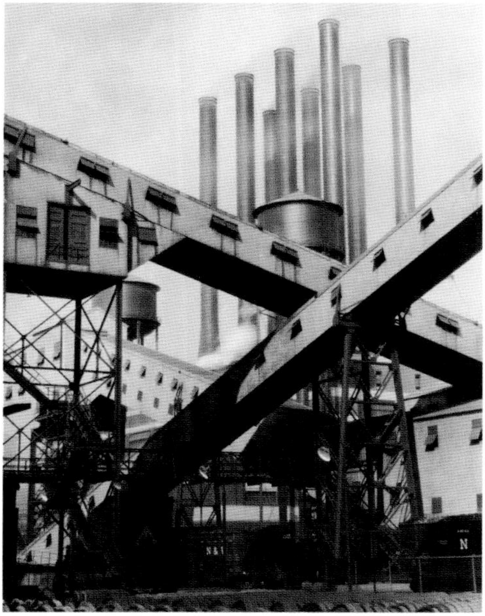

Converging verticals can be hard to avoid when shooting buildings, especially with wide-angle lenses, and they can be very distracting and spoil an otherwise perfect photograph. Charles Sheeler demonstrates how to cope with this problem to great effect in this famous study of the industrial might of America. Try not to tilt the camera too far from vertical, keeping the plane of the back of the camera as parallel to the face of the building as possible. Moving further away and shooting on a shorter focal length can help to correct this. Large-format field cameras have parallel movements known as 'rise', 'fall' and 'shift' that move the lens up, down and sideways relative to the centre of the camera back. Tilt-shift lenses are also available for SLRS that replicate the movements of a field camera, but they are specialized and expensive. Some cameras have gridlines in the viewfinder too that can be used to line up verticals and horizontals precisely; combined with a tripod this can produce perfect results.

Photography is always manipulation

David LaChapelle *Lost and Found*, 2012

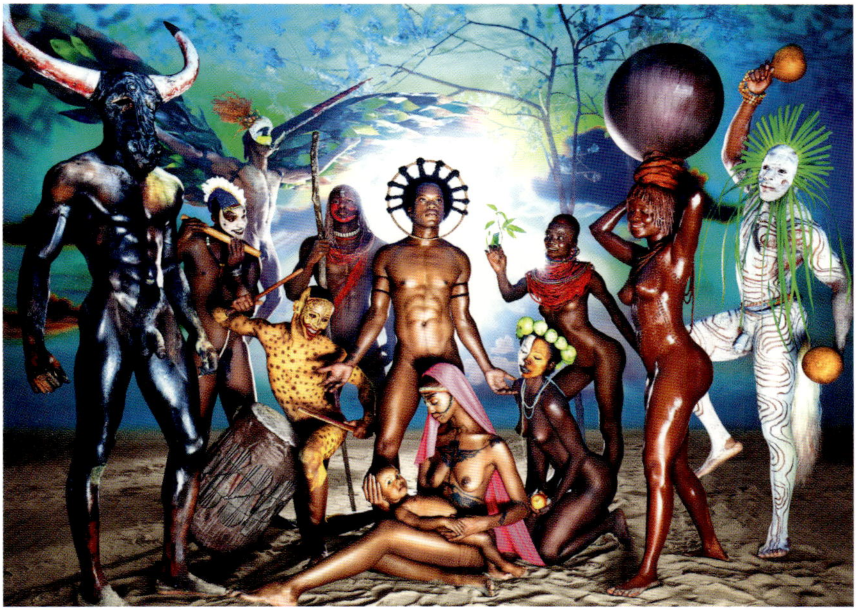

David LaChapelle's complex and colourful tableaux are full of wit and social commentary, as well as penetrating studies of the reality behind the façade of celebrity. His images are highly stylized and staged, and he accepts that his control of the scene makes a personal statement, claiming that 'people say photos don't lie. Mine do. I make mine lie.' He further notes that every image is the result of an intervention by the photographer, and to pretend otherwise is a failure to recognize the photographer's own prejudices, noting that 'the minute you point a camera at something, you are manipulating the image, because you are cropping out whatever is to the left and right of it. The minute you put a light on someone, you are manipulating the image.' The important element here is to be aware of our own position and to question it.

Make a list

Tony Ray-Jones *The City, London*, 1967

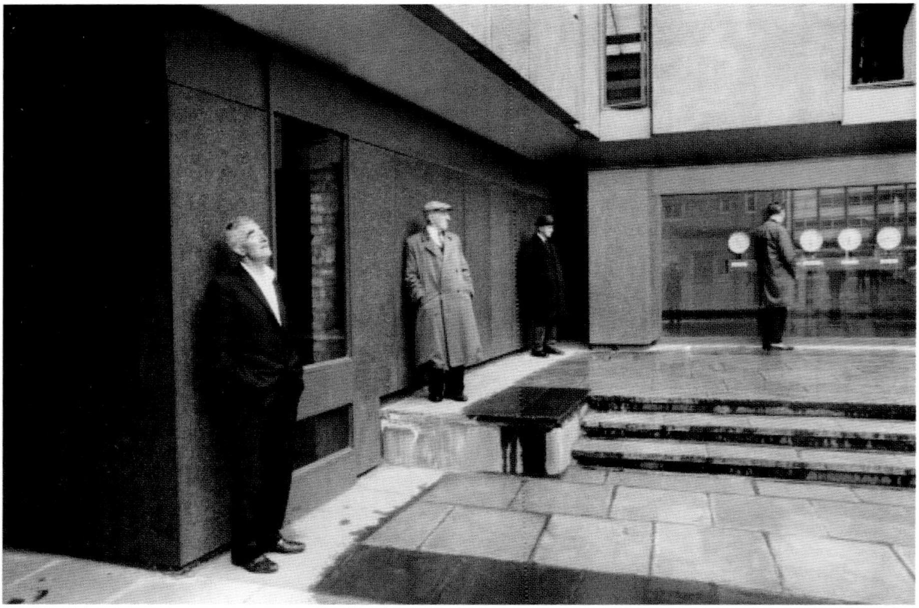

Tony Ray-Jones is one of the most influential British photographers, whose legacy of witty and intelligent street photography can be seen in the work of Martin Parr, Brian Griffin and Paul Reas. He was an obsessive photographer, and his notebooks are full of lists of potential ideas for projects and images. He set for himself this valuable list of reminders:

1. Be more **aggressive**
2. Get more **involved** (talk to people)
3. Stay with the subject matter (be **patient**)
4. Take **simpler** pictures
5. See if everything in background relates to subject matter
6. Vary compositions & **angles** more
7. Be more aware of **composition**
8. Don't take **boring** pictures
9. **Get in closer** (use 50mm lens)
10. Watch camera **shake** (shoot 250 sec or above)
11. Don't shoot too much
12. Not all eye level
13. No middle distance

Stare

Walker Evans *Corrugated Tin Façade, Moundville, Alabama*, 1936

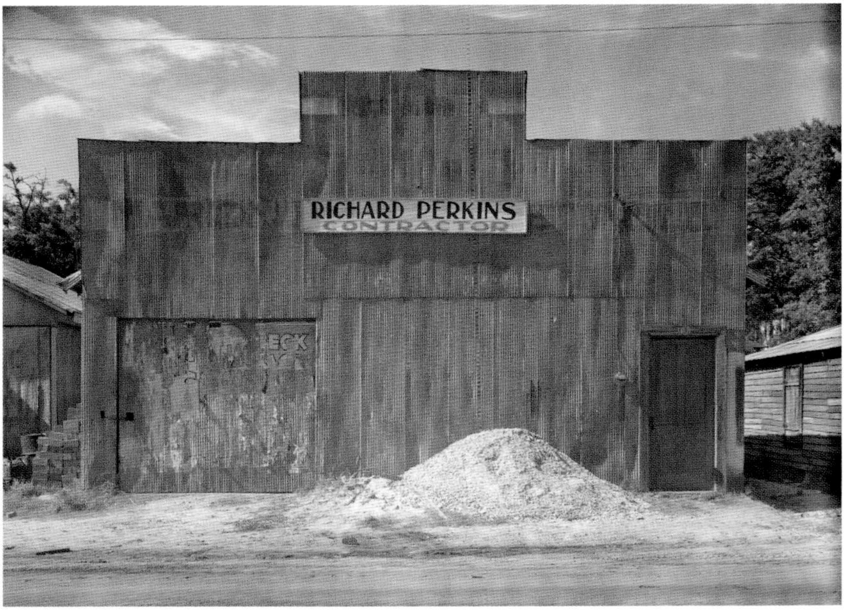

Walker Evans was a master of quiet observation, of letting the subject speak for itself in a seemingly transparent way that actually masked a powerful personal vision and intellect. His advice goes to the very essence of photographic seeing: 'Stare. It is the way to educate your eye, and more. Stare, pry, listen, eavesdrop.' Often deceptively simple, his photographs demonstrate the power of presenting the world as it is, of really looking with an intense and selective gaze, devouring the world around him. His pronouncement that 'the artist's eye must be hungry, and my eye is hungry' encourages us to go out into the world with a voracious appetite for celebrating those moments of encounter between our eyes, our brains and the world.

Compose from the outside in

David Hockney *Pearblossom Highway 1*, 1986

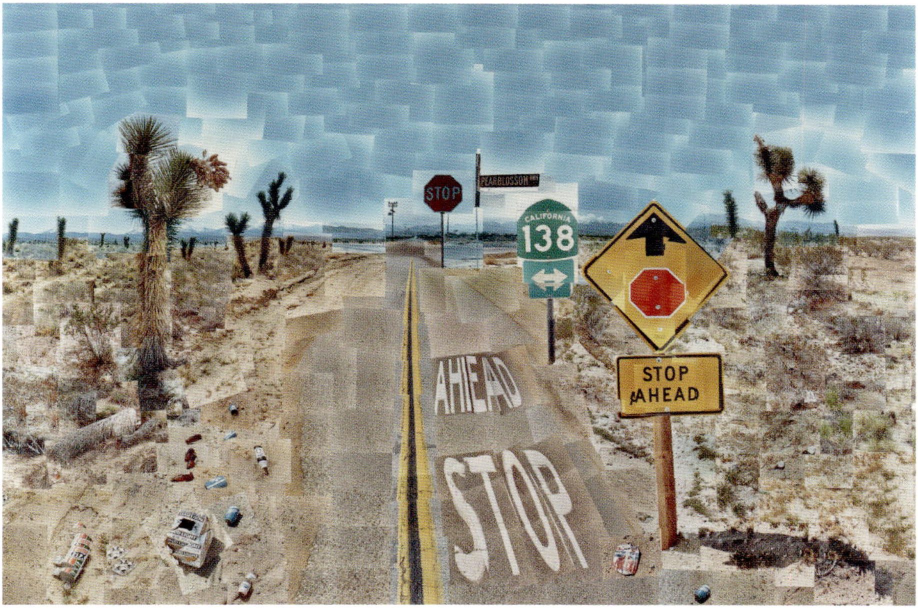

The artist David Hockney has explored how photography and painting relate to each other, in particular by using a technique of collaging together multiple images to create a composite whole. He stresses that whatever you include in the central part of the image is held there by the borders of the frame itself, arguing that the 'one cardinal rule of photography is that when you pick up the camera and look at things through it, you are very, very deeply conscious of edges. It is the edges that make the composition in a photograph and it is what you leave there that will enable you to see things in the middle.' To practise this, go out to shoot and concentrate specifically on exactly where you are positioning the frame, so that you are making a decisive crop of the scene: compose from the outside of the frame inwards instead of from the centre outwards.

The portrait is not the person

Rineke Dijkstra *Kolobrzeg, Poland, July 26*, 1992

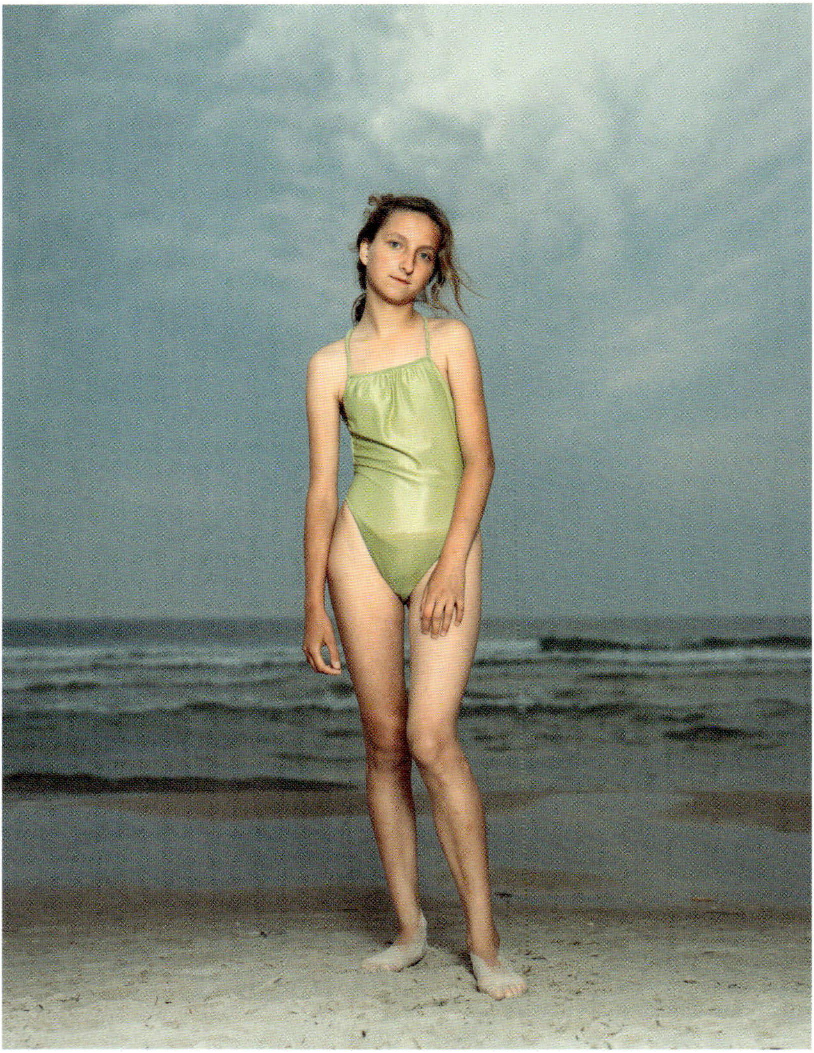

'When you take a photograph of somebody you have a relationship with the picture, not necessarily with them. Most of the people you don't see ever again.'

The Dutch portrait photographer Rineke Dijkstra is known for her penetrating studies of youth, shot on a large-format camera. She maintains that the photographic encounter always carries with it a sense of an abstracted reality, arguing if 'a photo will always tell the truth, as it captures only a fraction of a second'. The intervention of the photographer into the situation enlarges or emphasizes a certain moment, making it another reality. She observes how she aims to show things you might not notice in normal life. 'I always look for glimmers of individuality by concentrating on subtle gestures, poses and expressions. Just in these unguarded moments I find a certain truth that inhabits somewhere between the posed and the natural.' Once the image has been made, what lives on is not necessarily the meeting itself, but the visual record of it. 'When you take a photograph of somebody you have a relationship with the picture, not necessarily with them. Most of the people you don't see ever again.' Be aware of the fleeting nature of photographic portraiture, and that your image is a version of your experience of the person, not the person themselves.

Shoot manual

Paul Lowe

'Switching to manual, at least for a while, will make you a better photographer by making you much more aware of how the camera controls can be used creatively.'

Although all modern cameras have very sophisticated auto and program exposure modes, it is still important to understand how the shutter, aperture and ISO all relate to each other, and to take creative charge of the decisions about how they interact with each other to create the final photograph. Automatic programs are designed to produce a 'perfect' exposure, but this will always be based on averages; if you want to have full control of the photographic process then shooting on manual is the only way to go. You can choose if you want the image to be dramatically darker and underexposed for a low-key effect, or overexposed for an ethereal feeling. Additionally, you can decide exactly how much depth of field you want by selecting the best aperture yourself, or control blur and motion by adjusting the shutter speed. Switching to manual, at least for a while, will make you a better photographer by making you much more aware of how the camera controls can be used creatively.

Work the subject

Alexander Rodchenko *Pioneer*, 1930

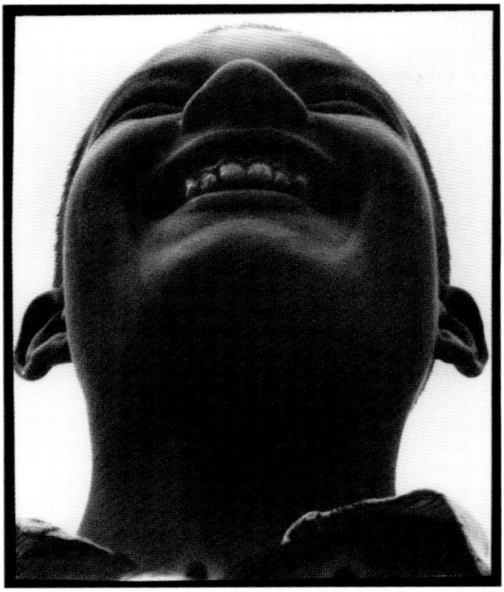

'Take different shots of a subject, from different points of view and in different situations, as if one examined it in the round rather than looked through the same keyhole again and again.'

One of the founders of Constructivism, the avant-garde Russian polymath artist Alexander Rodchenko was one of the earliest proponents of how the 35mm Leica camera liberated photography from the static feel imposed by the larger plate cameras. He looked for unusual angles and viewpoints, exploring how the freedom of movement of the new format allowed him to present new and often radical perspectives on everyday life. He encouraged the photographer to 'take different shots of a subject, from different points of view and in different situations, as if one examined it in the round rather than looked through the same keyhole again and again'. His advice is sound: actively challenge yourself to find a new vantage point from which to shoot. Surprising and visually arresting patterns and shapes can emerge when the world is seen from a different position to that of eye level.

Use a tripod

Simon Norfolk Simon Norfolk at work photographing archaeological remains below the Old City with the Arab neighbourhood of Silwan in the distance, 2019 (photograph by Samir Al-Sharif)

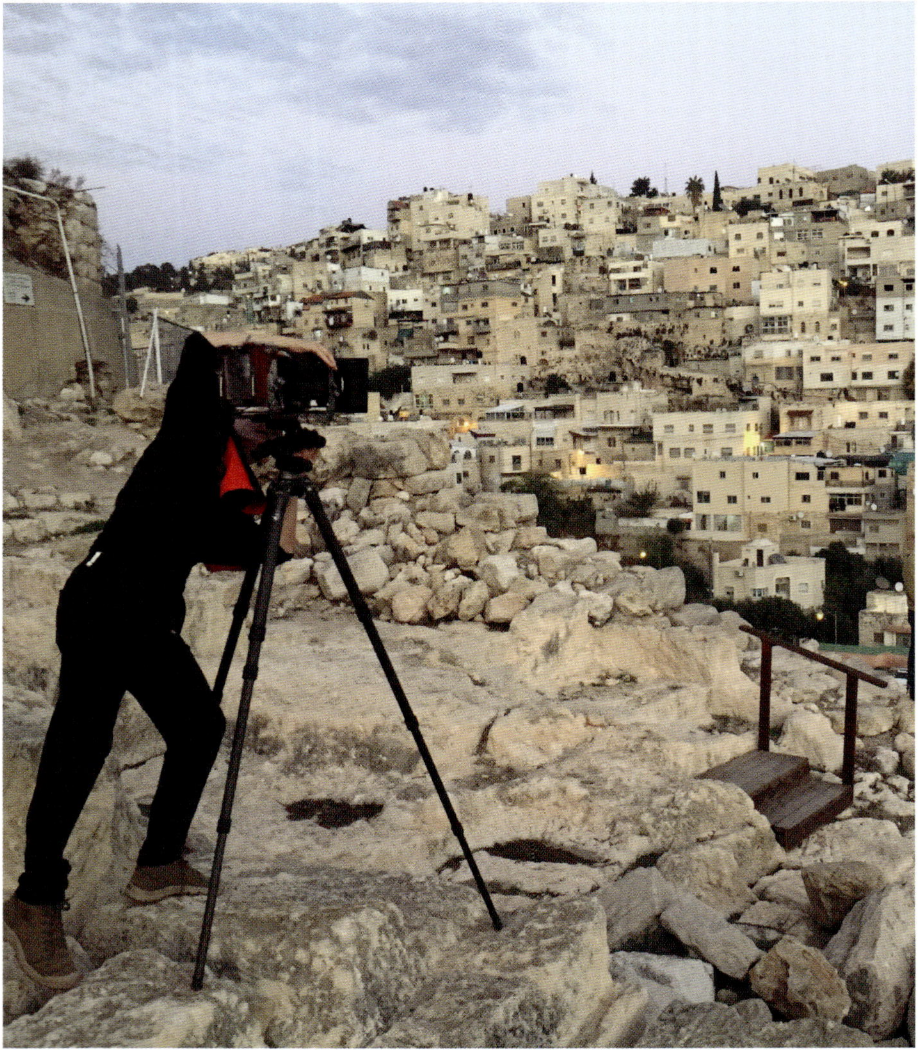

'Using a tripod will slow you down, and make you consider all the aspects of the photographic process more carefully.'

A tripod is a very useful accessory, and not just to keep the camera still to avoid camera shake. It will transform your ability to shoot in low light, allowing exposures of seconds, minutes and even hours. A moonlit scene can be transformed into an extraordinary landscape by using a long exposure on a tripod, or you can create time-lapse sequences that show the passage of light across the scene. A tripod will also give you sharper images, even at higher shutter speeds, by supporting the camera and making it more stable – longer telephotos often have tripod attachments on the lens itself for better balance.

More importantly, however, using a tripod will slow you down, and make you consider all the aspects of the photographic process more carefully, helping you to think about the relationship between shutter speed, aperture and depth of field, and take more care and precision over your composition and framing. Going out on a shoot with your digital SLR on a tripod, imagining it is a large-format plate camera, is a fantastic discipline to really make you strive for perfection in your image-making. Shooting on a tripod can also transform the dynamics of a portrait session by making the whole process more of a formal performance.

See like a child

Rinko Kawauchi *Untitled*, from the series *Utatatne*, 2001

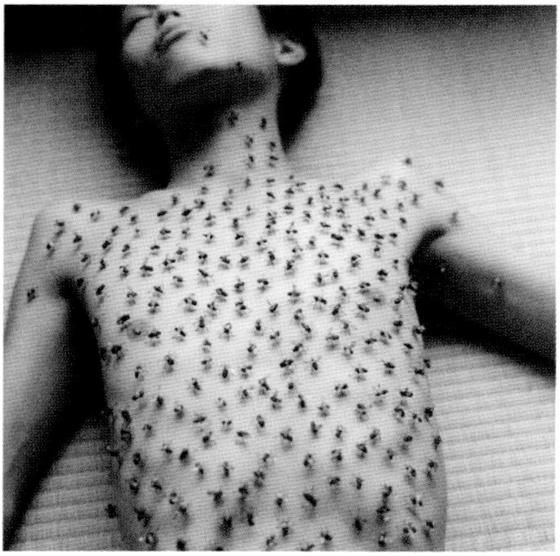

'Part of the photographer's job to see more intensely than most people do.'

One of photography's greatest assets is its ability to make us see things that are otherwise unobserved. As Bill Brandt observed, it is 'part of the photographer's job to see more intensely than most people do. He must have and keep in him something of the receptiveness of the child who looks at the world for the first time or of the traveller who enters a strange country.' Some photographers seem to be able to tap into another level of consciousness and find surprising moments in the everyday, like the Japanese photographer Rinko Kawauchi. She attributes a large part of her unique perscnal vison to this childlike perspective, observing how 'I stare at ants gathering around sugar, or when I seek shelter from the ra n, I gaze upon snails. These are things which you often do when you are a child aren't they? I have a very similar sensibility to that.' Cultivate this sense of innocence in your work, and try to look at the world around you with the sense of wonder of an infant discovering it for the first time.

The camera sees everything

Berenice Abbott *Herald Square in New York*, 1935

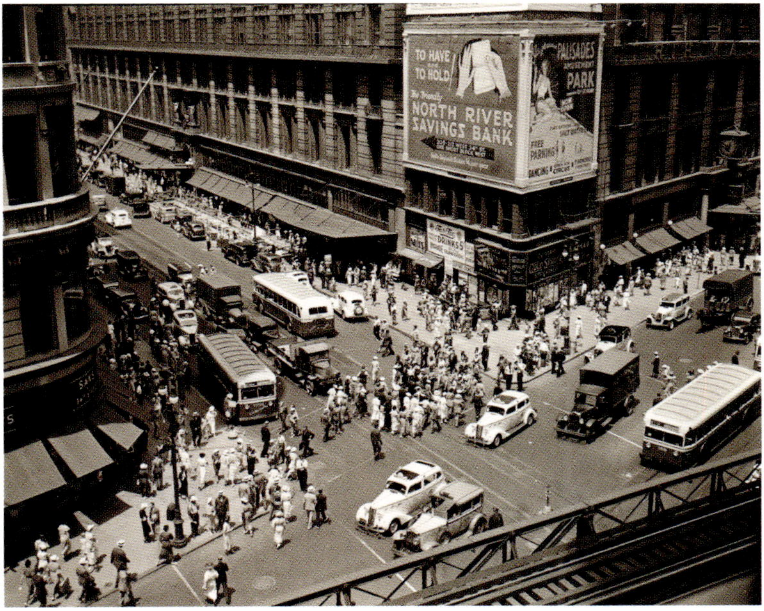

When we see the world we often do not look intensely at all of its detail and complexity. The human eye is fallible, and we tend to see only what we want to see: our attention is drawn to the obvious and to what we are directly interested in. The camera lens, however, records everything in front of it with equal regard and clarity. To become a good photographer, you need to learn to see like the camera, aware of every relationship between foreground, mid-ground and background that may not be immediately apparent to the human eye but will be glaringly obvious in the final photograph. As the renowned American photographer Berenice Abbott reminds us, 'what the human eye observes casually and incuriously, the eye of the camera notes with relentless fidelity'. When you are shooting, scour the frame for every tiny detail and make 100 per cent sure that you want it in your picture: as far as possible everything that is included – or excluded – in the frame should be a deliberate, conscious choice.

The best zoom lens is your legs

Ernst Haas *Revolving Door*, 1975

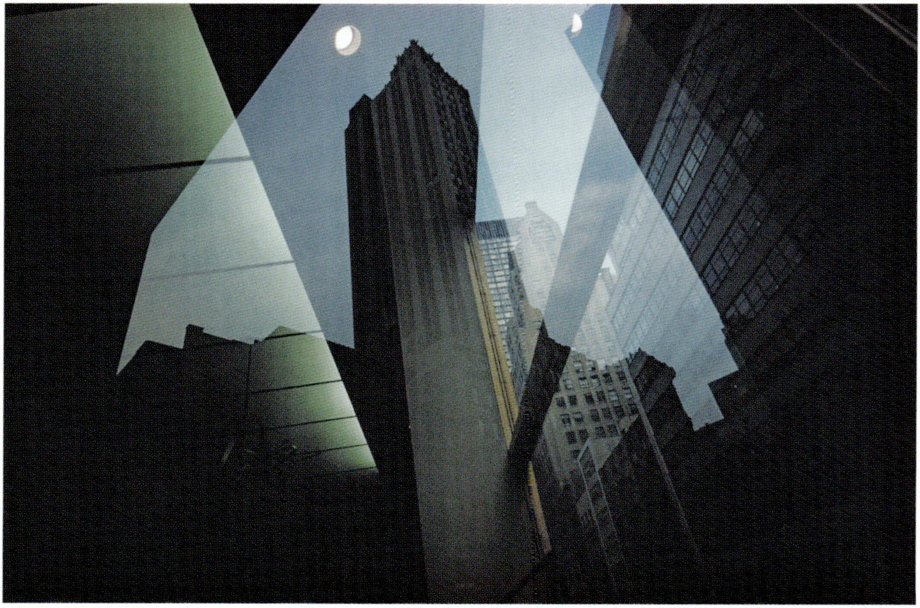

Modern zoom lenses are marvels of quality and convenience, allowing you to change the viewpoint and perspective of the camera over a huge range in a fraction of a second. However, they can make for lazy photography, where you just stand in one place and allow changing the focal length to determine the image. Ernst Haas, a master of the technique of photography, argued that the photographer should move themselves, not the lens, remarking: 'Best wide-angle lens? Two steps backward. Look for the "ah-ha."' Using prime fixed lenses can give you more discipline over your compositions as you have to consciously adjust your position to get the right framing, rather than zooming the lens in and out constantly, so that *you* make the picture, not the camera. If you only have a zoom lens, try taping it up at a fixed focal length and go out to shoot for a day to replicate a prime lens.

Find the emotion in the landscape

Aletheia Casey *After the Apology*, 2008

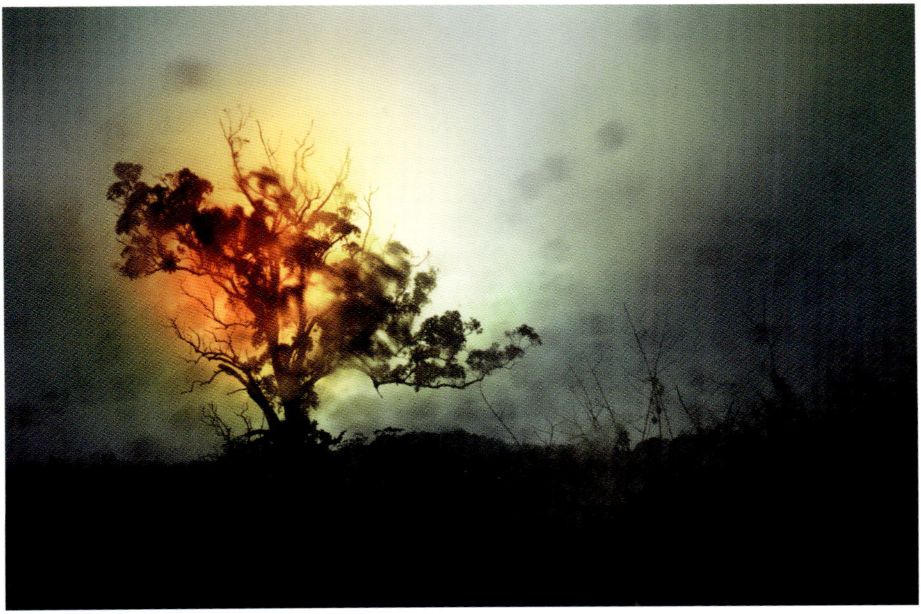

The Australian documentary photographer Aletheia Casey is known for her evocative and emotionally charged work, both in portraiture and landscape. But she doesn't treat them as disparate genres and approaches them both with the same attitude. When Casey shoots a landscape, she tries to focus on what is emotive about it, as you would a portrait.

A photographer needs to sit within the landscape and wait for the perfect moment to shoot – the perfect light. This is their opportunity to reflect on what makes the landscape so interesting and decide what the actual focal point of the photograph should be. When treating the landscape as you would a portrait, Casey thinks of the emotional focal point as the 'eyes' of the landscape. As the light and weather change, so does the scene, much like the expressions on people's faces. Casey argues: 'If you sit patiently and wait for the right moment the landscape will have an inherent emotive quality.'

Don't crop

Mary Ellen Mark *Children at Gypsy Camp, Barcelona, Spain*, 1987

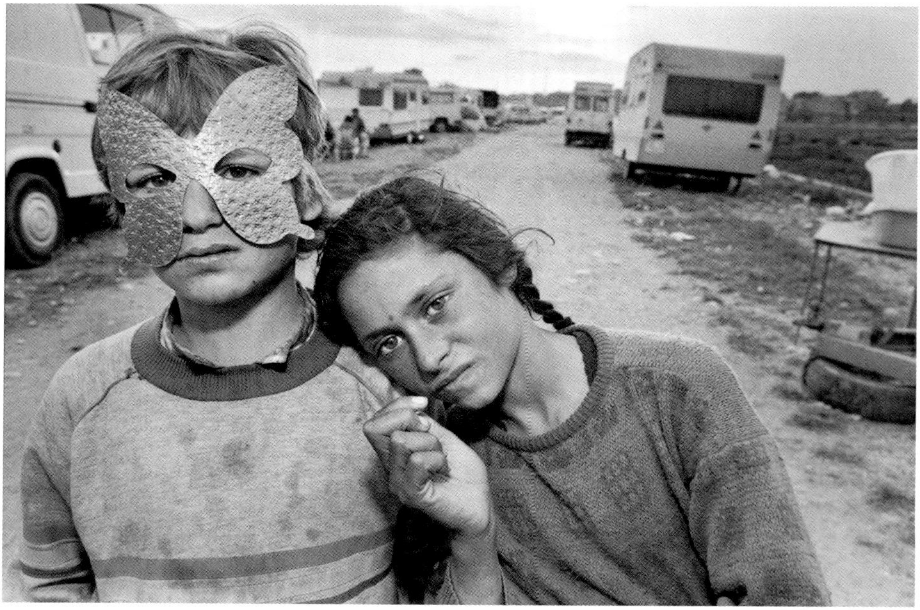

While the resolution of modern digital cameras is more than high enough to allow for cropping the image in post-production, in general it is better to get it right in camera at the point of exposure. Cartier-Bresson famously claimed never to crop his photographs, and his position was followed by the American documentary photographer Mary Ellen Mark, who noted that 'I don't crop my photographs. I consider the entire frame while I'm shooting. It's a discipline I learned when I began to photograph.' It's a discipline you should follow too: you can turn it into a game, where if you do not get exactly the frame you want with everything in the right place on the edges of the frame then you have failed, like trying to get a high score in a computer game. Over time, this self-control will help you become better at automatically scanning the edges of the frame to make sure no space is wasted.

Make quieter pictures

William Albert Allard *Buckaroo T. J. Symonds, IL Cow Camp, Nevada*, 1979

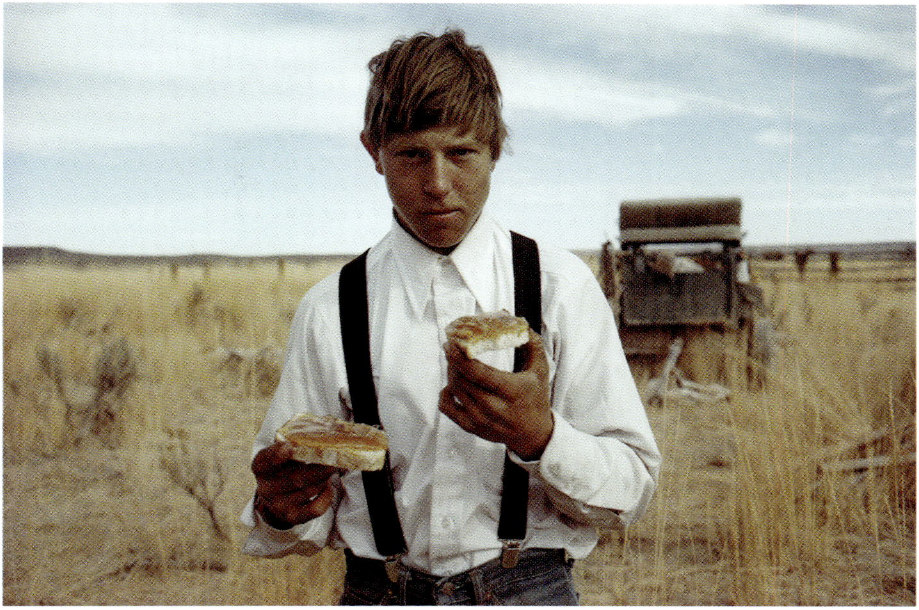

The photographs of William Albert Allard are full of visual and emotional subtleness, working their magic in a gentle way; they do not shout at the viewer with flashy technique or dramatic angles. Instead, they offer a calmer, more nuanced viewpoint, an effect that Allard consciously works at achieving, claiming that he believes 'in the resonance and staying power of quiet photographs'. He gives expert guidance on how to gain the acceptance of close-knit groups of people: 'If a subject has a delicate surface to it, you do not want to go charging in there. You need to establish some kind of presence and understanding.' Allow the subject the right to decide if they will let you into their lives. 'Photographing people requires a willingness to be rejected. So, I think the best approach is to be honest and direct.' When you are shooting in close proximity to people, take time to win their acceptance and then take time to slow down your photography, and quieten your images, avoiding excessive drama in technique.

Shoot RAW

Paul Lowe

'Shooting in RAW is the digital equivalent of having a negative stored in your filing cabinet in analogue photography.'

For the highest possible image quality, always shoot RAW files on your camera. RAW is a file format that captures all of the data recorded by the sensor, unlike JPEG, where information is compressed and lost to make the file size smaller. RAW will also capture much more detail in the image. For example, a JPEG records 256 levels of brightness, whilst RAW records up to 16,384 levels. You can adjust white balance and over- and underexposure more easily in RAW, and you have access to sharpening and noise-reduction algorithms in programs like Lightroom or Photoshop that are much powerful than those found in your camera. Non-destructive editing is also used on RAW files; when you make adjustments to the file, you're not actually doing anything to the original data, so if you change your mind in the future or want to try out different effects, the original file is preserved. Shooting in RAW is the digital equivalent of having a negative stored in your filing cabinet in analogue photography.

Elevate the banal

Lewis Baltz *Construction Detail, East Wall, Xerox, 1821 Dyer Road, Santa Ana*, 1974

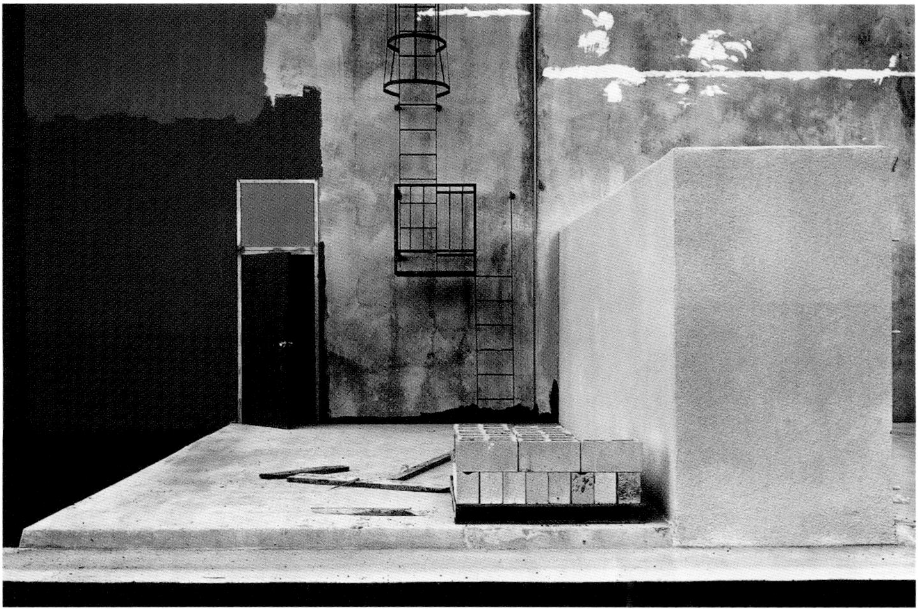

Lewis Baltz has been the supreme documenter of the non-spaces of America, transforming mundane and banal corners of the industrial and commercial landscape into abstract patterns that invite the viewer to look anew at the everyday. For Baltz, it was 'necessary to investigate photography, dismantle it, jettison all the non-essential components, and begin again with a stripped down but more powerful idea of what is, or could be "photographic"'. His photographs are of inherently real places, but they invite the audience to contemplate the image itself as an imaginative space, such that 'photographs no longer provoke a meditation upon external phenomena, but on the conditions of their own existence'. This idea that the act of photographing something can elevate it to the status of a valuable object is central to the medium's ability to make us notice things in the world that would otherwise go unperceived; as Baltz insists, 'everything is photogenic once it has been photographed'.

Drop the mask of the subject

Philippe Halsman Philippe Halsman photographing Salvador Dalí, 1954 (photograph by Yale Joel)

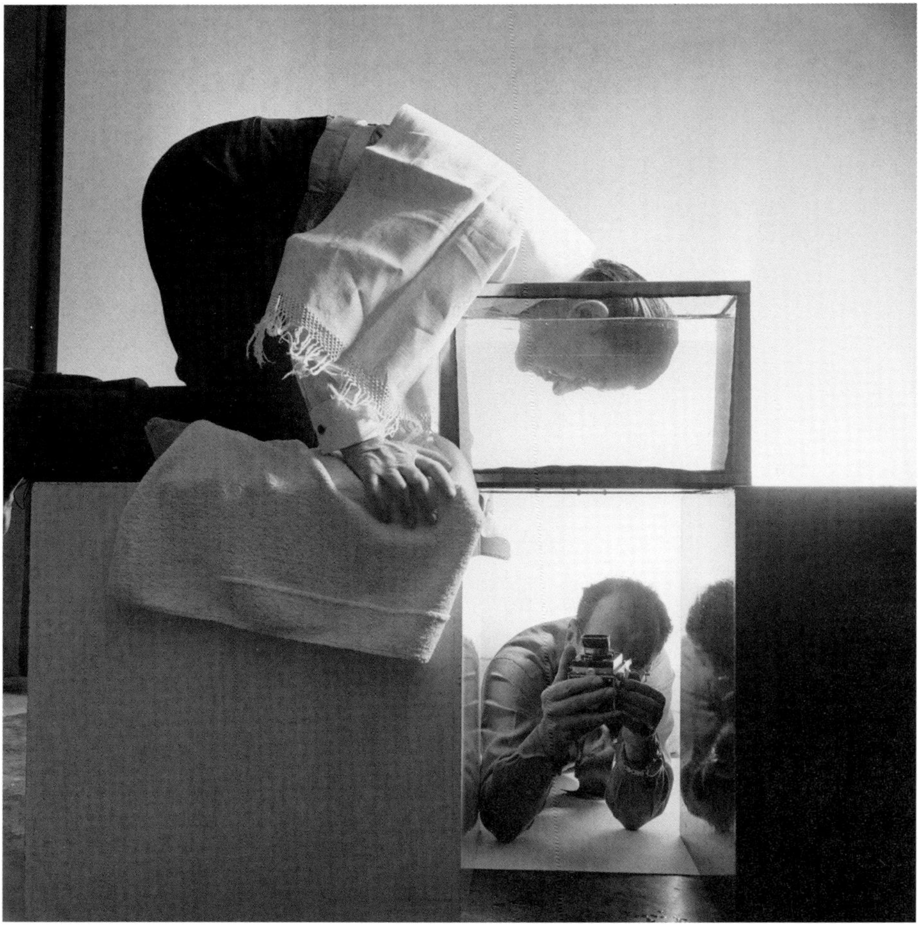

'I do not direct the sitter – the only thing I try is to help him over his fears and inhibitions. I try to capture what I feel reflects something of his inner life.'

Philippe Halsman explained how he always tried to find a way to connect with the inner life of his subjects, asserting that 'I do not direct the sitter – the only thing I try is to help him over his fears and inhibitions. I try to capture what I feel reflects something of his inner life.' However, he was a master of clever methods to find ways to probe deeper into his subject's personality, noting that 'most people stiffen with self-consciousness when they pose for a photograph. Lighting and fine camera equipment are useless if the photographer cannot make them drop the mask, at least for a moment, so he can capture on his film their real, undistorted personality and character.' Some of his techniques for achieving this included 'provoking the victim, amusing him with jokes, lulling him with silence, or asking impertinent questions which his best friend would be afraid to voice.' While this may be a little extreme for every portrait session, finding methods to break the ice with your sitter is vital.

Take bad pictures

Gueorgui Pinkhassov *Bluewater Commercial Center*, 1999

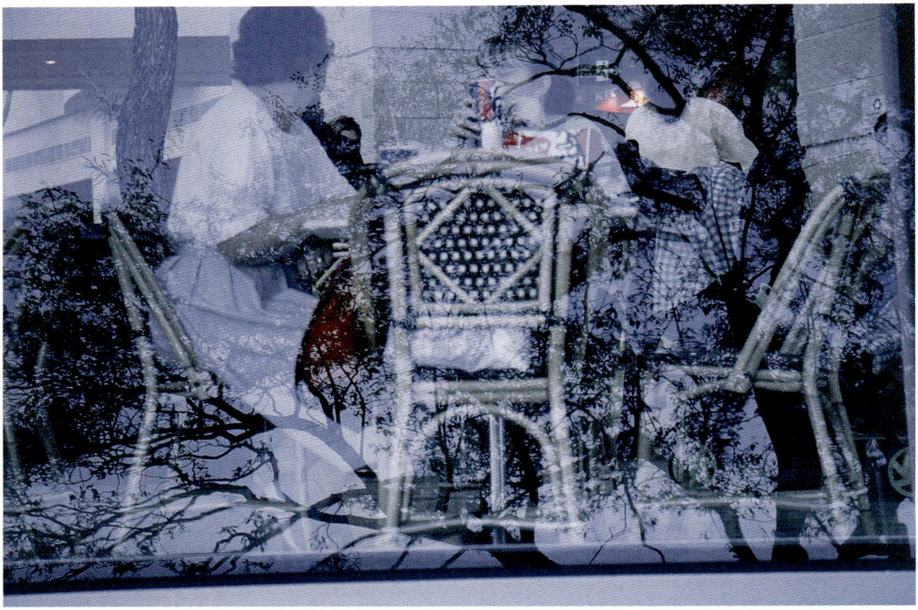

Magnum photographer Gueorgui Pinkhassov has a unique eye, always finding the strange and complex in everyday situations. A central part of his approach is to celebrate failure, seeing it as a route to a breakthrough in personal vision. He argues that 'great photos are born through accidents. Great photos happen when your value system changes and you see new values.' Pushing yourself to experiment with new visual strategies that may initially seem unsuccessful can lead to real breakthroughs, and he recommends not to be 'afraid to take bad pictures, because good pictures are the mistakes of bad pictures'. A key part of this is shooting a lot of pictures; as he notes, 'usually we take ten photos and throw out just a couple of them. But the result is much more effective if we take 100 photos and throw out 99 of them'. Really push yourself to see how the camera sees, responding intuitively to the world around you. A lot of your images will fail, but some will be spectacular successes.

Appreciate the colours of black and white

Anders Petersen *Lily Rose and Scar in Café Lehmitz*, 1970

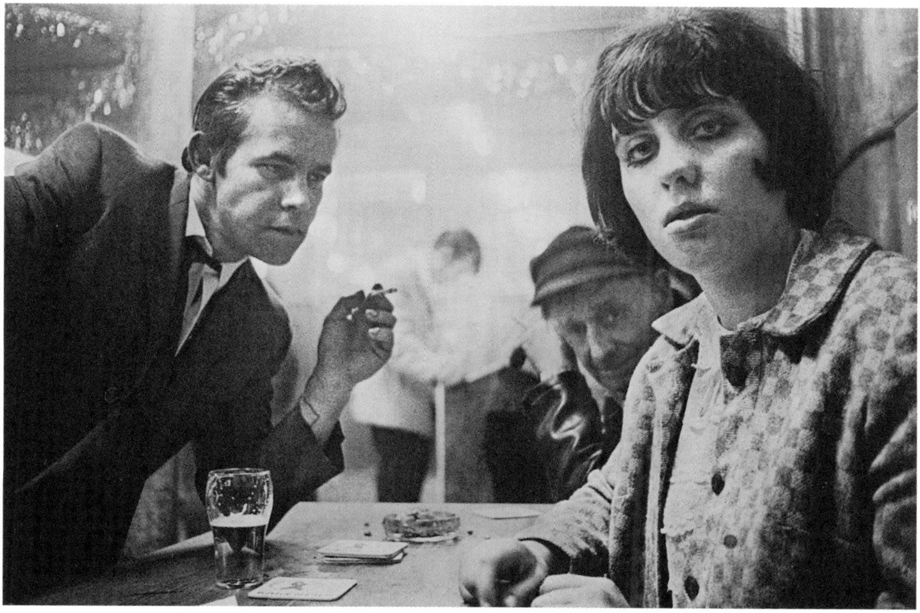

Anders Petersen's intimate documentation of the lives of the patrons of a late-night bar in Hamburg, Café Lehmitz, is full of emotion and the psychological drama of everyday life. Shooting in monochrome allows him to connect more with the subject: he argued that 'in black and white there are more colours than colour photography, because you are not blocked by any colours so you can use your experiences, your knowledge, and your fantasy, to put colours into black and white'. The abstraction of black and white helps him reach a deeper level of intimacy, claiming that 'I don't believe in reality really, it's a bluff. But I believe in a kind of reality that exists because of all the longing, dreams, secrets, nightmares, mostly longings. I think no picture is without longing.' Colour can be a distraction when you are trying to really engage with the lives of others.

Control your focus

Julia Margaret Cameron *Iago, Study from an Italian*, 1867

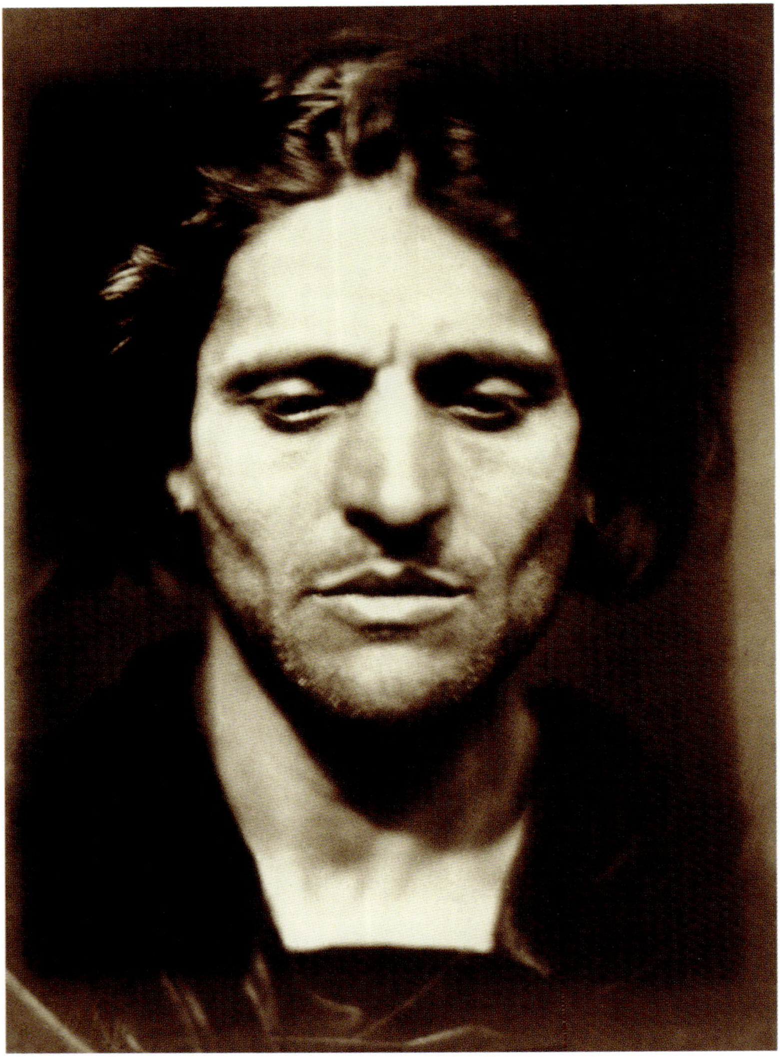

'From the first moment I handled my lens with a tender ardour, and it has become to me as a living thing, with voice and memory and creative vigour.'

One of the most creative controls we have is that of where we focus and how much depth of field we use. Combining a shallow depth of field with a careful choice of what to focus on can create images that really draw the viewer's eye to specific elements of the photograph. This can be very effective in portrait photography, and was a technique used by one the earliest masters of the genre, the English photographer Julia Margaret Cameron. She used a large-format 15" x 12" glass-plate camera with a Jamin Rapid Rectilinear lens, with a fixed aperture of f3.6 and a focal length of around 12", which had a shallow depth of focus at the close distances that she worked at. She instantly fell in love with the lens, exclaiming that 'From the first moment I handled my lens with a tender ardour, and it has become to me as a living thing, with voice and memory and creative vigour.'

Her first attempts with the camera were experimental, as she admitted: 'I believe that ... my first successes in my out-of-focus pictures were a fluke. That is to say, when focusing and coming to something which, to my eye, was very beautiful, I stopped there instead of screwing on the lens to the more definite focus which all other photographers insist upon.' But the effect, as in this powerful study of an actor based on the Shakespearean character of Iago demonstrates, was to concentrate our attention into an intense psychological portrait. She later challenged the conventions of sharp focus, by raising the question 'what is focus and who has the right to say what focus is the legitimate focus?' Think of this when you are deciding where to position your focal point and how much depth of field to use. Don't be a slave to auto focus and auto aperture selection.

Use photography as a weapon

John Heartfield *Adolf the Superman Swallows Gold and Spouts Junk*, 1932

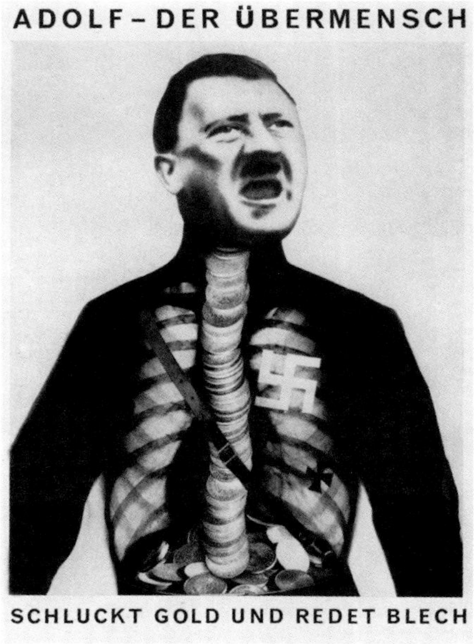

'If I assemble documents and juxtapose them with intelligence and skill, the effect of agitation and propaganda on the masses will be enormous.'

John Heartfield was a master of political photomontage and agitprop, and used his graphic skills to produce powerful images that criticized the Nazi regime in the 1930s. With its ability to combine images from different sources with text, the technique liberated him from the literal representation of politics to create satirical commentary on the rise of fascism and capitalism, as he explained, 'if I assemble documents and juxtapose them with intelligence and skill, the effect of agitation and propaganda on the masses will be enormous'. Heartfield's approach has been further developed by the British artist Peter Kennard, who has produced works supporting the Campaign for Nuclear Disarmament. Photomontage allows you to explore how combining images and text can be a powerful weapon in promoting a social or political cause.

Be selective

Berenice Abbott *Self-portrait*, 1945

'Selection of proper picture content comes from a fine union of trained eye and imaginative mind.'

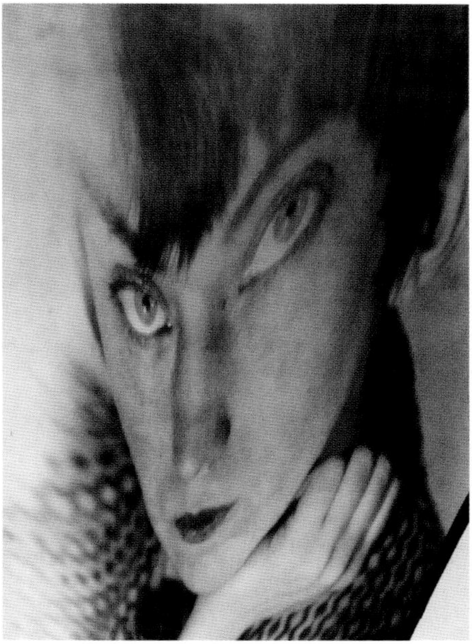

One of the key elements of successful photography lies in choosing what to actually include in the frame, and often, less is more. A compelling image, free from distractions, makes its point with clarity and forcefulness. For Berenice Abbott, this was a combination of both an aesthetic judgement and also an emotional one. She maintained that a photograph 'should be significant document, a penetrating statement, which can be described in a very simple term – selectivity'. She encouraged a focus on the 'kind of subject matter which hits you hard with its impact and excites your imagination to the extent that you are forced to take it'. When composing your photographs, really ask yourself if everything in the frame is contributing actively to the message or feeling you want the viewer to feel; if it isn't, leave it out and really concentrate on the essentials. Remember Abbott's advice that the 'selection of proper picture content comes from a fine union of trained eye and imaginative mind'.

Don't overthink

Manuel Álvarez Bravo *Daughter of the Dancers*, 1933

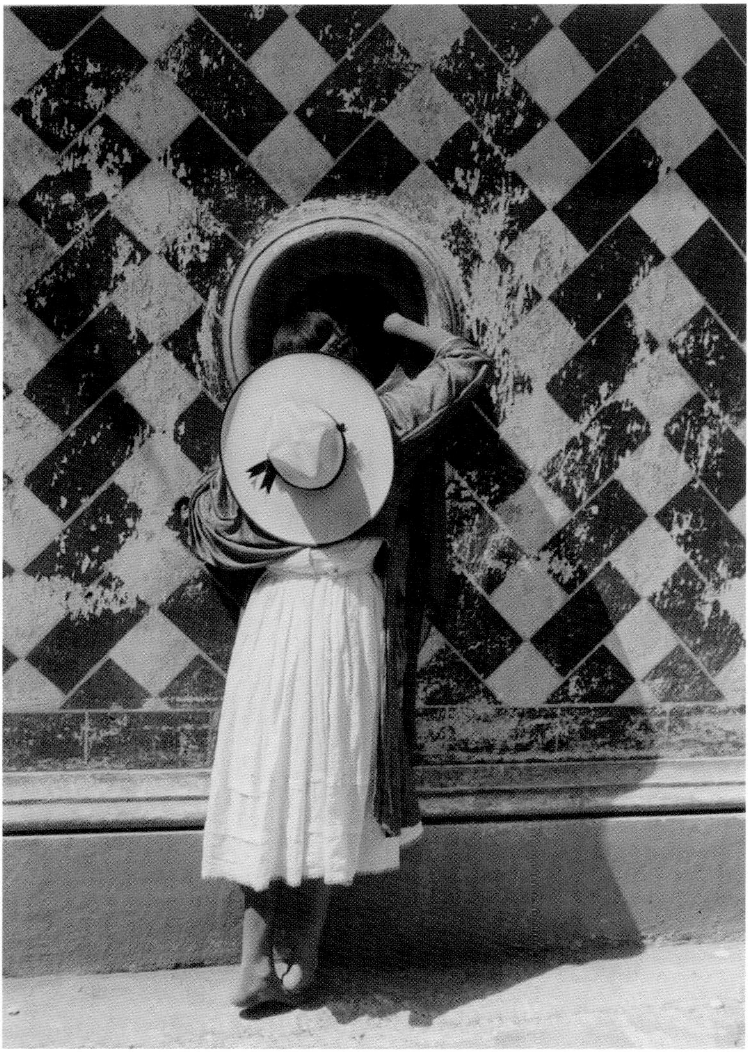

'Strange as it may seem, many photographers choose to use the eyes of another photographer, past or present, instead of their own. Those photographers are blind.'

Manuel Álvarez Bravo's work connected deeply with the spiritual and psychological life of Latin America, embodied in the sense of embodied magic realism found in the everyday life of Mexico. His philosophy was simple: don't overconceptualize the scene and 'shoot what you see, not what you think'. He felt that this allowed the situation to speak for itself, opening up a space where the viewer can create their own interpretations of the image, claiming that 'when one takes a photograph, one doesn't think about saying anything in particular. One doesn't think about making a statement but rather of creating something visual which later can bear a meaning that one didn't intend to transmit – depending on the viewer's interpretation but not necessarily on the photographer's.' Expanding on this, he also felt that too many photographers copied the works of others without letting their own vision guide them, arguing that a 'photographer's main instrument is his eyes. Strange as it may seem, many photographers choose to use the eyes of another photographer, past or present, instead of their own. Those photographers are blind.' While it is very useful to be aware of the canon of photography, you have to find your own unique way of seeing the world.

Journalists should be anarchists

Philip Jones Griffiths *Wounded Civilian, Vietnam*, 1967

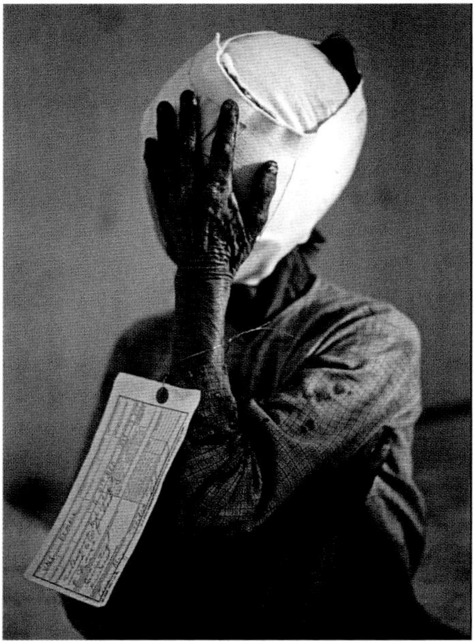

'Journalists should be by their very nature anarchists, people who want to point out things that are not generally approved of. It's by criticizing that society that humanity has made progress.'

The Magnum photographer Philip Jones Griffiths produced one of the most damning indictments of war and imperial folly in his book *Vietnam Inc.*, published in 1971. He made himself very unpopular with the authorities, following this dictum that 'journalists should be by their very nature anarchists, people who want to point out things that are not generally approved of. It's by criticizing that society that humanity has made progress.' He combined strong compositions with powerful situations, all supported by extended captions and text that collectively formed a devastating critique of the US military involvement in Southeast Asia. He succinctly summed up this combination as 'content alone is propaganda; form alone is wallpaper'. In photojournalism, visual impact is nothing without social relevance.

Work your eye every day

Eric Bouvet *South of Grozny, Chechnya*, 1995

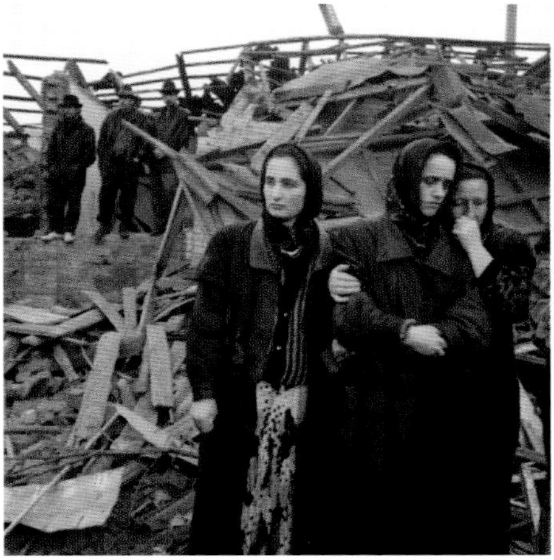

'We must work our eye, like a musician who repeats their scales every day. For us it's the same thing, no rest, no holidays.'

The French photojournalist Eric Bouvet is a great believer in keeping his visual chops sharp by regular and consistent practice. He insists that 'we must work our eye, like a musician who repeats their scales every day. For us it's the same thing, no rest, no holidays.' He even suggests that this can be done wherever and whenever you are: even if you don't have a camera, you can still mentally 'frame' the world around you and imagine what photograph you could take. You can turn this into a kind of game, by trying to guess the correct exposure for the scene in front of you, or the distance away from you something is, or visualizing what result the field of view of a particular lens would give you from your position. All these exercises will help you be faster and more instinctive when it really matters.

Tune in

Constantine Manos *Athens, Greece*, 2003

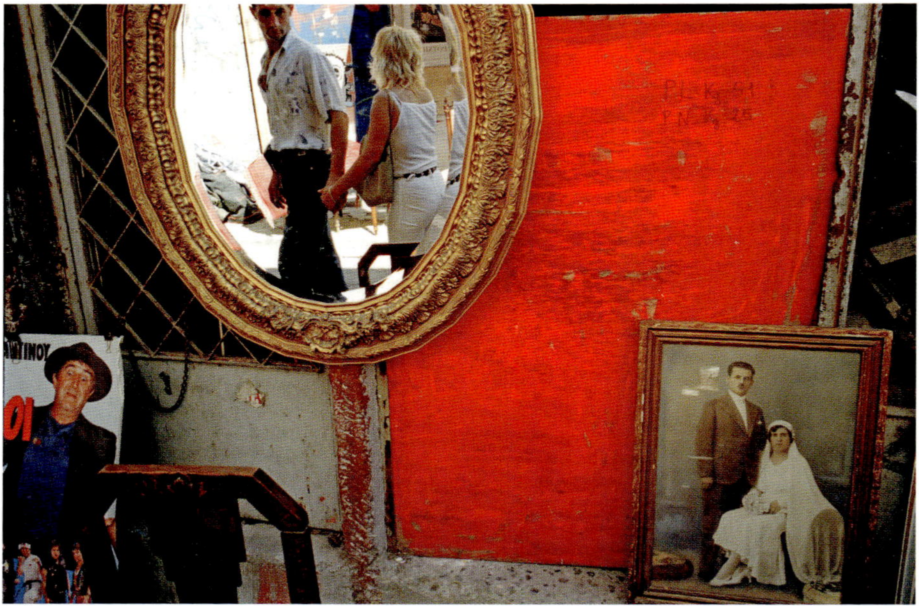

'Taking good pictures is easy. Making very good pictures is difficult. Making great pictures is almost impossible.'

The street photographer Constantine Manos makes a sobering point when he points out that if we follow the 'rules' of photography we might be able to get a decent picture in most circumstances but that to reach the highest level of image quality in terms of the combination of form and content is a very rare thing indeed. He reminds us that 'taking good pictures is easy. Making very good pictures is difficult. Making great pictures is almost impossible.' Working on assignment, you have to be able to consistently make good photographs, but every now and then the world gifts you that unique moment that makes a great image. Manos encapsulates this process by describing how the 'flow of people in a setting, their changing relationships to each other and their environment, and their constantly changing expressions and movements – all combine to create dynamic situations that provide the photographer with limitless choices of when to push the button. By choosing a precise intersection between subject and time, he may transform the ordinary into the extraordinary and the real into the surreal.' Try to tune into the flow of the world around you to be able to respond to it and recognize those transcendental moments when the magic really happens.

Get it right in camera

Paul Lowe

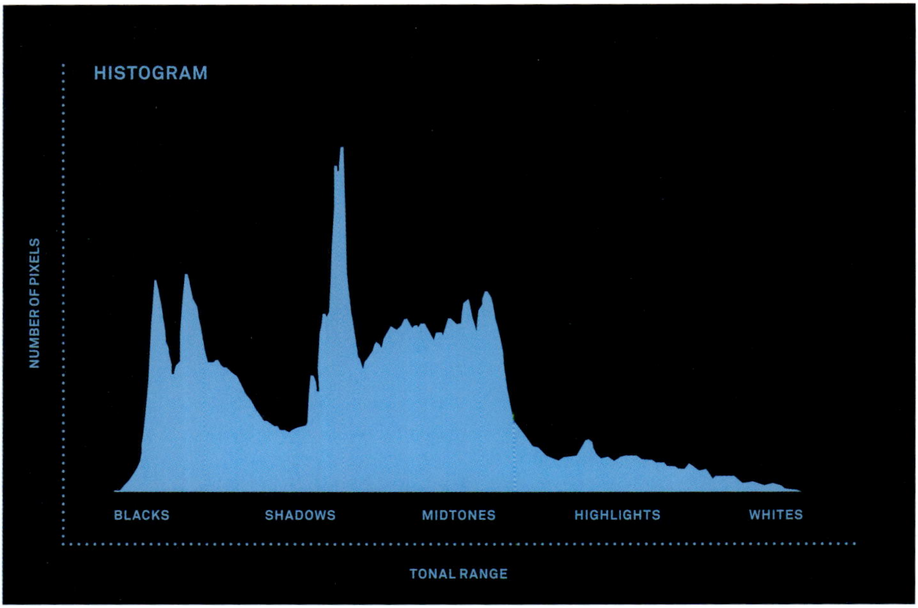

Digital editing and post-production software like Photoshop or Lightroom is now so powerful that a badly exposed file can be worked on to get a good final result. However, it is still better to get the exposure right in camera rather than relying on the software to fix an image with blown-out highlights or blocked-up shadows. In the days of film, especially colour transparency or slide, it was absolutely essential to make a perfect exposure: there was very little latitude to overexposure. Getting the best-quality initial image will allow you to get the best-quality final image after post-processing, as you will have a lot more usable information on the original file. Also, it will save time in post-production, as rescuing a bad exposure can be very time-consuming.

Be tenacious

Joe McNally *Donald Trump*, 1987

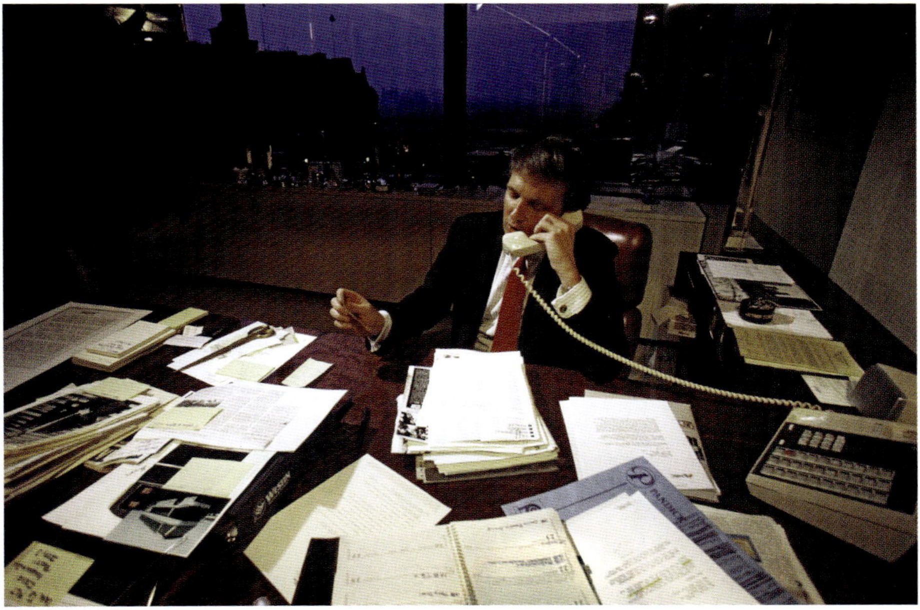

The American photographer Joe McNally is a master of light, and of the technical aspects of the medium, producing dramatic and visually arresting images from almost any situation. He puts a large part of his success down to simple hard work and graft, and not giving up, arguing that 'the qualities that I think get underestimated quite often are durability and tenacity and a willingness to just keep at it. Time spent behind the camera is just phenomenally important.' One vital piece of advice he gives is really worth adhering to: 'Don't pack up your camera until you've left the location.' In so many instances, an amazing picture opportunity presents itself out of the blue at the least-expected moment, and you have to be ready for it when it comes.

Master your technique so you can forget about it

André Kertész *Washington Square, Winter*, 1954

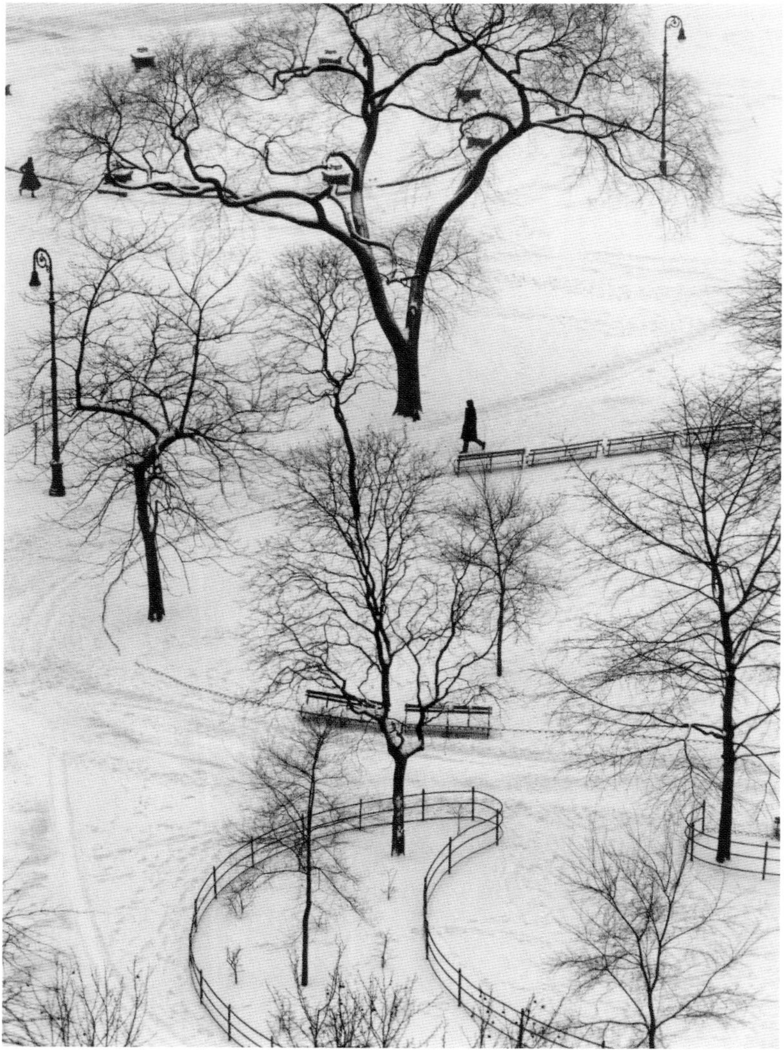

‘Technique is only the minimum in photography. It’s what one must start with. I believe you should be a perfect technician in order to express yourself as you wish and then you can forget about the technique.’

Understanding the four stages of competence is important if you want to take your skills as a photographer to the next level. You should be so familiar with your equipment that using it becomes second nature and you can work instinctively. As the Hungarian master photographer André Kertész tells us, ‘technique is only the minimum in photography. It’s what one must start with. I believe you should be a perfect technician in order to express yourself as you wish and then you can forget about the technique.’ Practise incessantly and regularly with all the camera controls so that you pass through the four stages, moving from unconscious incompetence, where you have no idea what you are doing wrong or why, to conscious incompetence, where you know what is wrong but still don’t know how to fix it, on to conscious competence, where you still really have to concentrate to get it right, until you finally reach the level of unconscious competence, or mastery, where the skill becomes second nature.

Seek clarity

Sam Abell *Ireland*, 1994

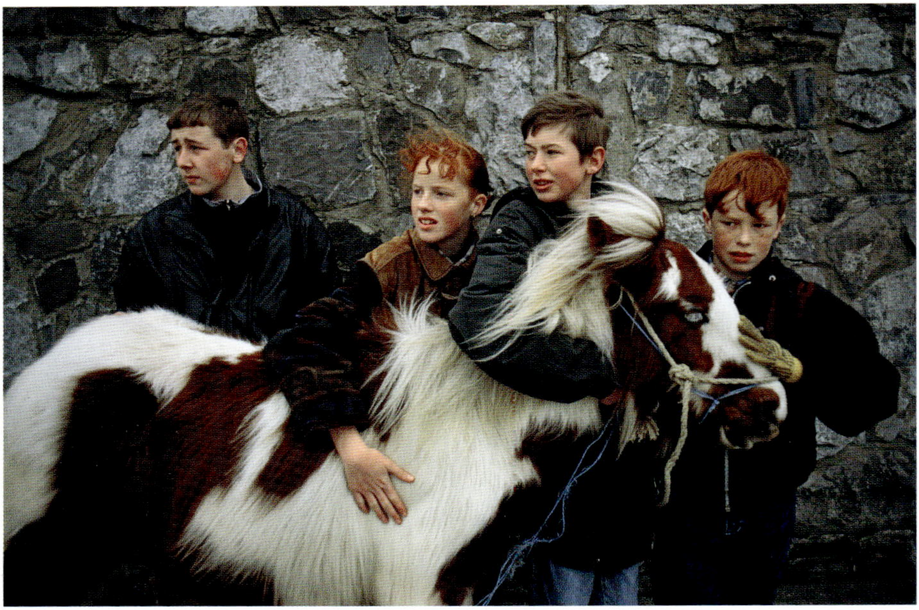

Sam Abell shot more than twenty stories for *National Geographic* over a thirty-seven-year career with the magazine, and is known for his quietly beautiful documentary images. Key to his approach is the search for those moments where the meaning of a situation is expressed most clearly, as he explains: 'My first priority when taking pictures is to achieve clarity. A good documentary photograph transmits the information of the situation with the utmost fidelity.' For Abell, this does not simply mean that the content of the photograph is evident, however, as he is also seeking to 'present an image that arouses the curiosity of the viewer or that, best of all, provokes the viewer to think – to ask a question or simply to gaze in thoughtful wonder'. For Abell, a great photograph is one that both informs and moves the viewer at the same time, the 'kind of picture that makes you want to pick up your own camera again and go to work'.

Make light your inspiration

Ruth Bernhard *In the Wave*, 1945

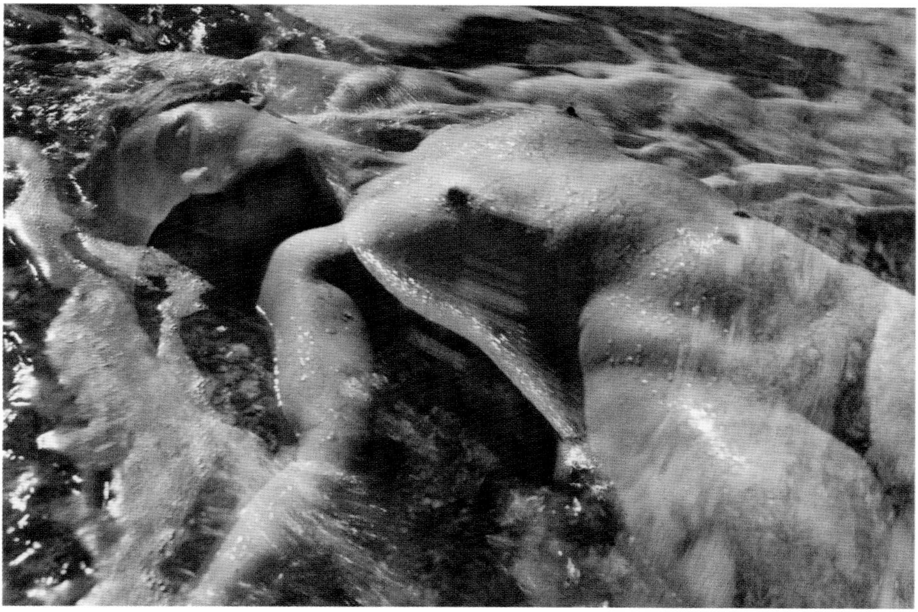

Ruth Bernhard was one of the most significant photographers of the nude, and revelled in the exploration of the infinitely changing qualities of light. She saw it as her 'inspiration, my paint and brush', noting how it formed the very basis of the structure of her photographs, as it 'caresses the essential superlative curves and lines'. She emphasized that in her work her aim, 'through the magic of light and shadow, is to isolate, to simplify and to give emphasis to form with the greatest clarity'. Learn to really look at light, how different sources create different effects from soft to hard, from dark shadows to full highlights. To improve your mastery of light, set up a simple tabletop still life, and experiment with how lighting it in different ways can radically change the subject depending on its intensity and direction.

Use north light

Irving Penn *Truman Capote, New York*, 1948

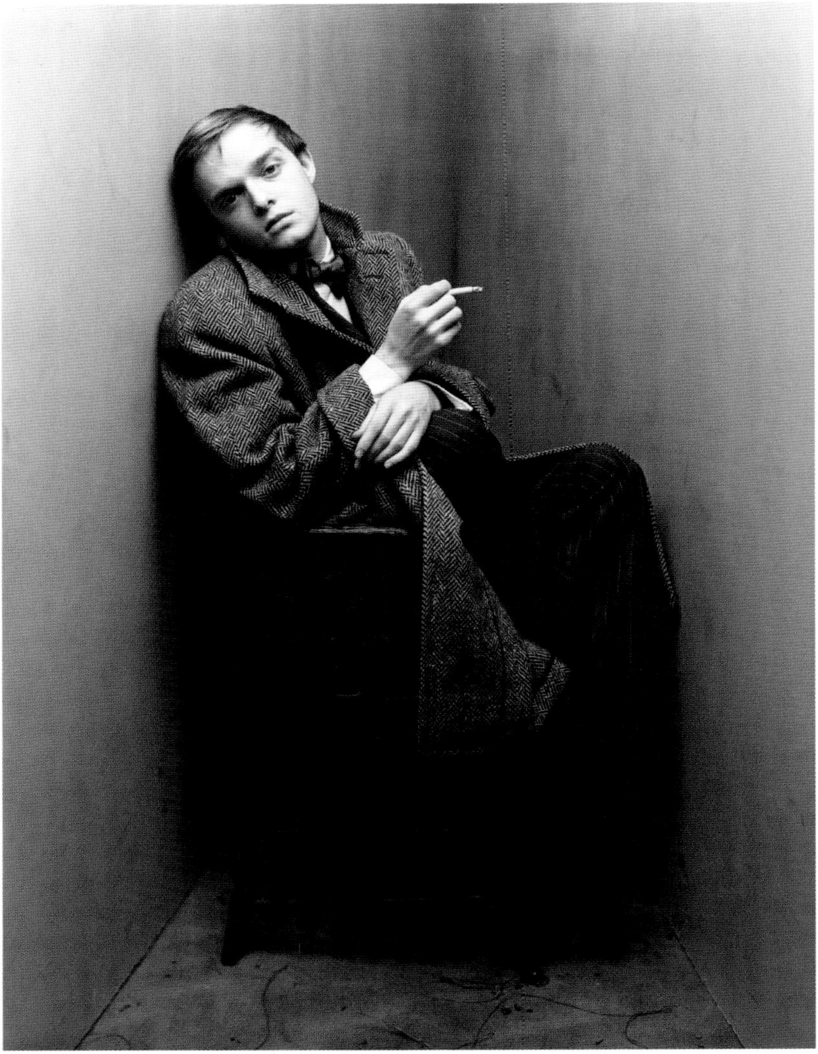

'It is a light of such penetrating clarity that even a simple object lying by chance in such a light takes on an inner glow, almost a voluptuousness.'

Ever since the earliest days of photography, when the passion for daguerreotypes led to purpose-built studios with huge glass roofs, 'north light' has been the standard for portrait photography. One of its leading proponents in the twentieth century was the American Irving Penn, who celebrated the 'sweetness and constancy to light that falls into a studio from the north sky that sets it beyond any other illumination. It is a light of such penetrating clarity that even a simple object lying by chance in such a light takes on an inner glow, almost a voluptuousness'. His trademark method of shooting his subject against a plain background, often backed into a corner of the studio, allowed him to explore the amazing way that north light gives a three-dimensional, solid quality to the subject. While building a north light studio is beyond most photographers, you can replicate the effect by shooting outdoors against a white background in open shade, or by using the biggest softbox you can find positioned above the subject.

Be a participant in the lives of others

Graciela Iturbide *Angel Woman, Sonoran Desert, Mexico*, 1979

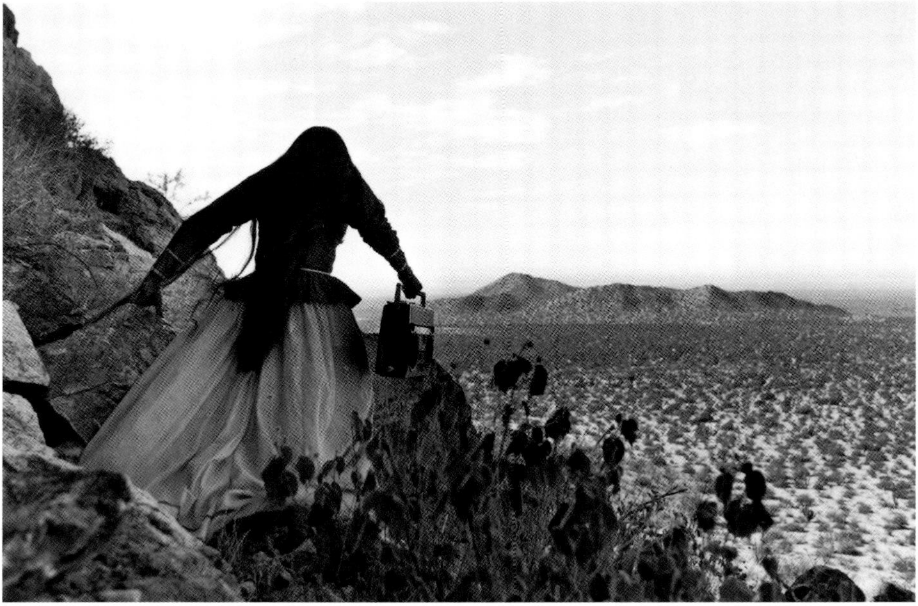

Graciela Iturbide is known for her comprehensive exploration of the spirit of Mexican culture. She feels that 'while using my camera I am, above all, an actress participating in the scene taking place at the moment, and the other actors know what role I play'. The camera can become almost invisible in such intimate situations, which can be akin to a theatrical performance: 'when I'm taking pictures I even forget that I have a camera. When I shoot I forget about everything. Light comes, death comes, people go in and out in costume – and it's like a play'. Shooting with a wide-angle lens allows her to get really close to her subjects, as she explains: 'I never use a telephoto lens. I need to be close to people. I need their complicity; I need them to be aware that I am there taking their picture.' Working with the minimum of equipment, just one camera and a wide-angle lens, and opening yourself up to be a part of the performance can be your passport into the lives of others.

Bend your knees

Vanessa Winship *Resident, Photographer Katie Troyer, Amish Community, Pinecraft, Florida, USA, February,* 2019

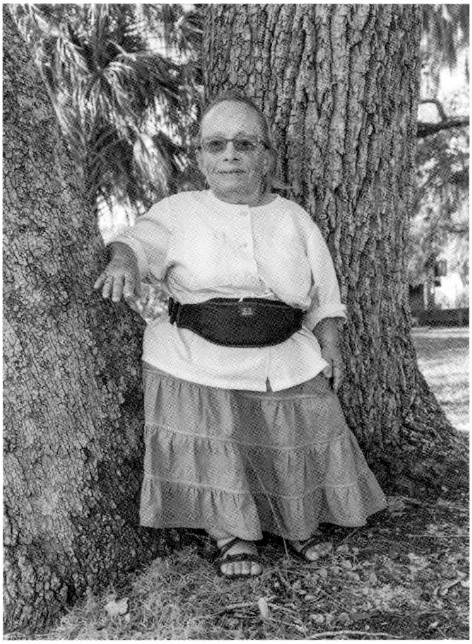

'Remember you're an animal that usually stands on two legs; crouch down and kneel sometimes; lie on the floor and feel how it is looking up from ground level.'

Vanessa Winship has a unique ability to connect on a deep emotional and psychological level with her subjects by finding points of contact between herself and the people she encounters, many of whom are strangers initially. She uses the simple metaphor of 'bending your knees' to signify not just the importance of moving your camera position to at or below eye level in order to connect with the subject, but also to think about how you relate to the person in front of you as an individual as well. She reminds photographers to 'remember you're an animal that usually stands on two legs; crouch down and kneel sometimes; lie on the floor and feel how it is looking up from ground level'. However, the idea also represents 'being flat on your back, the position of someone perhaps about to be kicked in the head, or down on your knees, down on your luck'. Think about how you can put yourself on the same level as your subject to make the connection between you all the more powerful.

Learn to love light

Lara Jo Regan *Octavia Butler, Legendary Science Fiction Writer and Winner of MacArthur Genius Grant, in Her Altadena, California Home*, 1998

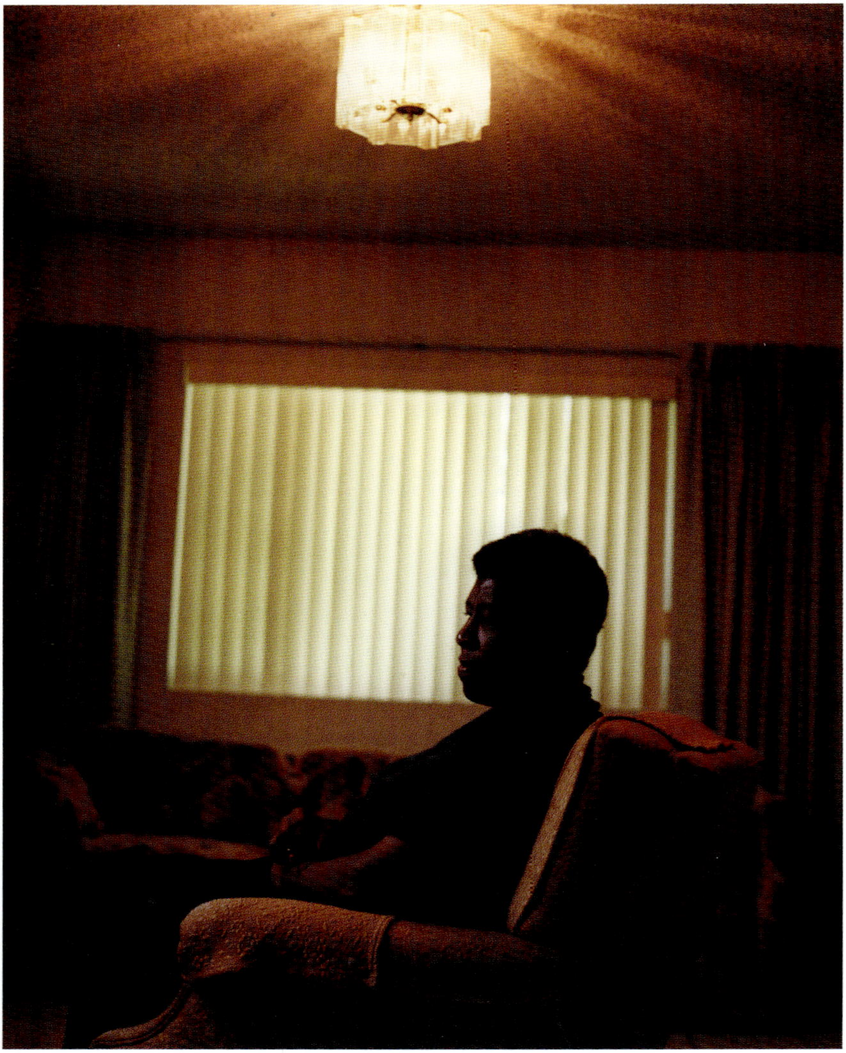

'Lighting is a beautiful language of the spirit in which you want to become as fluent and versatile as possible.'

The American documentary photographer Lara Jo Regan cautions against using a fixed approach to lighting your subject, and instead advises to respond to the light in the situation itself. She emphasizes that the 'mood and feeling of a photograph is profoundly affected by lighting', and cautions photographers to 'resist applying the same formulaic or trendy lighting techniques to everything you photograph. Both often have little meaningful relation to the nature of the subject and will dilute your opportunity for expression that is more thoughtful, dimensional and unique.' Light has its own energy and voice, and we should embrace its full potential to transform the image, recognizing that the 'interplay of luminosities has infinite possibilities. Lighting is a beautiful language of the spirit in which you want to become as fluent and versatile as possible.' When you are out shooting, really look at the light, observing how it changes depending on the source – deliberately go out in different lighting situations to learn how to really master the variety of moods that light can produce.

Be discreet

Henri Cartier-Bresson *Sunday on the Banks of the River Seine*, 1938

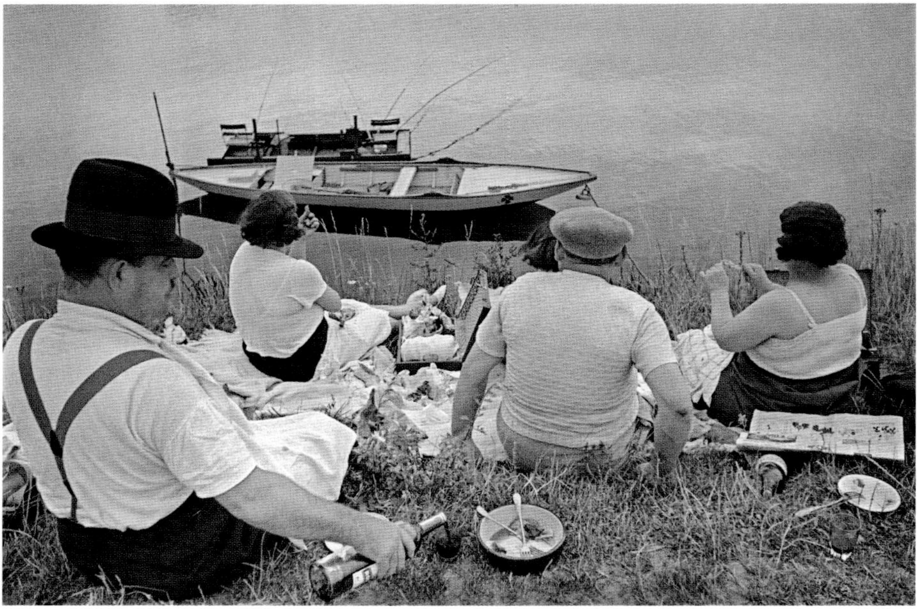

Henri Cartier-Bresson found in the 35mm Leica the perfect tool for his observational style of photography: it allowed him to shoot quickly and unobtrusively without being noticed. He pursued a delicate approach to the subject, advising that 'one has to tiptoe lightly and steal up to one's quarry; you don't swish the water when you are fishing'. He worked intuitively and spontaneously, but with great intelligence and formal control, counselling that one should 'think about the photo before and after, never during. The secret is to take your time. You mustn't go too fast. The subject must forget about you. Then, however, you must be very quick.' Perhaps his most poetic advice in this regard was concerning portrait photography, where he felt 'you have to try and put your camera between the skin of a person and his shirt'. Working with small rangefinder cameras or even a smartphone can allow you to be more discreet and to blend in with the crowds.

Shoot around the golden hour

Simon Norfolk *The City of Matera, Basilicata, Italy*, 2015

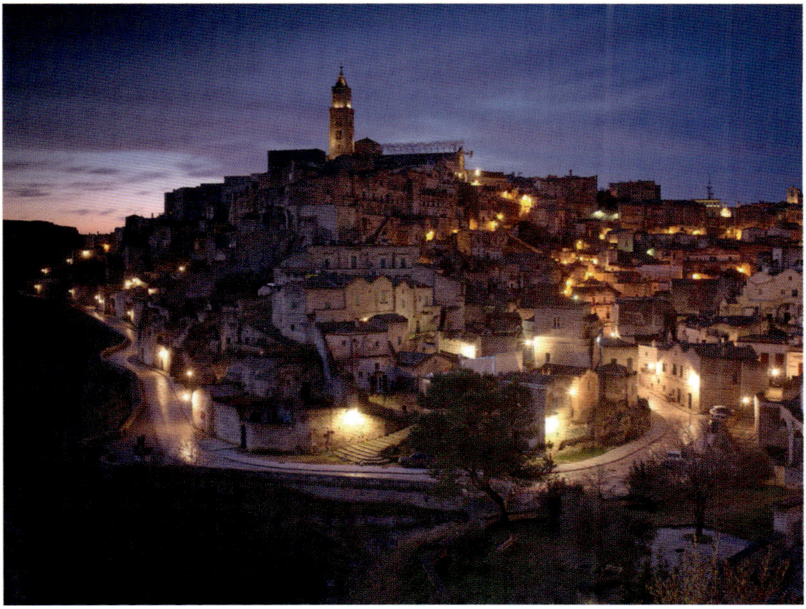

The 'golden hour' is the time just after sunrise or just before sunset, when the daylight is suffused with yellow and red, giving a warm atmosphere to light. The direction of the light is also low, bringing out relief in the scene and casting long, dramatic shadows that can be used to great effect as components of composition. Sometimes called '*National Geographic* time', as it is a characteristic look of many of the published photographs in the magazine, it is a great time to be out shooting as your images will really pop with saturated colours and strong delineations between light and dark. However, shooting in the 'blue hour' immediately before and after the golden hour can also make for wonderful images, as the soft, diffuse light can create an ethereal feel, and modern digital sensors can cope with the low light conditions. Simon Norfolk's image of the Italian hilltop city of Matera, shot with a tripod, illustrates this perfectly.

Work the edges of the situation

William Albert Allard *Cowboys Watching a Rodeo in Texas*, 1982

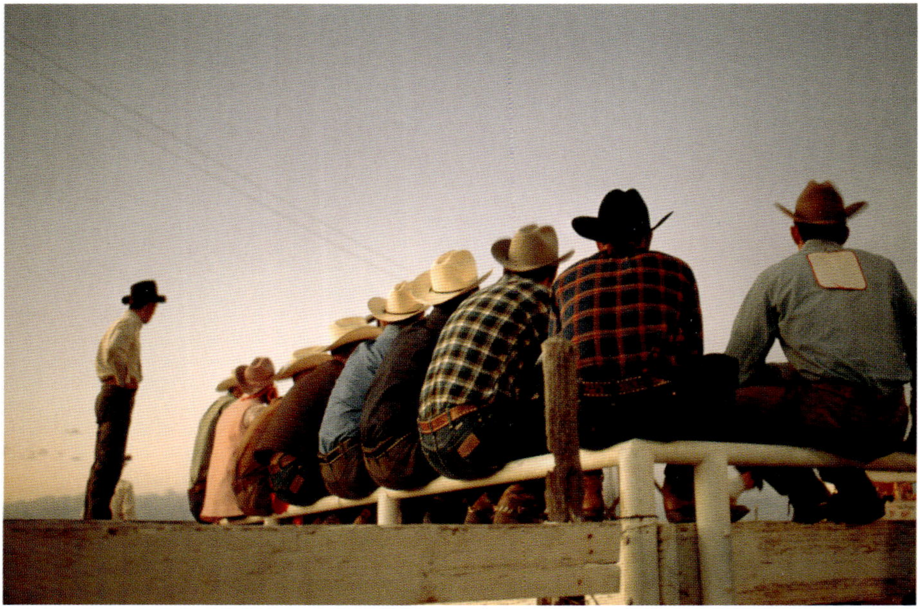

In his long career working mostly for *National Geographic* magazine, William Albert Allard has demonstrated time and again an extraordinary ability to penetrate to the emotional core of a story, finding those charged moments when the aesthetics of colour and form combine with the humanity of his subjects. Key to his approach is to look away from the main attraction. He feels that the 'best pictures are often on the edges of any situation. I don't find photographing the situation nearly as interesting as photographing the edges.' Deliberately turning away from the obvious can frequently be an effective way to find your own unique perspective; as Allard recommends, 'you've got to push yourself harder. You've got to start looking for pictures nobody else could take. You've got to take the tools you have and probe deeper.' If you find yourself in a situation with other photographers all shooting the same scene, consider quietly walking away to find your own viewpoint on the periphery.

The best images are both simple and complex

Anne Williams

'The most arresting, memorable and effective images simultaneously combine simplicity and complexity, both visually and in terms of understanding. They have an immediacy that engages the viewer, yet linger on, asking questions rather than providing answers. At its most basic level this often means that two or more ideas, feelings or aesthetics are rubbing up against each other in a surprising juxtaposition, the familiar within the unfamiliar or vice versa, leaving it for the viewer to resolve the possibly unanswerable riddle of their relationship. Text or captioning may either anchor or enhance the deferral of meaning. Subtlety and economy of means are the key.'

Anne Williams is one of the most influential educators and curators in British photography. She explains how the simplest images can carry a profound message.

Find the surprising in the ordinary

David Burnett David Burnett at impeachment hearing, 2019 (photograph by Chip Somodevilla)

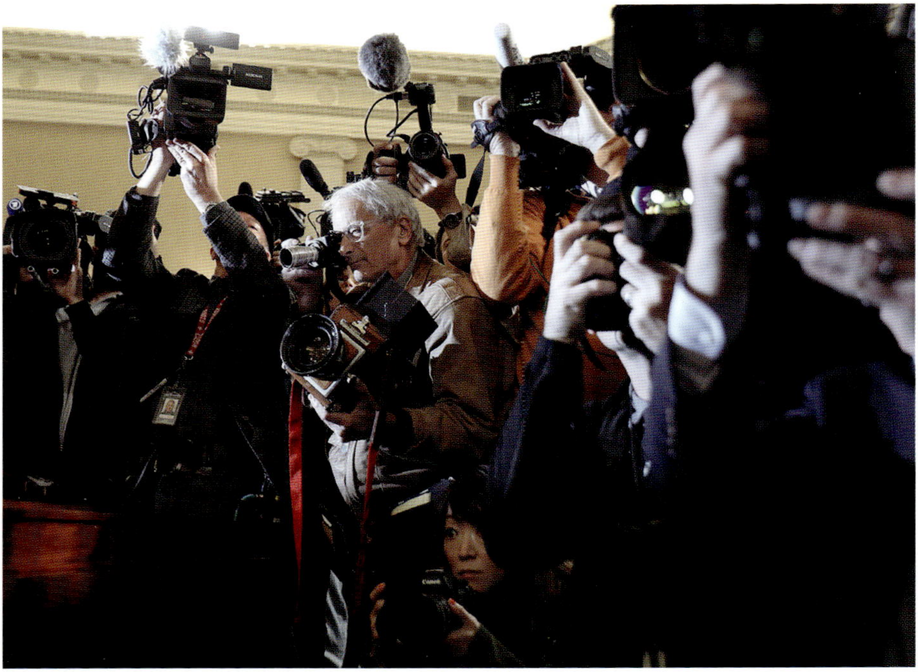

‘When you are shooting in the same place for a long time, you really have to push yourself beyond autopilot.’

David Burnett is one of the legends of photojournalism, and his work has featured in the world’s leading magazines since the 1970s. He is a master of finding ways to make the obvious seem different and unusual, challenging himself to find new interpretations of familiar subjects, feeling that the ‘eye and the brain react to the foreign, so when you are shooting in the same place for a long time, you really have to push yourself beyond autopilot’. One of the best examples of how he has applied his creativity to a well-known situation lies in his ongoing coverage of the Olympics, which he has been photographing since the Los Angeles Summer Games of 1984. Driven by his desire to ‘find some other technique or physical location that might yield the picture that is a little surprising’, unlike all of the other conventional sports photographers with their super-long telephotos and motor-driven digital cameras, Burnett has returned to using a camera from a previous generation. His 1940s Speed Graphic 4" x 5" takes single sheets of film, and he uses its shallow depth of field when shooting wide open to create these extraordinary landscapes of the sport, where the action seems frozen as if from a child’s-eye perspective. Think how you can use a technique or camera position to make the familiar seem strange and exciting.

Use prime lenses

Paul Lowe

'Their greatest benefit is they make you aware of exactly the field of view of that particular focal length, and understand how it translates the world around you into a photograph.'

Prime lenses have a fixed focal length, and offer some significant advantages over zooms. Although modern zooms are very high quality, and can cover an extraordinary range, they do have their drawbacks. A prime lens will usually be faster, lighter, more compact and generally have a better image quality. Some exotic fixed lenses like the famous Leica Noctilux-M 50mm can have maximum apertures as wide as f 0.95, and f 1.4 is increasingly common for wide angles like 35mm. These wider apertures allow shooting in very low light, and can make dramatic portraits where the shallow depth of field throws most of the image out of focus, concentrating attention on just the eyes of the subject. Prime lenses will also generally be sharper, and suffer less from distortion, vignetting and chromatic aberration. But their greatest benefit is that they make you aware of exactly the field of view of that particular focal length, and understand how it translates the world around you into a photograph.

Blur is your friend

William Klein *Dance in Brooklyn*, 1955

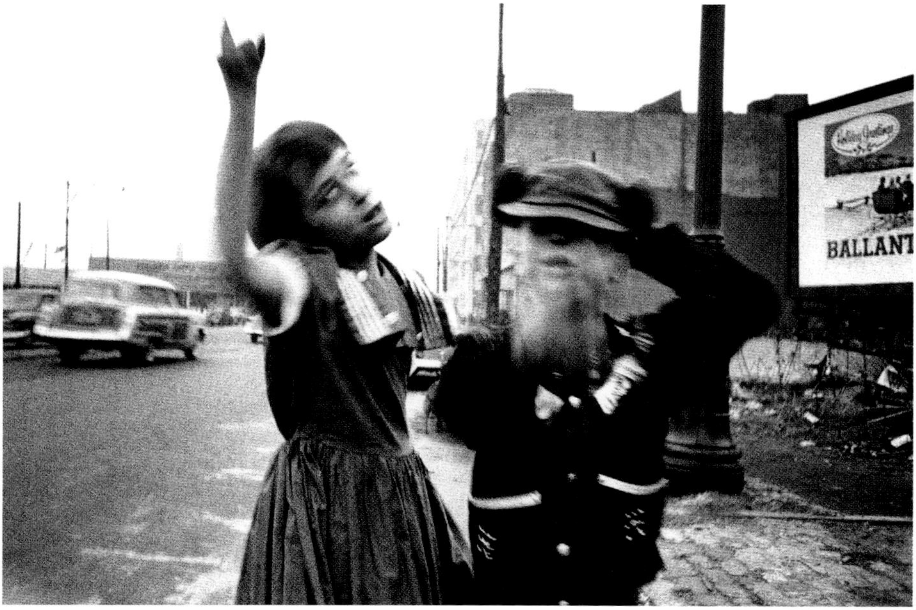

One of the main variables in photography is the shutter speed; normally when there is movement in the situation we want to keep this high to freeze motion and get a sharp image. However, deliberately using a slower shutter speed of over 1/30th of a second can be used to create a visceral sense of the energy of the scene. William Klein used this to great effect in his groundbreaking work in New York in the 1950s, where he broke the conventions of the day to produce grainy images with high contrast and dramatic angles, giving a sense of urgency and drama. He claimed that movement is part of the energy of the city, and that capturing it on film was an essential part of documenting urban culture, noting that 'if you look carefully at life, you see blur. Shake your hand. Blur is part of life.' Experiment with how different shutter speeds create varying degrees of blur and find your 'sweet spot' where the distortion is sufficient to give a sense of energy but still retain the trace of the subject.

Remember that photography is both easy and difficult

Edward Steichen *Greta Garbo*, 1928

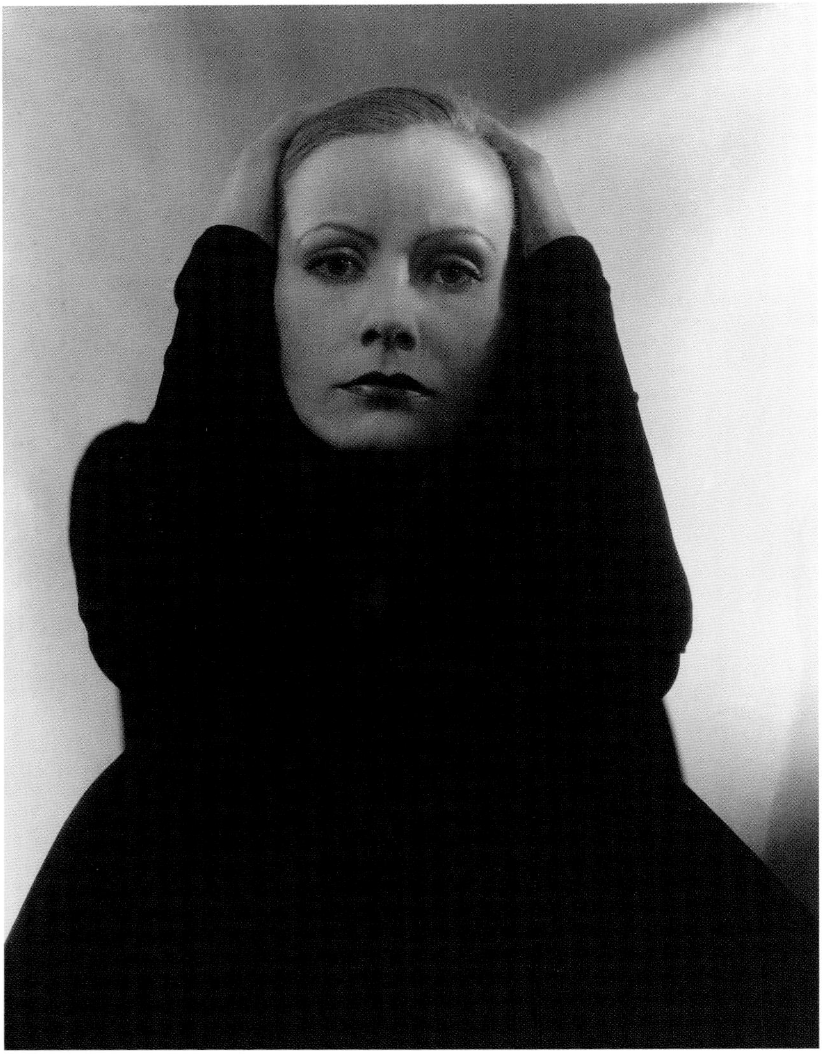

'[The photographer is the] only image-maker who begins with his picture completed. His emotions, his knowledge, and his native talent are brought into focus and fixed beyond recall the moment the shutter of his camera has closed.'

Everyone thinks they are a photographer, just because they have a camera – or now, a smartphone. Taking a picture is as simple as pointing the automatic apparatus at the scene and pressing the button. Or is it? As the master American photographer and editor Edward Steichen noted, photography is a 'medium of formidable contradictions. It is both ridiculously easy and almost impossibly difficult.' He pointed out the contradiction that although 'its technical rudiments can readily be mastered by anyone with a few simple instructions' the challenge lies in fixing the moment forever in the frame. Unlike an artist, who 'begins with a blank surface and gradually brings his conception into being', Steichen noted that the photographer is the 'only image-maker who begins with his picture completed. His emotions, his knowledge, and his native talent are brought into focus and fixed beyond recall the moment the shutter of his camera has closed.' Being able to previsualize how the camera optics and controls will translate the three-dimensional world into two dimensions is a skill that needs to be practised and honed; you really need to know the controls of your camera inside out to be able to use them instinctively.

Search for every detail

Francis Frith *Egypt Temple*, 1858

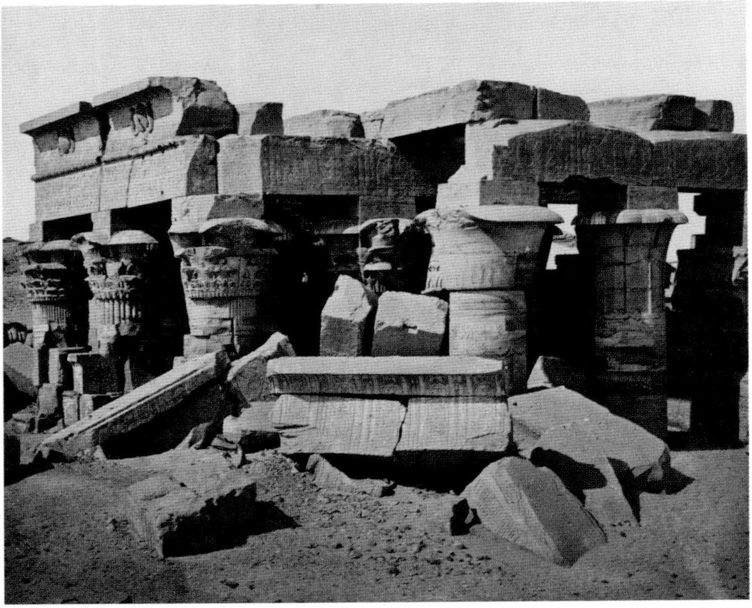

One of the greatest attributes of the camera is its ability to record every aspect of a scene in almost infinite resolution. The celebrated photographic explorer, Francis Frith, writing in 1859, pointed out that 'every stone, every little perfection, or dilapidation, the most minute detail, which, on an ordinary drawing, would merit no special attention, becomes, on a photograph, worthy of careful study'. He went on to explain that this level of accuracy offered the opportunity for the viewer to scan the resulting image at their leisure, noting that 'very commonly, indeed, we have observed that these faithful pictures have conveyed to ourselves more copious and correct ideas of detail than the inspection of the subjects themselves had supplied'. Putting your camera on a tripod, as Frith would have done, and looking very carefully through the lens to scour the frame for every minute detail will help you develop the skill to see as the camera sees.

Strip it back to the essentials

Richard Avedon Richard Avedon in his New York studio, 1975 (photograph by Jack Mitchell)

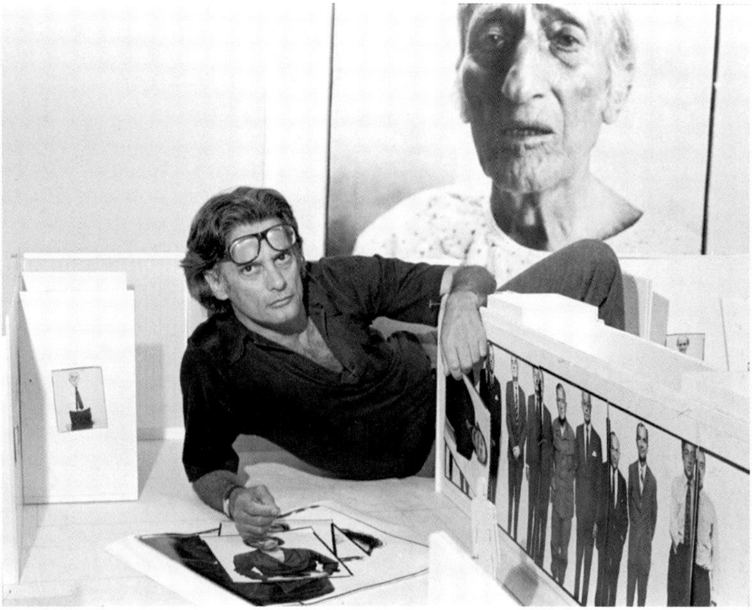

Richard Avedon had an extraordinary talent to reach into the core of a person through the simple act of gazing hard at their face. His approach was minimalist, stripped back to the essentials of the camera, the subject and the photographer, as he explained: 'I've worked out a series of no's. No to exquisite light, no to apparent compositions, no to the seduction of poses or narrative. And all those no's force me to the "yes." I have a white background. I have the person I'm interested in and the thing that happens between us.' The intensity of this encounter allowed him to find in people's expressions an expression of their character: as he simply but profoundly expressed it, 'Faces are the ledgers of our experience.' The discipline and simplicity of isolating a subject against a white background forces you to really try to connect with the sitter.

Use a shutter speed faster than the focal length of your lens

Paul Lowe

'Practise your slow shutter technique and you will be amazed at how low you can go.'

To avoid camera shake and blur, the general rule is to set your shutter speed to at least one stop faster than the focal length of the lens you are using. So, for example if you are shooting with a 135mm telephoto, use a shutter speed of at least 1/250th, and ideally higher. However, with careful bracing of your arms, or using something like a table to support you, and controlling your breathing, you can get away with slower speeds. This is especially true with wide-angle lenses that are more forgiving of camera shake. Practise your slow shutter technique and you will be amazed at how low you can go, especially if your lens has image stabilization built into it.

Work fast

Jacques-Henri Lartigue *My Cousin Bichonnade*, 1905

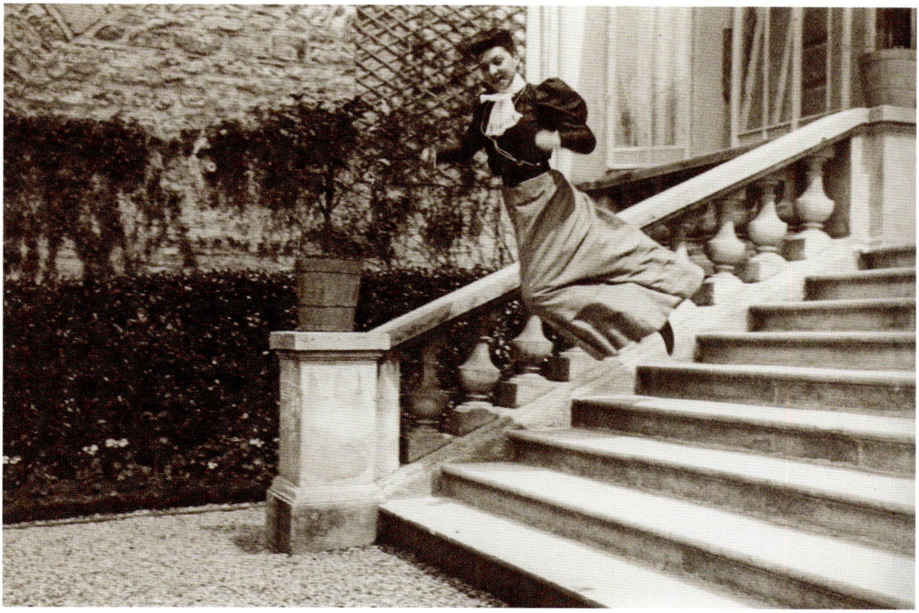

Being able to work a situation efficiently and quickly is a vital skill for photojournalists, street photographers, and sports photographers. The Frenchman Jacques-Henri Lartigue had an enviable ability to capture fast-moving action, especially given that he used a glass-plate camera and a Kodak Box Brownie. His golden rule was: 'Work fast. As for framing, composition, focus – this is no time to start asking yourself questions: you just have to trust your intuition and the sharpness of your reflexes.' Even if you are not an aspiring action photographer, shooting sports can be a very useful way to develop your reflexes, as can working in crowded situations like festivals or fairs where people are constantly on the move. Also try shooting while you yourself are moving, so that you are constantly having to adjust focus and composition while traversing space.

Be patient

Alfred Stieglitz *Winter, Fifth Avenue*, 1893

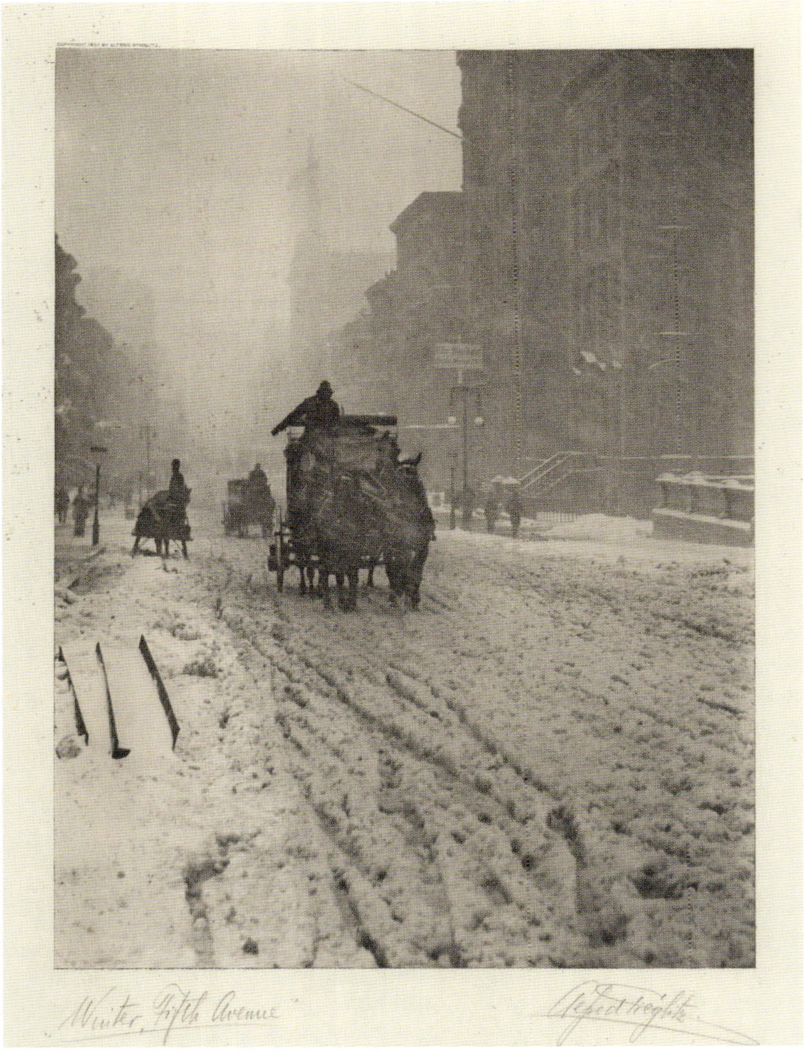

'In order to obtain pictures by means of the hand camera it is well to choose your subject, regardless of figures, and carefully study the lines and lighting. After having determined upon these watch the passing figures and await the moment in which everything is in balance; that is, satisfies your eye. This often means hours of patient waiting.'

Alfred Stieglitz was one of the leading proponents of photography as an art form, and he extolled the virtues of patience in writing about one of his most celebrated images. 'In order to obtain pictures by means of the hand camera it is well to choose your subject, regardless of figures, and carefully study the lines and lighting. After having determined upon these watch the passing figures and await the moment in which everything is in balance; that is, satisfies your eye. This often means hours of patient waiting. My picture, *Fifth Avenue, Winter* is the result of a three hours' stand during a fierce snow-storm on February 22nd 1893, awaiting the proper moment. My patience was duly rewarded. Of course, the result contained an element of chance, as I might have stood there for hours without succeeding in getting the desired pictures.'

Walk a lot

Alex Webb *View from a Barbershop near Taksim Square*, 2001

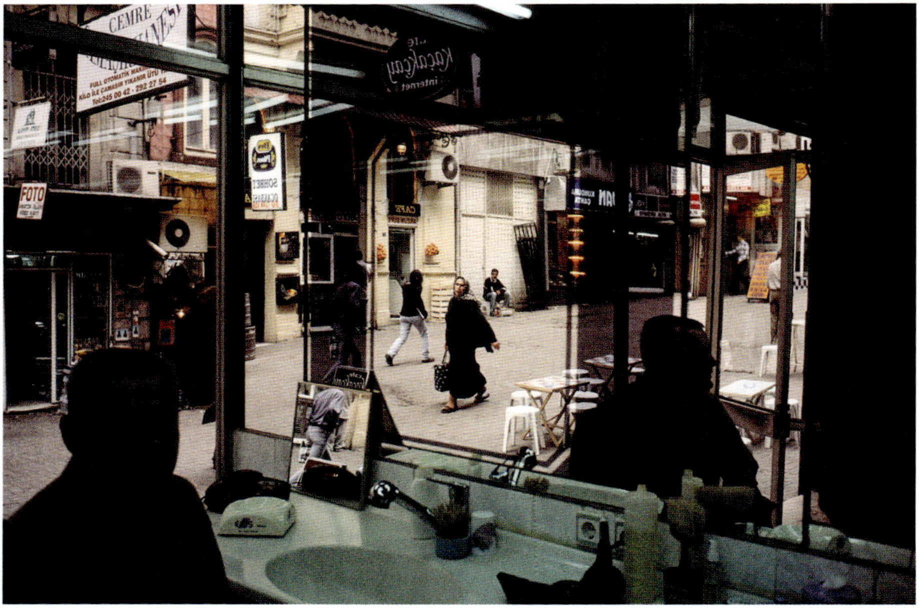

One of the greatest exponents of colour photography, Alex Webb has a deceptively simple methodology, as he explains: 'I only know how to approach a place by walking. For what does a street photographer do but walk and watch and wait and talk, and then watch and wait some more, trying to remain confident that the unexpected, the unknown, or the secret heart of the known awaits just around the corner.' Webb opens himself up to the process of being on the street, explaining that unlike 'traditional photojournalists who arrive with an idea of what they are going to produce or what the editor wants' he prefers to 'approach a subject very much as a street photographer and a wanderer, without preconceptions. I try to leave it extremely intuitive and exploratory.' Adopt Webb's philosophy, and think of yourself as a *flâneur* seeking those surreal and unexpected moments that reveal something of the character and culture of a place in a way that could not be preordained or predicted.

Innovate

Alexey Brodovitch *Harper's Bazaar* layout meeting, 1952 (photograph by Walter Sanders)

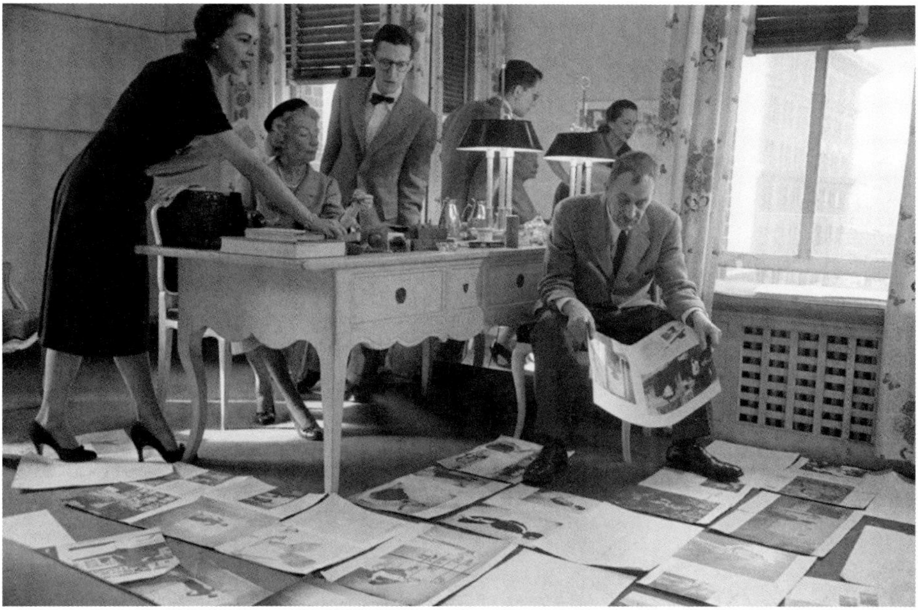

Alexey Brodovitch was one of the most influential figures in modern photography, who brought an innovative and fresh vision to his role as art director of the fashion magazine *Harper's Bazaar* from 1934 to 1958. He was also a hugely respected teacher, with his students including Diane Arbus, Eve Arnold, Richard Avedon, Lisette Model, Garry Winogrand and Tony Ray-Jones. His advice to photographers he assigned was simple: 'Astonish me!' He recognized that a lot of photography had become formulaic and repetitive, noting that 'the disease of our age is this boredom and a good photographer must successfully combat it. The only way to do this is by invention – by surprise.' Follow his guidance that 'When you look into your camera, if you see an image you have ever seen before, don't click the shutter', and seek out your own unique personal response to the scene: don't slavishly copy others.

Form and content are indivisible

Henri Cartier-Bresson *Brussels*, 1932

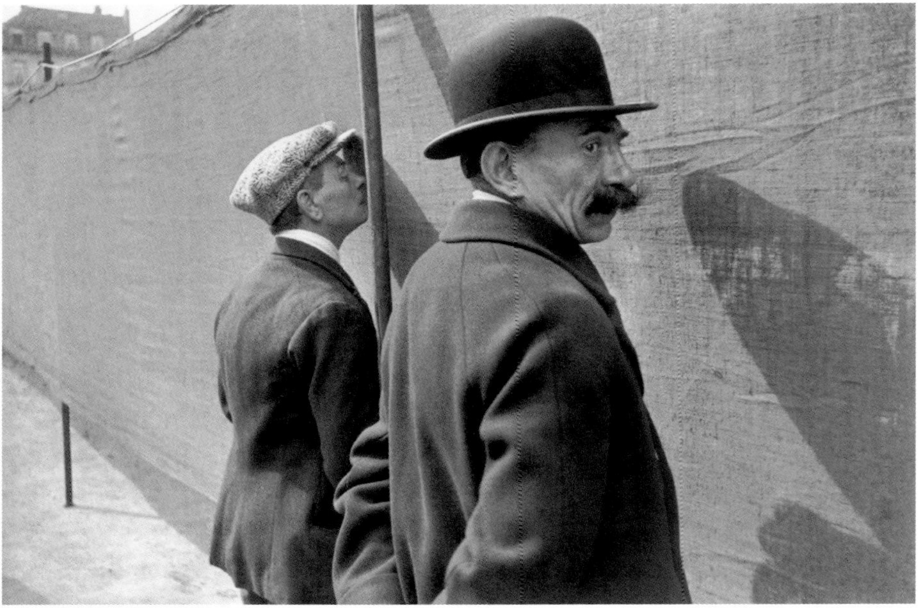

Originally titled *Images à la Sauvette* ('Images on the Run'), Cartier-Bresson's book *The Decisive Moment* is widely considered to be one of the most important photobooks of the twentieth century. Described by Robert Capa as 'a Bible for photographers', the book encapsulated Cartier-Bresson's humanistic aesthetic.

'To me, photography is the simultaneous recognition, in a fraction of a second, of the significance of an event, as well as of a precise organization of forms which give that event its proper expression. I believe that through the act of living, the discovery of oneself is made concurrently with the discovery of the world around us which can mould us, but which can also be affected by us. A balance must be established between these two worlds – the one inside us and the one outside us. As the result of a constant reciprocal process, both these worlds come to form a single one. And it is this world that we must communicate. But this takes care only of the content of the picture. For me, content cannot be separated from form. By form, I mean the rigorous organization of the interplay of surfaces, lines and values. It is in this organization alone that our conceptions and emotions become concrete and communicable. In photography, visual organization can stem only from a developed instinct.'

The best camera is the one you have with you

Ed Kashi Ed Kashi shooting with his iPhone, Saint-Brieuc, France, 2016

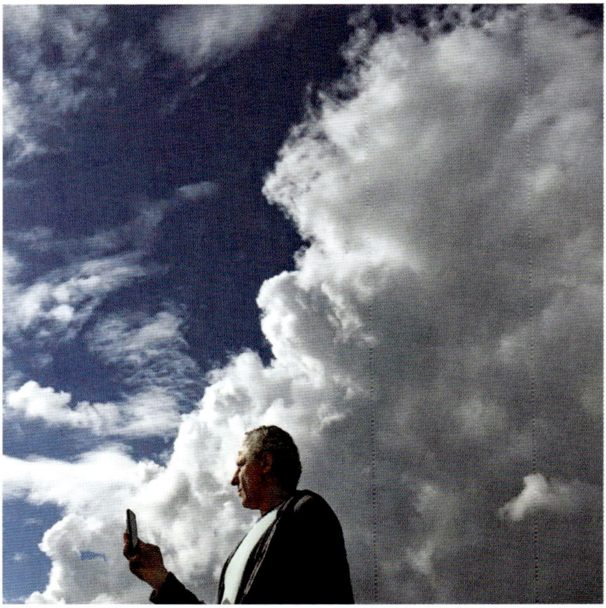

Modern smartphones have sensors that more than equal the best digital SLRs of a generation ago, and can produce very high-quality results. Ed Kashi uses his phone regularly, reminding us that 'with mobile photography you always have a camera in your pocket. Smartphones today are powerful tools for creating both stills and video of high quality.' They also offer advantages over conventional cameras in that they are more discreet and therefore they 'can also be an effective tool when trying to stay low profile'. He advises that you should 'always keep your phone charged and with enough space to capture images, especially if you get the chance to be a citizen journalist, but also just to capture daily life'. Smartphones are now fully capable of professional-quality results, so don't dismiss them as just for selfies and snapshots.

Learn to master flash

Paul Lowe *Chechen Women Praying on the Road Facing Russian Soldiers in Order to Stop their Advance on the City of Grozny*, 1994

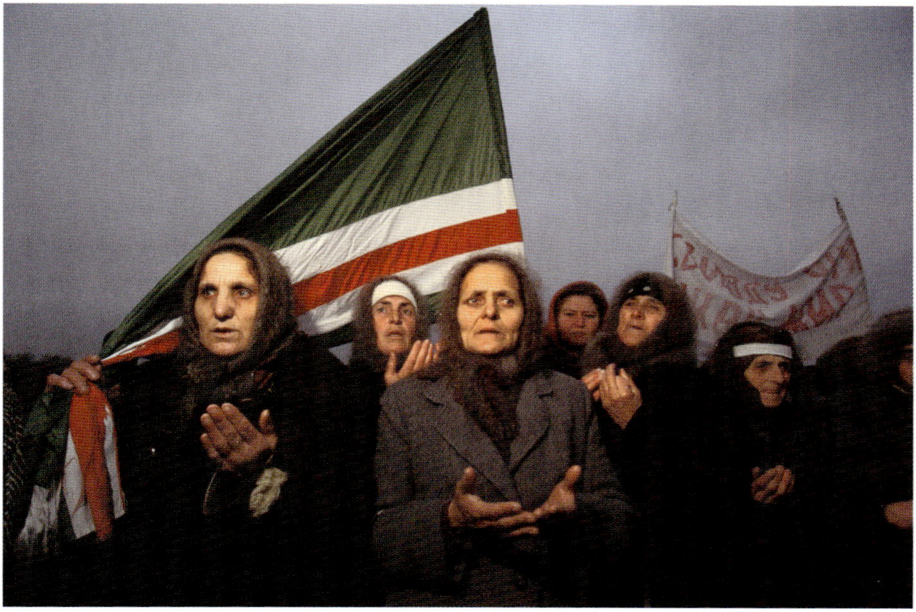

Sunshine in your pocket might be one way of describing the usefulness of flash, and is the key to understanding how to use it. Flash can be used to give a hard, directional light or a soft, gentle illumination. Try to avoid using the flash mounted directly on the camera, as it gives hard edges, is very contrasty, flattens out the subject and can cause red eye. Direct flash is useful, however, when it is used as a fill light to reduce the contrast in a backlit subject such as someone standing with their back to the sun. The best thing is to get the flash off the camera on a cord and use it from the side, holding the flash in one hand and the camera in the other. This will give an interesting, directional light that will give much more depth to the image. The other main way to use flash is to bounce it off the ceiling or walls of the room you are in. This gives a soft, overall light that fills the whole space. Learning how to use flash creatively will transform your ability to work in a wider range of lighting situations.

Being a Photographer

Find pictures everywhere

Elliott Erwitt *USA, New York City*, 1953

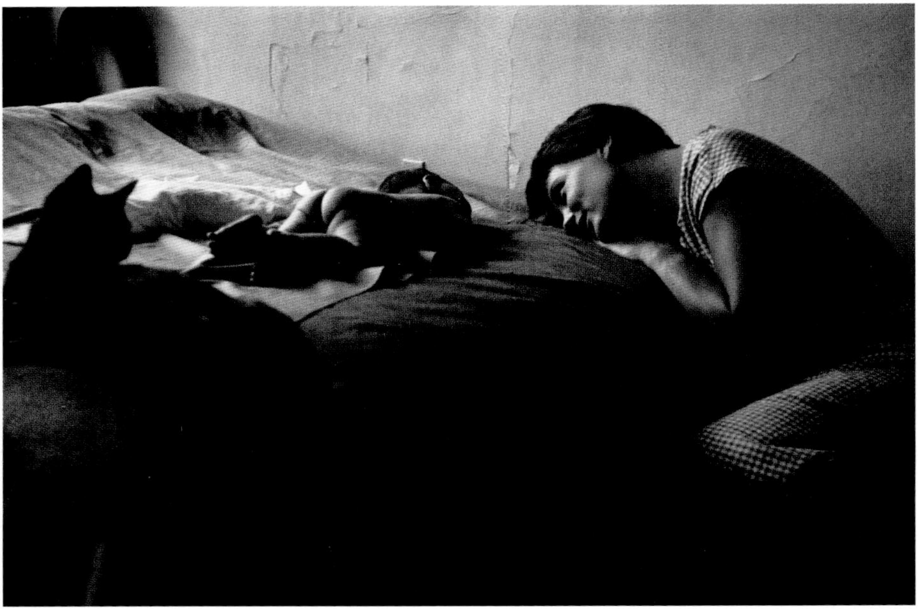

Erwitt is one of the greatest proponents of the deceptively simple act of photographic observation, remarking that for him 'it's just seeing – at least the photography I care about. You either see or you don't see.' His advice is to remain open to the infinite potential of the everyday, arguing that 'you can find pictures anywhere. It's simply a matter of noticing things and organizing them. You just have to care about what's around you and have a concern with humanity and the human comedy.'

Erwitt's work is worthy of careful study to see how he is able to find the human element in almost any situation, no matter how banal. Really push yourself to think about the world around you in terms of connections between the elements of the frame, finding juxtapositions and contrasts that create meaning.

Break through barriers

Martine Franck *France, Provence. Town of Le Brusc. Pool Designed by Alain Capeilleres*, 1976

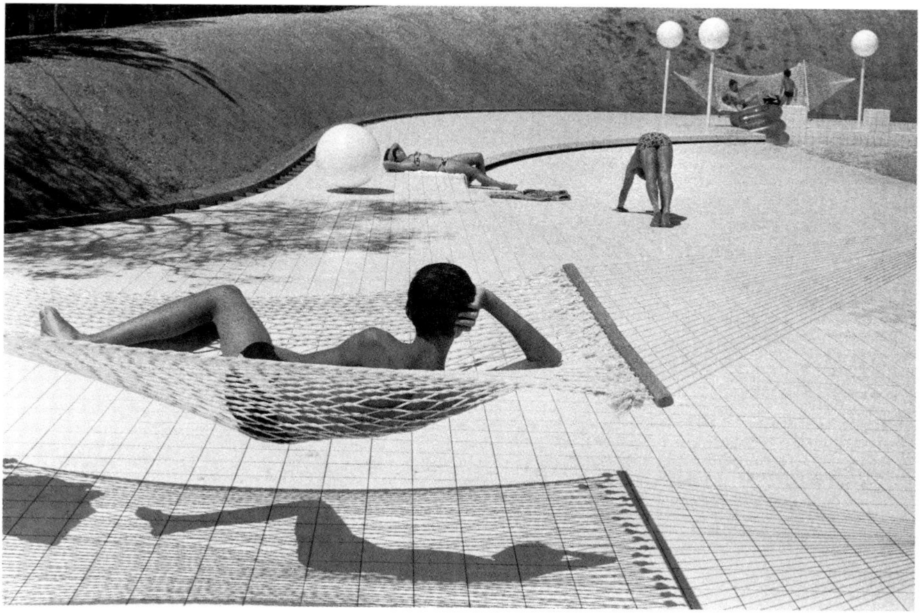

The Magnum photographer Martine Franck used photography as a way to overcome her shyness, recalling that she 'found talking to people difficult; a camera in hand gave me a function, a reason to be somewhere, a witness, but not an actor'. She explains how photography can be a vehicle to break down barriers:

'The camera is in itself a frontier, a barrier of sorts that one is constantly breaking down so as to get closer to the subject. In doing so, you step over your limits; there is a sense of daring, of going beyond, of being rude, of wanting to be invisible. To cross on to the other side, you can only get there by momentarily forgetting yourself, by being receptive to others; hence, as a photographer, I am in two different worlds at once. That is all I can really say about what I feel when photographing – the rest remains in the domain of the unconscious. Transgression is the word I have been searching for all along.'

Collaborate with your sitter

Aletheia Casey *Ella in Callala Bay*, 2018

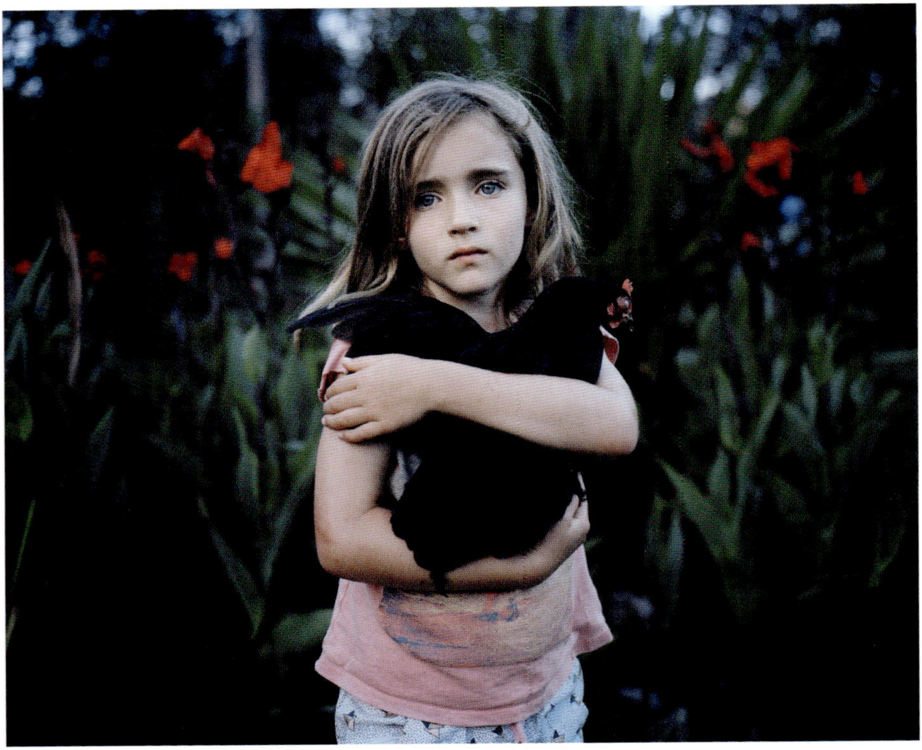

‘Humans unconsciously mimic each other – from facial expressions to moods and body language. Children do this with parents and carers, and adults also unconsciously ‘copy’ the facial expressions and body language of others. This is particularly true in the process of portraiture. […] As a photographer, you need to be aware that the sitter will unintentionally and unconsciously mimic you. A portrait is about the relationship between the photographer and the sitter. A successful portrait is a collaboration, where aspects of you are reflected within the sitter, and where, if you have the insight, you can reach parts of a person often kept hidden.’

Aletheia Casey is an accomplished portrait photographer who uses composition, colour and framing to create powerful character studies with a deep psychological connection to her subjects. She explains how the interaction between photographer and sitter is vital to making a successful portrait.

Take sides

Danny Lyon *Demonstration Turned Violent as Police Forcibly Remove Protestors and Use Tear-gas*, 1964

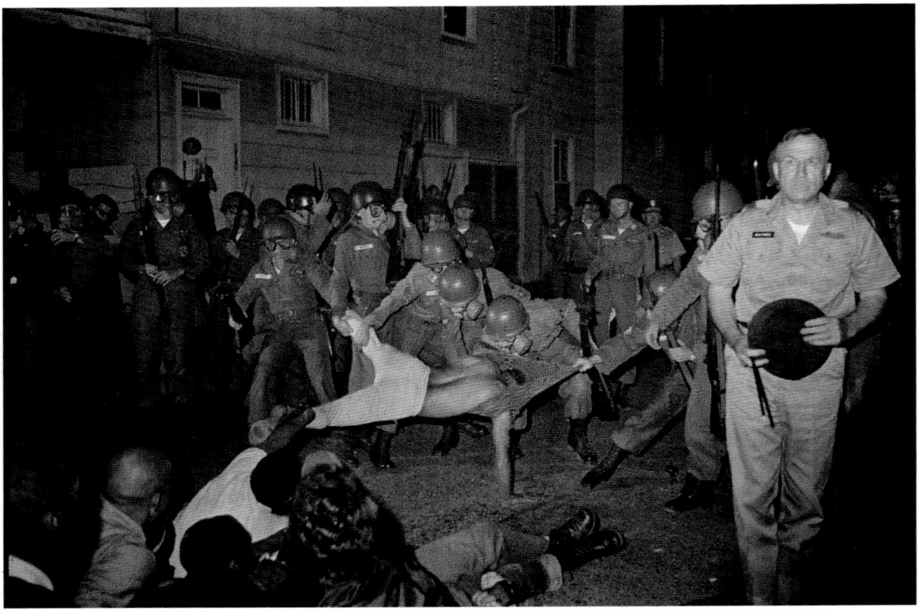

Danny Lyon was the first staff photographer for the Student Nonviolent Coordinating Committee (SNCC), one of the most significant American civil rights organizations of the 1960s. His unflinching coverage of the struggle against segregation and for the rights of African Americans was a major landmark in committed advocacy photography. Lyon was often in the thick of the protests, but did not stand on the sidelines. Instead, he insisted that the 'most unsafe place to be, whether people are using rocks or bullets, is between the lines. You must choose a side, if for no other reason than to have a firm spot on which to stand and a moment's peace to focus.' He also remarked: 'I feel totally responsible for what I see. I feel totally responsible for what I photograph.' Think carefully about your own politics when working in this field, be aware of your prejudices and preconceptions, but also allow what you believe is ethically right to guide your alignment.

Always expect the unexpected

Louie Palu *Kandahar, Afghanistan*, from *Front Towards Enemy*, 2017

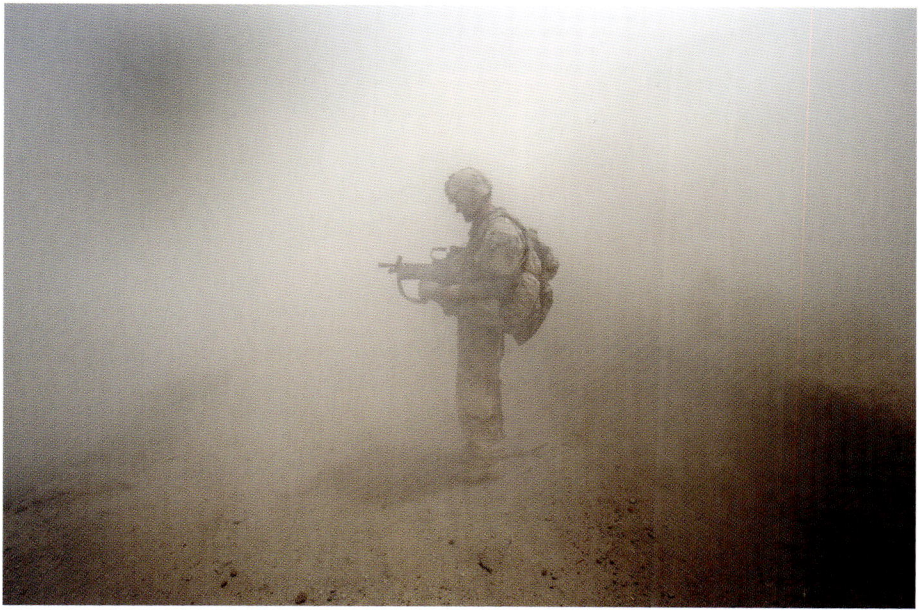

Louie Palu is a Canadian documentary photographer and film-maker known for covering social-political issues, including war and human rights. He covered the war in Kandahar, Afghanistan, between 2006 and 2010 and the drug war on the US–Mexico border between 2011 and 2012. He writes:

'The thing I plan for the most before and during an assignment is what will happen when everything goes wrong. First, how will I get my photography back on track and second, how I will keep my morale high and continue to nurture the creative side when things don't go as planned or there is a major unexpected roadblock. Believe me, in a war zone things going wrong is a daily event. In fact some of my best images have come out of adversity but then having a plan to correct the problem.'

Play with preconceptions

Philip-Lorca diCorcia *Brent Booth; 21 Years Old; Des Moines, Iowa; $30*, 1990

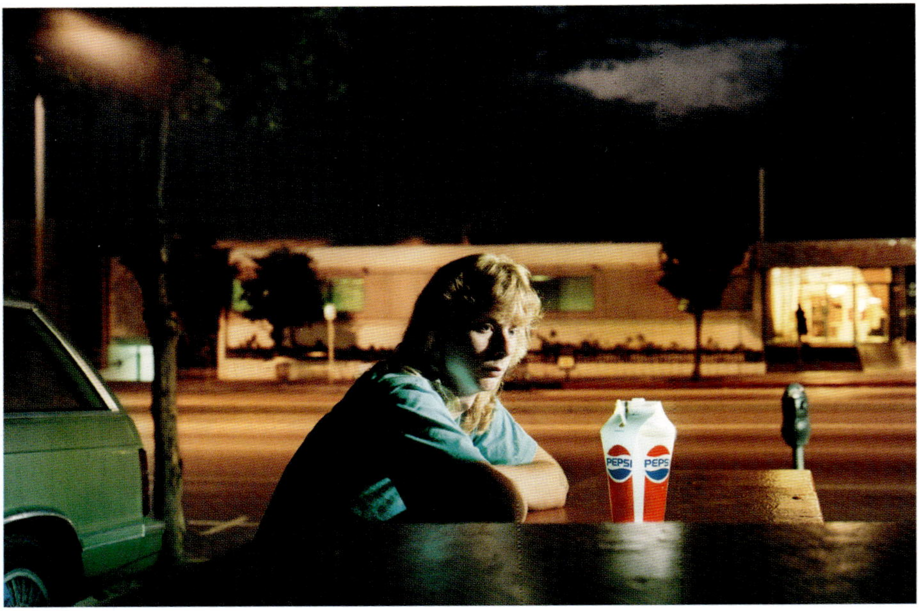

Philip-Lorca diCorcia's work balances on the tightrope between reality and fiction, with his images drawing on a range of visual and psychological sources to create complex fables about the human condition. He actively plays with the presumptions and preconceptions of the visual grammar of the medium, and then subverts them, so what we see is not quite what we get. His observation that 'photography is a foreign language everyone thinks he speaks' reflects on the contradiction that it appears on the surface to be a deceptively simple act yet is a complex and nuanced practice that has a complex set of codes and structures. He explains how 'photography . . . unites the obvious and the unconscious at the level of the liminal – the border between what we see and what we suspect'. His work speaks to the way in which the photograph can tap into a space between the word and the image, creating layers of meaning and interpretation that often remain difficult to articulate but are undoubtedly present.

Break the rules one at a time

Sara Terry *Prayer for the Dead, Srebrenica Widow*, 2015

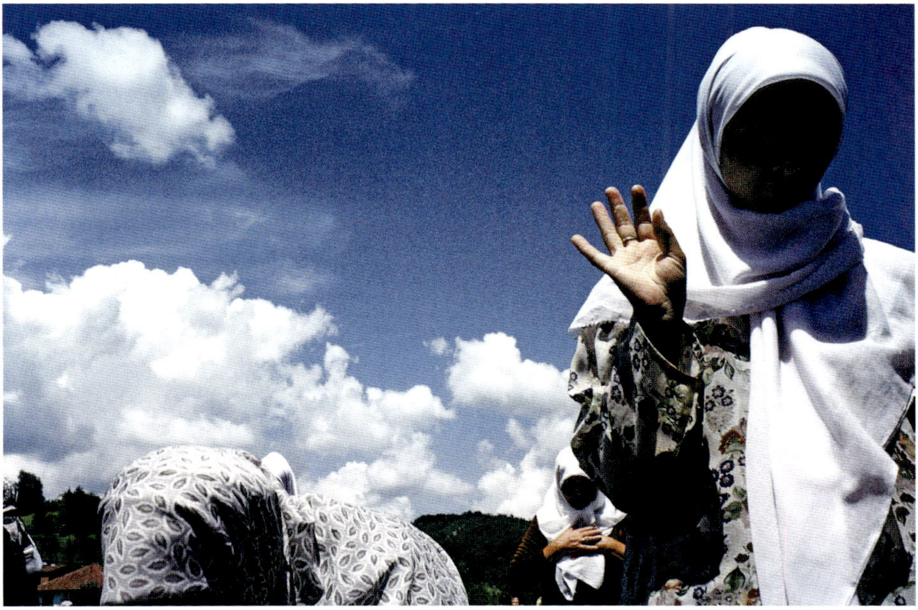

Sara Terry came into photography and documentary film-making from journalism after a long career as a writer, and argues that you have to learn how to master the basics of the craft pf photography to then allow you to find your own unique personal voice:

'Learn the rules. Learn composition and the rule of thirds, and how to properly manually expose and focus. Study the masters – when you find a photo that intrigues you, spend time with it. Think about where the photographer had to stand to make that picture, what obstacles they might have had to overcome, the source of the light and what it does to the frame. Live the rules until you have integrated them into your practice, into the ways that you see and make photos. And then break them. One at a time. See what happens – and then choose for yourself the rules you keep and the new ones you create.'

Look inside yourself

Roger Ballen *Dresie and Casie, Twins, Western Transvaal*, 1993

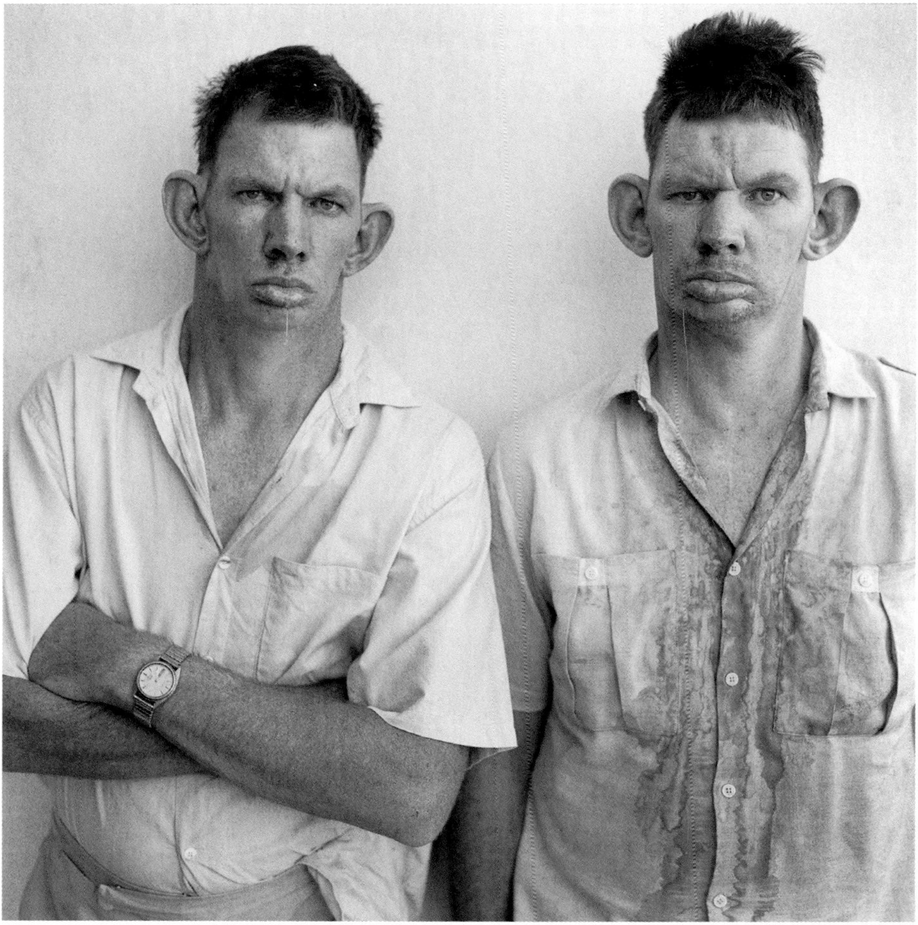

‘Because photography is such an easy medium to master technically, especially with today’s cameras, people don’t realize that it’s not just being able to pick up a camera.’

Roger Ballen’s powerful psychological studies confront the viewer with troubling questions about South African society. However, he argues strongly that the images emerge from his own desires as much as from his subjects, feeling that his ‘purpose in taking photographs over the past forty years has ultimately been about defining myself. It has been fundamentally a psychological and existential journey.’ He feels that the photographer needs to reflect on their own experiences and motivations to fuel their work, instructing us of the ‘need to travel deep inside yourself to create a good picture’. The apparent simplicity of the technology masks the real complexity of picture making: ‘Because photography is such an easy medium to master technically, especially with today’s cameras, people don’t realize that it’s not just being able to pick up a camera. When I lift that camera up to take a picture, I’ve gone through thousands of steps to get to that point. That’s what you’re really seeing; it’s a complex view of the world, through my imagination, through my experiences’.

Photograph with all your ideology

Sebastião Salgado *Refugees at the Korem Camp, Ethiopia*, 1984

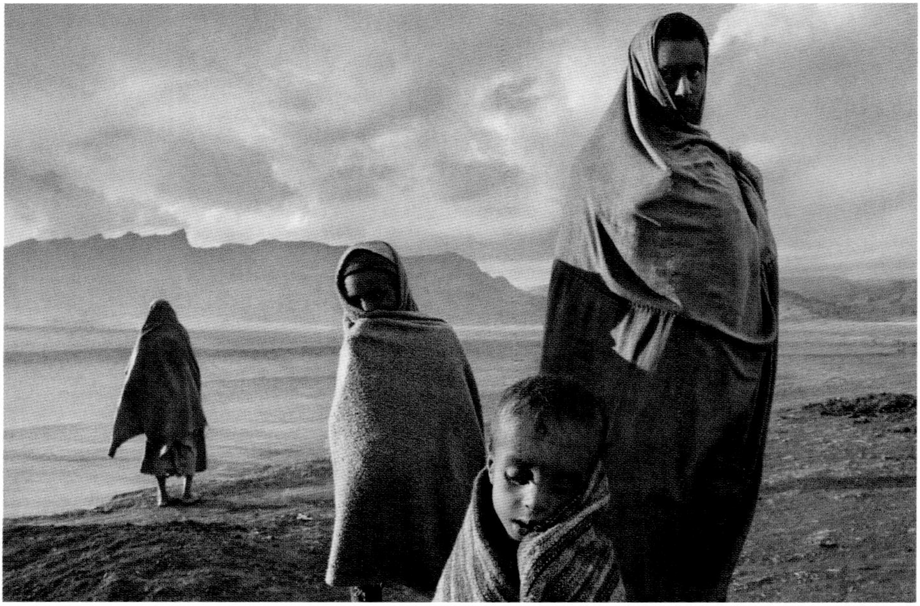

Over the last four decades, Sebastião Salgado has become one of the world's leading documenters of the impact social and economic change has had on both the human and natural world. Throughout all of this, he has sought to be respectful of his subjects. 'If you take a picture of a human that does not make him noble, there is no reason to take this picture.' He argues that you have to have a strong point of view, an ideology, and that this will come through in your work, but there is a point at which the work becomes collaborative: 'When you spend more time on a project, you learn to understand your subjects. There comes a time when it is not you who is taking the pictures. Something special happens between the photographer and the people he is photographing. He realizes that they are giving the pictures to him.' The act of photography is an exchange between you and your subject: allow them the space to express themselves as dignified human beings.

Work at the boundaries

Sally Mann Photographer Sally Mann relaxes with her dog 'Honey', 2004 (photograph by Michael Williamson)

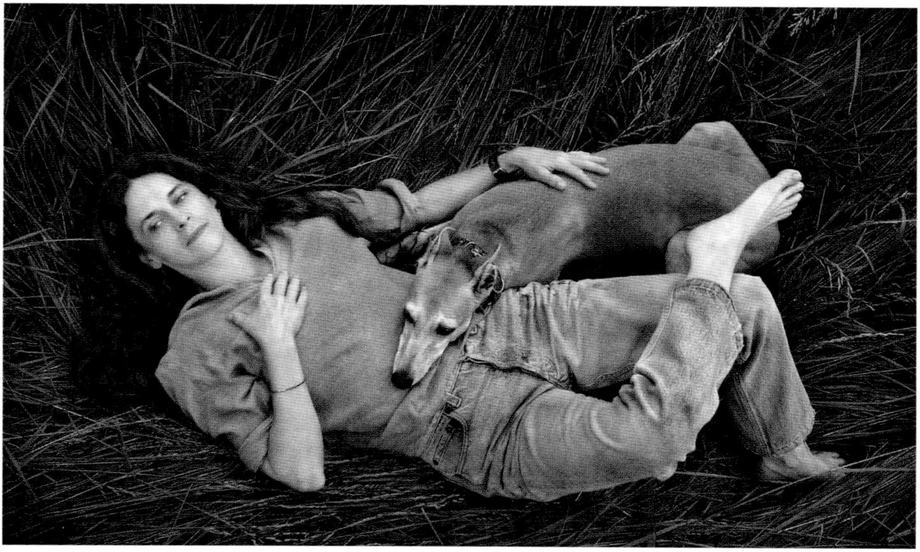

Strong emotionally and psychologically charged pictures often come from moments where the photographer's presence has intervened into the situation perhaps a little bit harder than it should in order to get that heightened energy into the image. In her intimate and intense body of work, Sally Mann acknowledges this tension by declaring that 'exploitation lies at the root of every great portrait, and all of us know it. Even the simplest picture of another person is ethically complex.' Indeed, it is exactly in this working at the boundaries that the encounter can generate the most powerful photographs, as she argues: 'if transgression is at the very heart of photographic portraiture, then the ideal outcome – beauty, communion, honesty, empathy – mitigates the offense'. It takes experience in working closely with others to hone our sense of how far it is appropriate to push a situation, but you often have to go that bit further than you might think appropriate to get the best pictures.

Finding your personal vision is hard

Chuck Close

'I think that while photography is the easiest medium in which to be competent it is probably the hardest one in which to develop an idiosyncratic personal vision. It is the hardest medium in which to separate yourself from all those other people who are doing reasonably good stuff and to find a personal voice, your own vision, and to make something that is truly, memorably yours and not someone else's. A recognized signature style of photography is an incredibly difficult thing to achieve . . . Photography is not an easy medium. It is, finally, perhaps the hardest of them all.'

Chuck Close bridges the worlds of fine art and photography with his large-scale portraits, so is well qualified to comment on how difficult it can be to find your own unique style.

Find the extremes

Lauren Greenfield *Jackie and Friends with Versace Handbags at a Private Opening at the Versace Store, Beverly Hills*, 2007

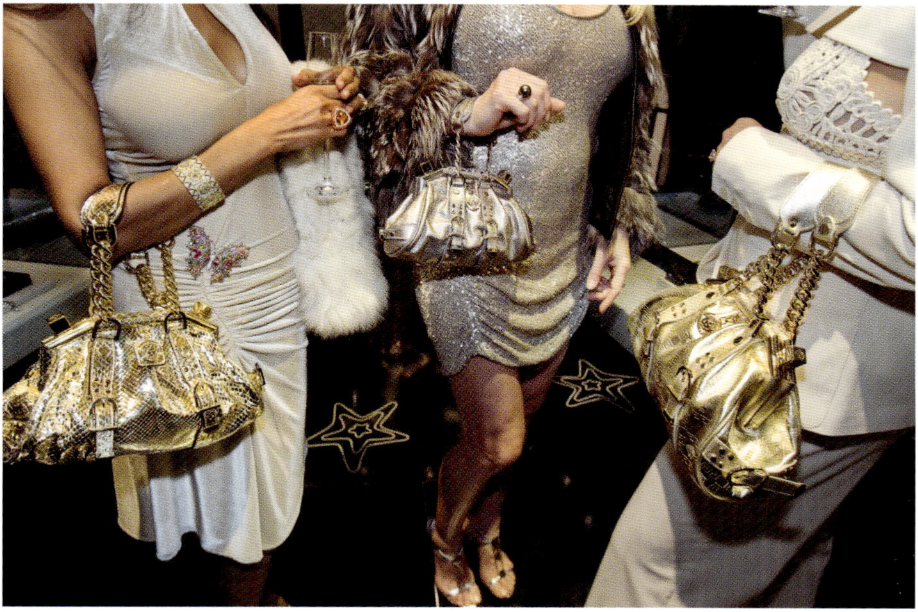

Photography often depicts those living on the edges of humanity, whether rich or poor. For the American documentary photographer Lauren Greenfield, this is a successful strategy, using them as a mirror to reflect on the rest of society. She explains how 'I've often used the extremes in my work to comment on the mainstream. I think that sometimes a subject that I'm working on, like popular culture, is so present all around us that they're hard to see. It's like: How do you see the air you breathe? How do you see how it affects you?' She has explored the lives of the wealthy in the United States, and has developed an aesthetic that combines saturated colours and flash to highlight the excess of their lives. She is 'constantly trying to deconstruct what I see and to show its beauty and its attraction. I use bright colours and strobes to get that full reflection. I want to acknowledge and reference the attraction of wealth. But I'm also looking for the layer that reveals how wealth doesn't fulfil its promise.'

Listen

Giles Duley *Shamah Darweesh, over 90 Years Old, from Homs*, 2016

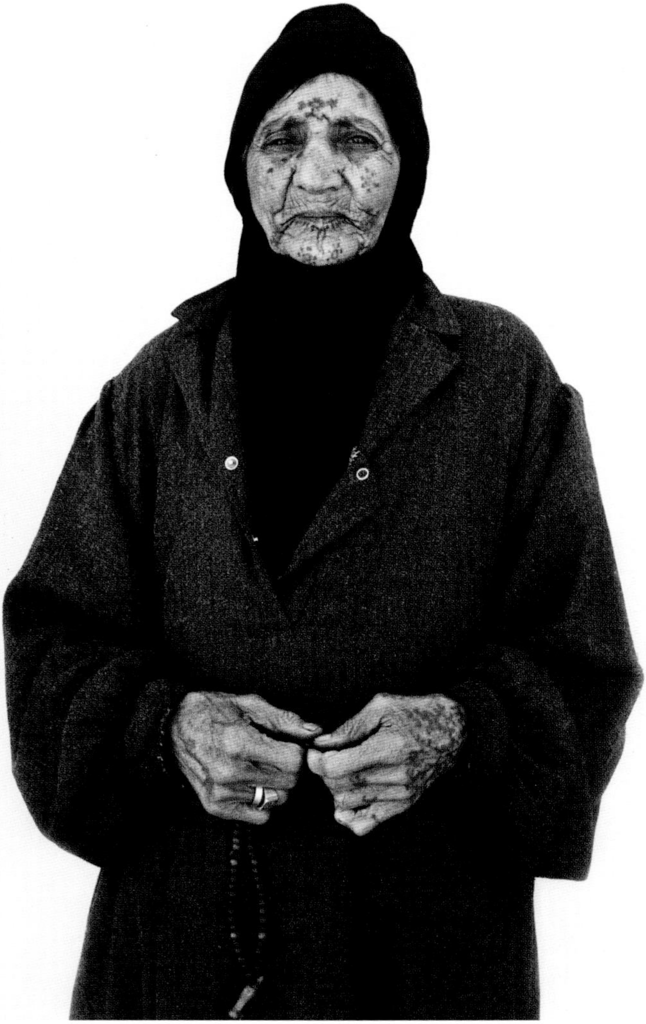

'Listen. It may be a strange thing to say to a photographer. But to really capture somebody's story, you must listen to it first. Too many photographers turn up and meet the person looking through the viewfinder, they already think they know what the image will be. For me that's wrong – I have to listen first, understand the story – then maybe I'll find a way to tell it. Don't make photographs because you think it's what others want to see – shoot what you love, what you are passionate about, what you know.'

In 2011, Giles Duley lost both legs and his left arm after stepping on an Improvised Explosive Device (IED) in Afghanistan whilst photographing those caught up in the conflict. He was told he would never walk again and that his career was over. However, characteristically stubborn, Duley told his doctors 'I'm still a photographer,' and returned to work in Afghanistan less than eighteen months later. He has been working on a long-term project, *Legacies of War*, documenting post-conflict societies, and offers this heartfelt advice on how to photograph people in intimate situations.

Shoot what you love

Joe McNally *Thi Kim Phuc Phan and Son*, 1995

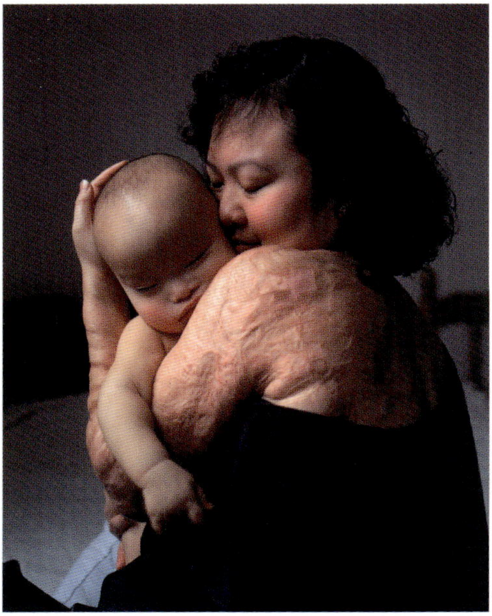

'Always remember to make room to shoot what you love. It's the only way to keep your heart beating as a photographer.'

The veteran photographer Joe McNally has shot a vast range of assignment photography, from photojournalism and news to sports to advertising and commercial assignments. From all of this experience, his key advice is to always ensure you create a space to photograph what you really care about. 'No matter how much crap you gotta plough through to stay alive as a photographer, no matter how many bad assignments, bad days, bad clients, snotty subjects, obnoxious handlers, wigged-out art directors, technical disasters, failures of the mind, body, and will, all the shouldas, couldas and wouldas that befuddle our brains and creep into our dreams, always remember to make room to shoot what you love. It's the only way to keep your heart beating as a photographer.'

Learn to let go

Maggie Steber *Haitian Soldiers Go after a Small Boy Trying to Steal a Box of Food Aid*, 1986

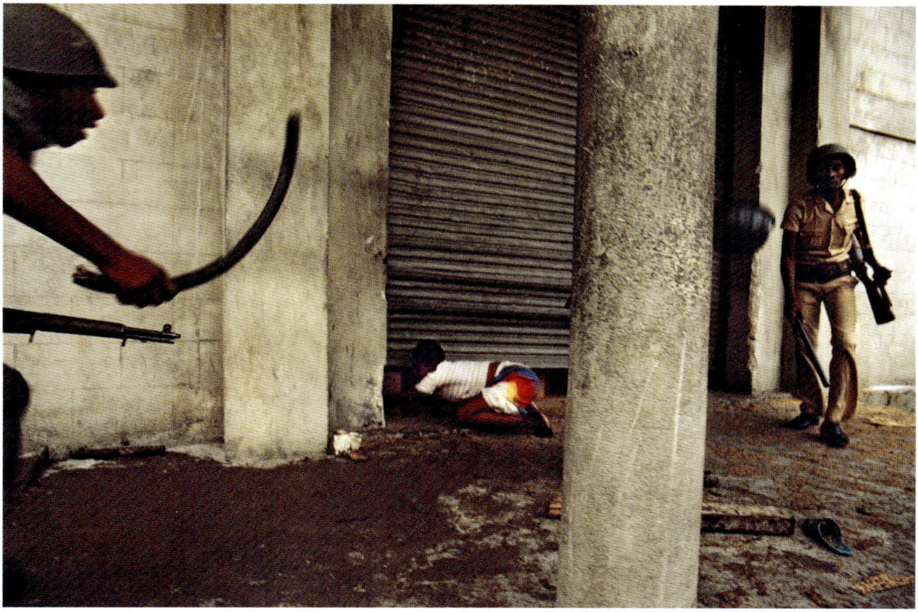

No matter how much we as photographers try to control our images, from how we frame and edit them, to what platforms we distribute and disseminate and publish them on, we have to accept that at a certain point we have to surrender our control over how the viewer will respond to them, and accept that they will create their own meanings and interpretations of them. This inevitability is well summed up by Maggie Steber, who observed that 'Photographs are like our children. We put the best of ourselves into them – the best of our vision, our minds, our hearts – and then we send them out into the world. At some moment, perhaps the moment we click the shutter, they are being released. From that moment on, they don't really belong to us any more.'

Six rules

Chris Steele-Perkins *Oxford Students under Hypnosis at Spring Ball*, 1989

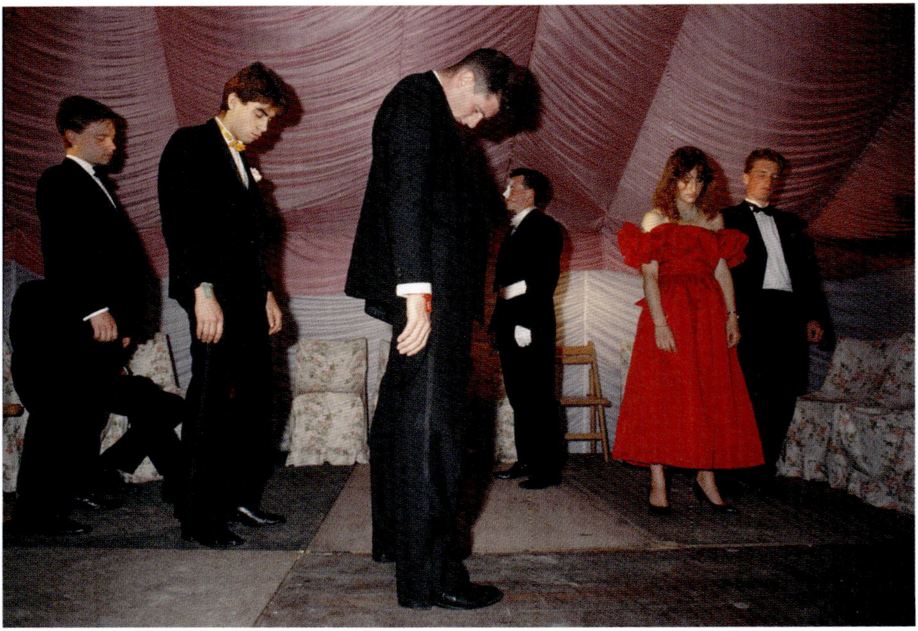

1 Never think photography is easy. It's like poetry: it's easy enough to write a few rhymes, but that's not all it takes to write a masterpiece.

2 Study photography and what other photographers have achieved. Learn from them but don't try to be the same as them.

3 Photograph things you really care about, not things you feel you ought to.

4 Take photographs in the way you feel is right, not the way you think you ought to.

5 Be open to criticism, it can be really helpful, but stick to your core values.

6 Take photographs, lots of them. Be depressed by them, take more. Hone your skills and get out in the world and interact.

Award-winning photojournalist and documentary photographer Chris Steele-Perkins has been a member of Magnum Photos since 1979 and offers this valuable advice to aspiring photographers.

Always carry your camera no matter what

Lara Jo Regan *School Girls, Los Angeles, California*, 1993

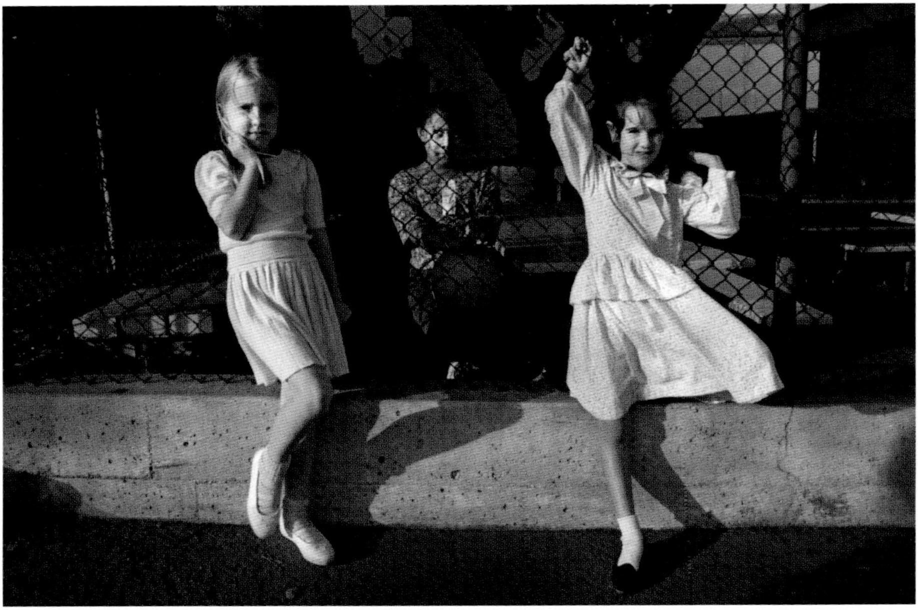

Lara Jo Regan's work combines painterly aesthetics with sociological observation, and she has turned her camera to a wide range of subjects, from a long-term documentary of Southern California to her pet dog, Mr Winkle, who became one of the world's first viral Internet sensations and achieved international cult popularity after she created a witty series of photographs of him posed in comic situations.

‘If you aspire to be a serious street photographer carry your camera with you everywhere, even if you’re not in the mood or it detracts from your outfit. Amazing moments typically present themselves at the most unexpected and inconvenient times. When they do, make a wholehearted effort to document them, no matter how tired, shy, lazy or preoccupied you feel. If you are driving during such sightings, park and drag yourself and your gear out of the car. Unless you figure out the mysteries of quantum physics, you will never be able to travel back in time for a second chance to capture what you saw. What photography has going for it that no other art form does is its relationship with time, its magical ability to freeze a moment so it can be shared with countless others. I’m still haunted by the sublime moments I skipped out on sanctifying. Now they live only in my mind, forever trapped.’

An image should always be critically informed

Gemma Marmalade *Seed Series (Green Fingered)*, 1976

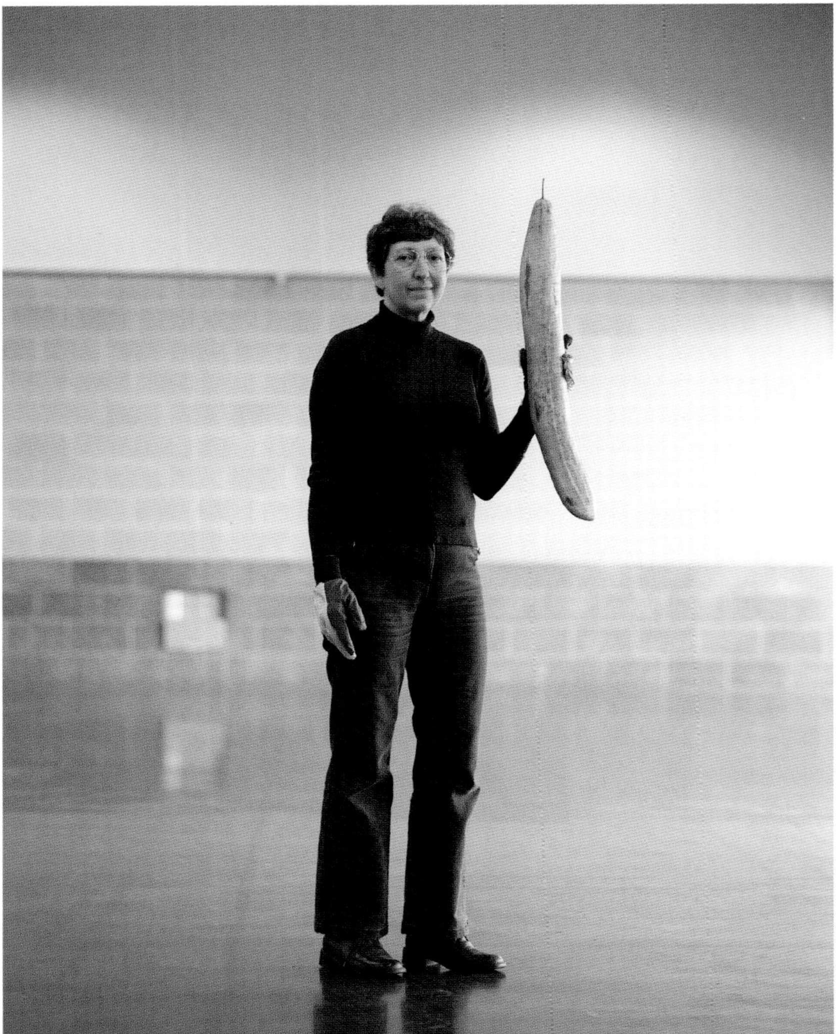

The photographer and educator Gemma Marmalade argues for the value of academic substance to bodies of photographic work.

'It is an important distinction that any image be fully understood in terms of where it sits in the context of politics, histories, philosophies and other cultural influences of which it is made. It is also of equal merit that any value attributed to it ought to evidence engagement with such matters. No image is made in a vacuum and the photographer's awareness and receptivity to the undeniable influences straddling over the frame is in direct correlation to its visual efficacy. Academic discussion of the image is often unfairly marginalized as elitist; somehow sabotaging instinctive creative process. Yet I find the symbiosis of tuning strategic academic research study with a process of responsive making an illuminating and ultimately satisfying process. The image is unconsciously infused by these authorities and often induces opportunity for innovation and originality. Only by standing on the shoulders of giants, as the metaphor suggests, does the vanguard of progress occur, visual or otherwise. Given the universality of visual communication, especially in an image-saturated world, the author bears a responsibility to use their platform with purpose both aesthetically and critically.'

Record the relationship

Susan Meiselas *Essex Junction, Vermont. 1973. Lena on the Bally Box*, 1973

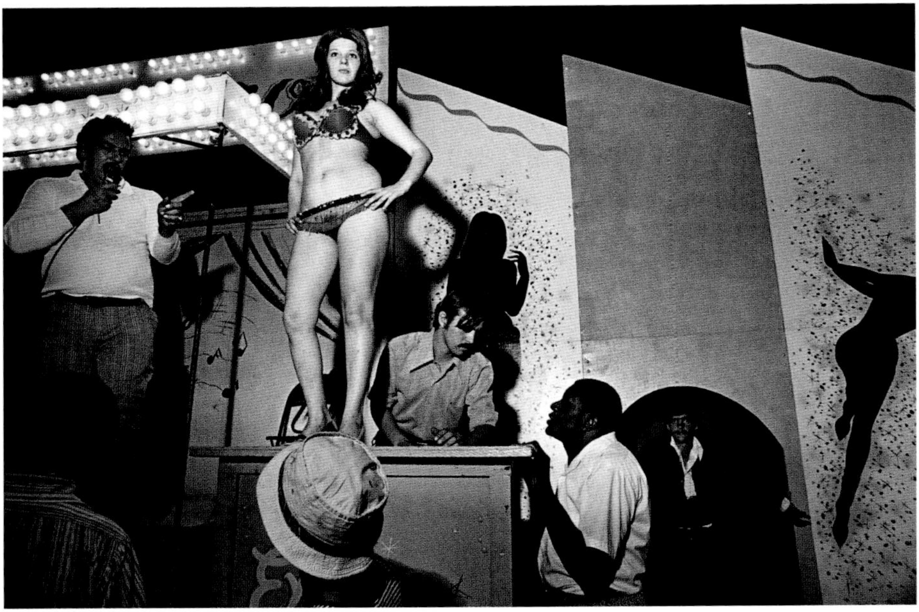

Susan Meiselas is one of the greatest documentary and photojournalistic photographers whose work spans decades of covering human rights issues. From her *Carnival Strippers* series in the 1970s to her epic project on the Kurds, she has been fascinated by the encounter between herself and the world, asserting that the 'camera is an excuse to be someplace you otherwise don't belong. It gives me both a point of connection and a point of separation'. She aligns herself as a storyteller who uses a camera, but seeks to expand from the visual to other forms of evidence, expressing that she is 'deeply interested in the photograph as a record of an encounter and enjoy putting myself in a timeline of image-makers, alongside other travellers, such as anthropologists, colonists, missionaries, even tourists'. Think about how you can expand the immediate moment of making the picture into a broader context that reveals more about the experience of being there to others.

Hear through your eyes

Paul Caponigro *Rock Wall No. 2*, 1977

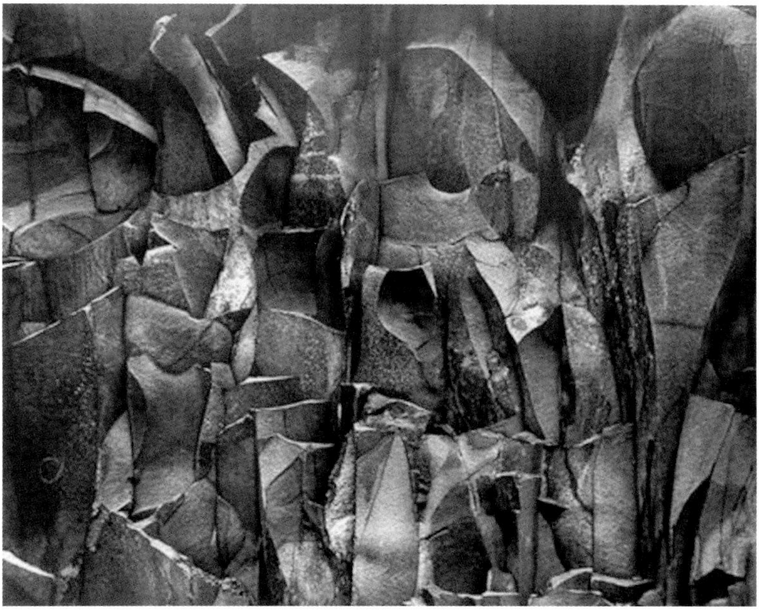

Paul Caponigro saw the creative impulse as rooted in the desire to 'make sense of random and often unrelated details', feeling that for him photography provided an 'intersection of time, space, light, and emotional stance'. He poetically expressed the relationship between the craft and technique of the photographic process and the expression of emotion, relating how he saw the 'materials of photography as being a type of terrain. Emulsions, liquid developers, silver salts, and fixers interact, and I construct a landscape that I need to first explore in my mind's eye if I am to make it manifest as an artful image in silver'. Following from this premise, he argued that if the photographer could 'recognize the life of the materials' in this way, it would open up the possibility of a heightened sense of awareness of the world, and enable them to 'hear through the eyes'.

Find a subject you care about

Mark Power *Scarborough*, from *The Shipping Forecast*, 1993

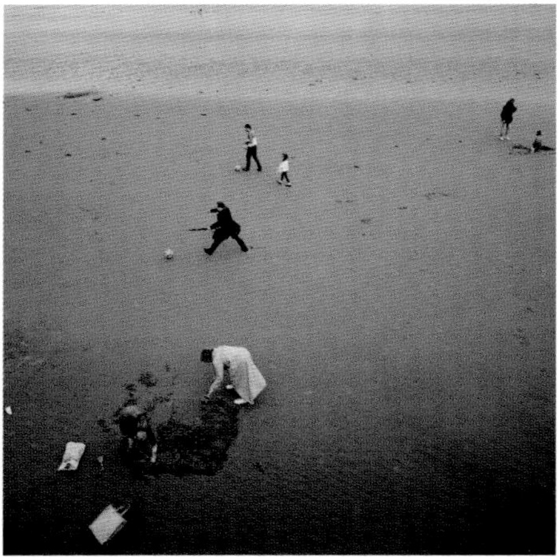

'If you have something to say, and even better you have an innovative way of saying it, then opportunities are out there.'

The Magnum photographer Mark Power believes that in today's competitive market although there are far more people trying to 'be photographers' than there were in previous generations, there are also far more opportunities. To stand out in the crowd, simply having 'good pictures' is no longer sufficient; today, he argues, 'it has to be about ideas, and about the intent of the work. If you have something to say, and even better you have an innovative way of saying it, then opportunities are out there.' Above all, you have to be passionate and committed to your project, and he urges photographers to 'find a subject you care about, something that moves you. Something which stirs your rawest emotions. And then have patience.'

Just do it

Chloe Dewe Mathews *A Young Woman Bathes in Crude Oil at the Sanatorium Town of Naftalan*, 2010

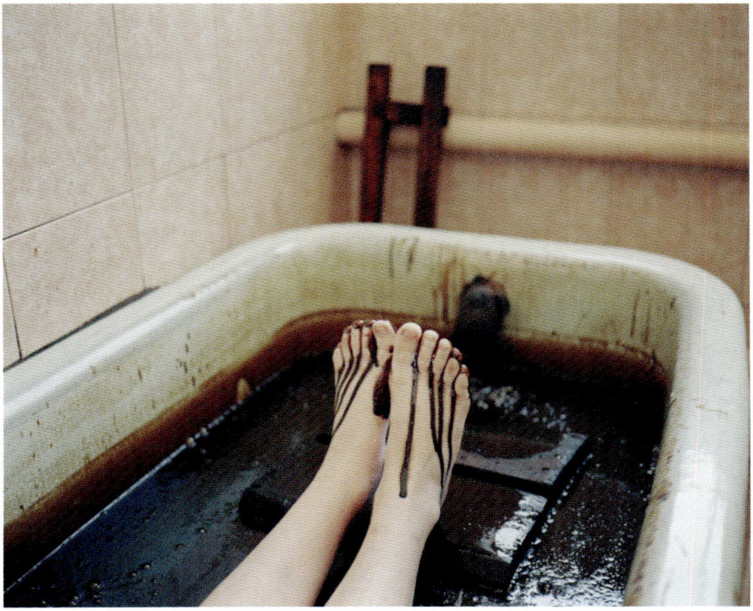

Chloe Dewe Mathews has worked on long-form documentary projects on Hassidic Jews, the Caspian Sea and the sites of executions of deserters from the First World War. Her advice on starting a large project is to simply throw yourself into the work, exhorting photographers to 'Just do it! Don't spend weeks and months chatting about what work you plan to do, considering if it's a good enough idea, because it is in making that the work evolves.' Her motivation comes from a sense of wanting to be surprised by the world, and she advises against having preset concepts before embarking on a project, as 'If you go into a project already with an agenda, you often miss the most interesting things that are happening.' Push yourself to commit to a project and just get shooting, and make yourself open to the serendipity of the world around you and the visual and storytelling opportunities it offers.

Put the camera down

Léonie Hampton *Glass Darkly #1*, from the series *Mend*, 2017

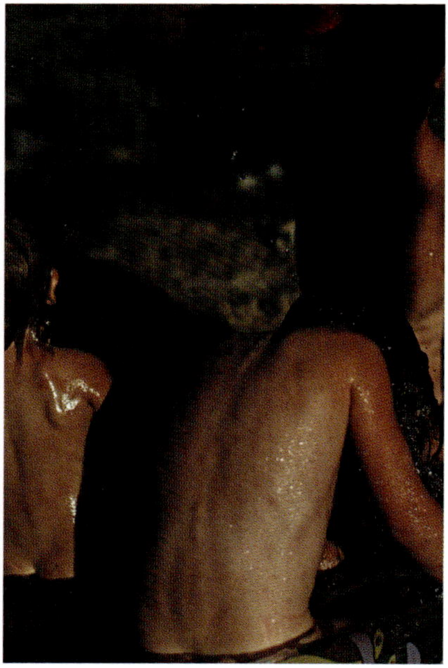

'Remember that photography is simply a tool to communicate what you feel, what you see and what you want to say.'

For more than a decade, Léonie Hampton has been documenting her relationship to her family, and their collective attempts to clear her mother's house, which had become overwhelmed by objects. Combining photography, film and sound, *In the Shadow of Things* is an attempt to 'navigate the tide of emotions that erupted when this landscape of possessions was disturbed'. In documenting this complex network of close relationships, she learnt to 'remember that photography is simply a tool to communicate what you feel, what you see and what you want to say'. There were times when she felt she could work freely and record what was happening, but others when she simply had to experience it without any barriers, and realized that 'sometimes it is best to put the camera down, be present and connect to what is there more deeply'.

Be curious

Eve Arnold *Marilyn Monroe*, 1960

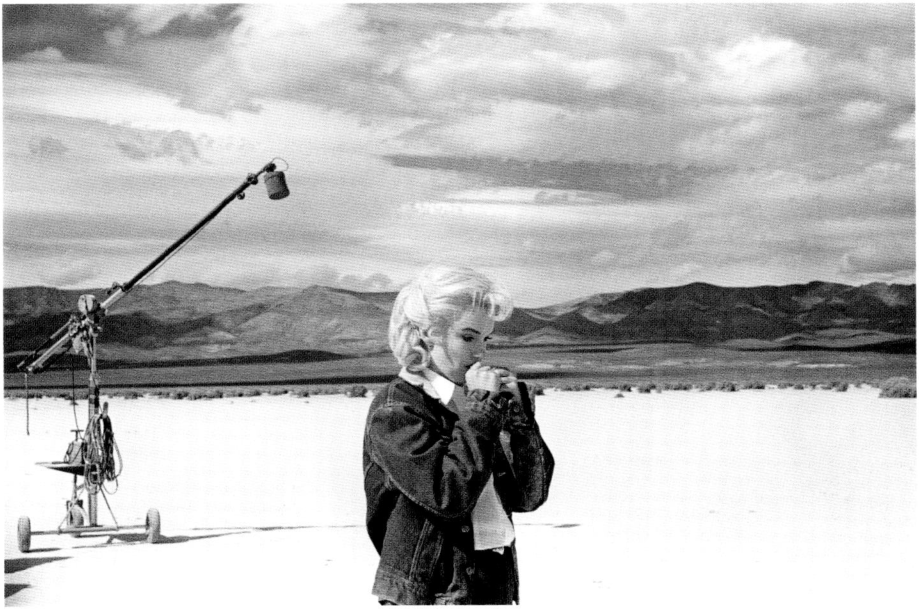

Eve Arnold's recommendation that an 'overwhelming curiosity and a good digestion' were the essential attributes to be a good photographer was deceptively simple. For Arnold, 'my passport was my camera', and it allowed her access to the most intimate moments in the lives of ordinary people and celebrities alike. Her friendship with Marilyn Monroe was the epitome of her working method, she saw the act of photography as an exchange between herself and a subject willing to open up for the camera, describing how what she tried to do was 'to involve the people I was photographing. To have them realize without saying so, that it was up to them to give me whatever they wanted to give me ... if they were willing to give, I was willing to photograph.' The camera can provide the opportunity to share extraordinary moments of connection between you and the world if you are both inquisitive and sensitive.

Figure out what you are about

Tina Barney *Family Commission with Snake*, 2007

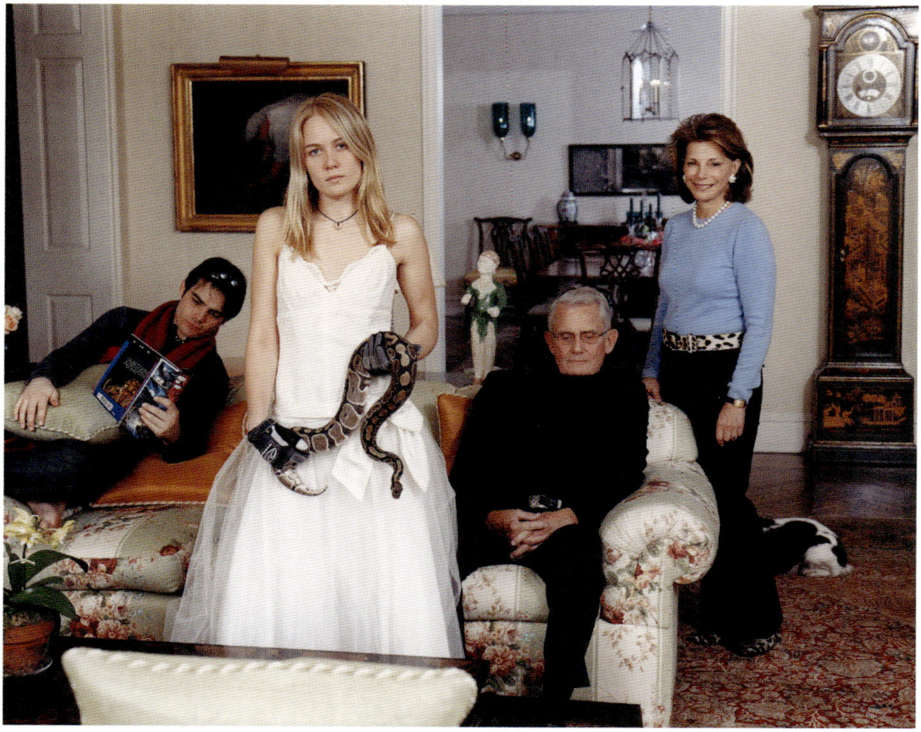

'I know now that before I take a picture I have to be sure how I feel about the subjects. What I don't know is if I should explain to them what I'm doing while I'm photographing them.'

Tina Barney has chronicled the lives of the well-to-do citizens of New England and New York for decades, building up a composite portrait of these families, often over generations. Her large-format camera allows her to achieve a high level of detail to capture their environments as well as lending a formality to the aesthetics of the image with its painterly overtones. She maintains that having a point of view is vital, asking yourself what you find important as a point of departure for your interactions with the world, and recommends sitting down with 'a pencil and paper and think about what your life is about. What you are about. Don't even take a camera into your hands before you figure that out.' This will then in turn inform how you relate to the people and situations you shoot, even if you keep your own feelings somewhat hidden from them, as she reveals: 'I know now that before I take a picture I have to be sure how I feel about the subjects. What I don't know is if I should explain to them what I'm doing while I'm photographing them.' Establish in your own mind exactly what you are interested in, what motivates and drives you, well in advance of actually going out to make pictures.

Photographs are mysteries

Diane Arbus Photographer Diane Arbus poses for a rare Portrait in the automat at Sixth Avenue, New York, *c.*1968 (photograph by Roz Kelly)

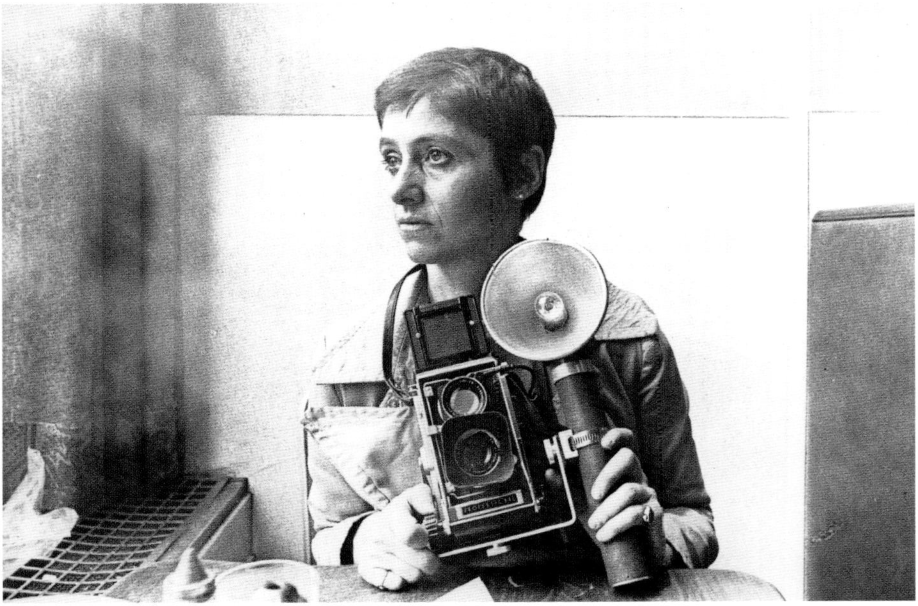

One of the most influential photographers of all time, Diane Arbus penetrated into the complex lives of others, especially those on the margins of society. She saw the camera as a passport to enter into places she would otherwise be unable to see, arguing that 'If I were just curious, it would be very hard to say to someone, I want to come to your house and have you talk to me and tell me the story of your life. I mean people are going to say, You're crazy. Plus, they're going to keep mighty guarded. But the camera is a kind of license.' Having gained access, she was able to make complex character studies that reward repeated viewing, drawing the viewer into imagining the things that the image suggests but leaves unsaid; as she insightfully remarked, 'the photograph is a secret about a secret, the more it tells you the less you know.' The medium is often at its best when it tells us something, but not everything, about a subject, leaving room for the imagination to fill in the gaps of representation.

Work without preconceptions

Jocelyn Bain Hogg *Millie and Mrs Ansell, the Bon Accord Nursing Home, Hove*, 1983

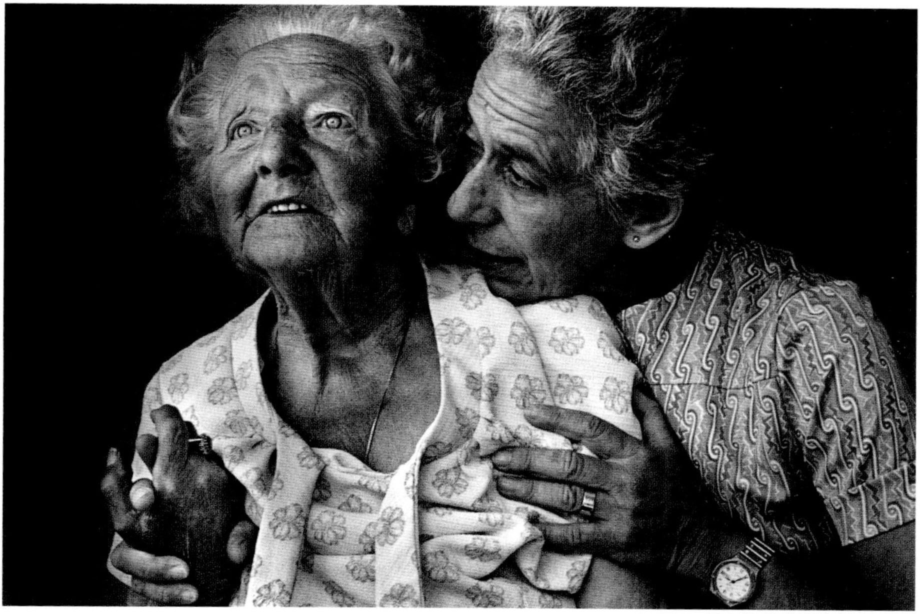

Jocelyn Bain Hogg has worked with subjects from all walks of life, from the elite of high society and celebrity culture to East End villains. His guiding principle in working with such a wide range of different social and political positions is to always have an open mind, and to 'treat everyone you photograph without pre-judging them, thus dignifying their humanity, and work on all projects without preconceptions'. He asks 'What right have we to assume anything anyway? The minute we do, a paradigm shifts and any semblance of documentary veracity is out of the window.' We are all human and have our own opinions and influences but for Bain Hogg it is essential to approach every subject without prejudice and on their own terms.

Read more

Tod Papageorge *Central Park*, 1979

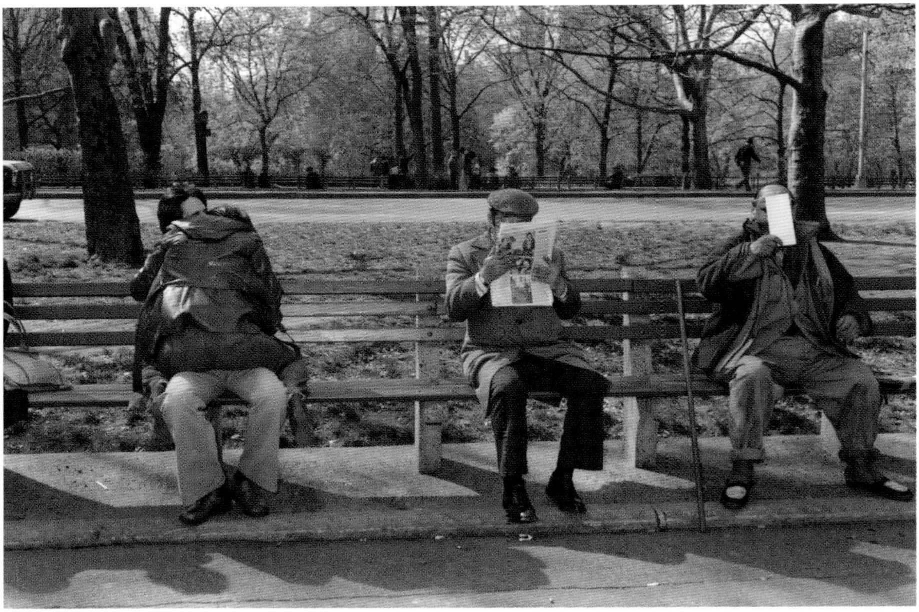

Tod Papageorge is one of the most significant American photographers and educators, who was the influential director of the graduate photography department at the Yale University School of Art. His reworking of the dictum by Robert Capa is a call for photographers to think more deeply about their work. Papageorge sees parallels between writing and photography, calling into question the latter's apparent veracity by calling it a 'fiction-making medium'. As an English literature major he 'recognized in photography a way of making poetry without the terrible agony of putting words together, thinking in my delusion that photography would be easier, and never suspecting that it was harder, or at least as difficult'. His advice is to treat a photograph like a text, and to ask 'if you're reading a photograph as a tale, then what does that have to do with whatever was out there in the world?' Thinking about how poetry and literature operate as imagined versions of the truth can help liberate your work from the literal.

It’s not your story

Edmond Terakopian *A Woman Prays in an Armenian Church in Gyumri, for the Souls of Those Who Died in the Armenian Earthquake*, 1988

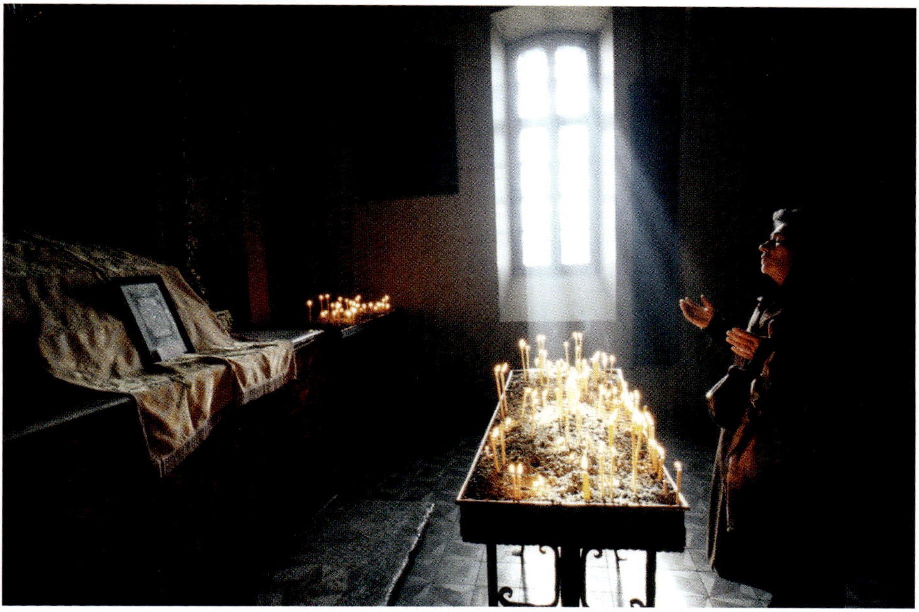

The award-winning photojournalist Edmond Terakopian reminds us that, when documenting other people’s lives, especially in situations of distress, ‘it’s not your story, it belongs to your subject. You must never forget that.’ He feels that although you have to be tough-skinned you also have to retain a core of respect, noting that ‘you have to be hardened in order to function in the job though perhaps it’s more accurate to describe this as concentration. You cannot be side-tracked. You’re there with a purpose; to tell the story, to share with the world what’s happening.’ He also feels he has to make that connection with people. ‘Honesty and openness inspire respect, and that in turn provides opportunities. Only then can I find the small moments and unusual events that properly characterize a story.’ His mantra for how to approach his photography is one all photojournalists could adhere to: ‘Humanity is the foundation of any image. Then comes the journalism aspect, and then the photography.’

Never give up

Swarat Ghosh *A Rickshaw Puller Trying to Fix His Mini Rickshaw at the Old City of Hyderabad, India*, 2019

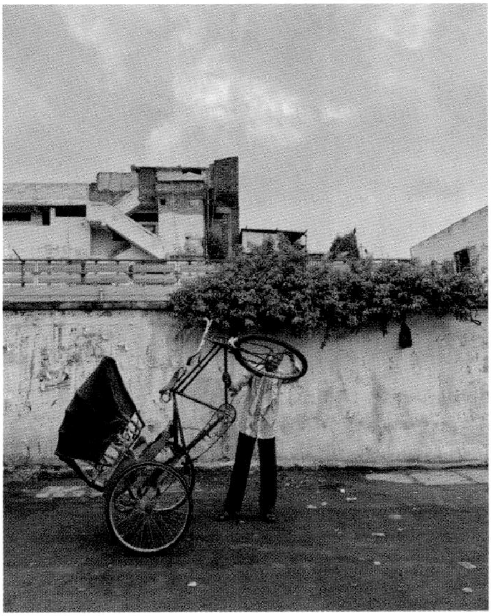

'Always [be] on your toes as luck or god might favour you with a little surprise on the very next moment.'

The Indian street photographer Swarat Ghosh is a great believer in the virtues of patience when out shooting, as a situation that promises little visually can suddenly be transformed by a change in light or in the geometry of figures moving through the frame. He explains how 'on the streets every day brings new challenges and you have to cope with that' and that you should never give up on a scene and be 'always on your toes as luck or god might favour you with a little surprise on the very next moment'. For Swarat, shooting great street photographs is 'all about the timing and observations' so you have to be persistent and focused on those tiny details and moments that can transform a photograph from the mundane to the extraordinary.

Know who you are

Bénédicte Kurzen

'Ask yourself: what kind of photographer am I? As Henri Cartier-Bresson told us, the magic of photography is creating a straight line between your heart, your brain and your eyes. Finding which part of the triangle feeds the other one, and what is our unique alchemy to combine these elements, will define which kind of photographer we are. We all have a trigger, a spark which will open the Pandora's box of our obsessions and our curiosity and make the camera the extension of our inner voice. Some photographers will be intellectually stimulated, others will consider photography as an emotional journey, or even a pure visual exploration.'

Bénédicte Kurzen is a French photojournalist and documentary photographer known for her work covering conflicts and socio-economic changes in Africa. She won a World Press Photo Award for her collaborative project with NOOR photographer Sanne De Wilde for *Land of Ibeji* in 2019.

Immerse yourself in your subject

Daniel Meadows *Foster Mother and Children*, 1972

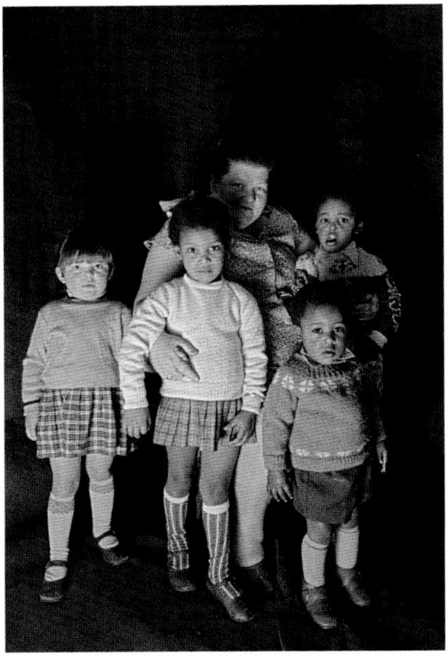

'Nothing must be more important than your work. Work by yourself and be disciplined.'

Daniel Meadows has sustained an exceptionally long career in photography, often returning to subjects and people he first photographed in the 1970s to see how they look today. He maintains that total commitment and immersion to a project is needed, suggesting that you 'live close to it, as close as you can and in a way that's sustainable. Nothing must be more important than your work. Work by yourself and be disciplined. Do it for at least eight hours every day and do it as well as it can be done.' Finally, his sobering yet probably realistic closing comments are: 'Don't expect anyone to be interested in what you've done for at least twenty years.'

Be consistent

Dorothy Bohm *Paris*, 1953

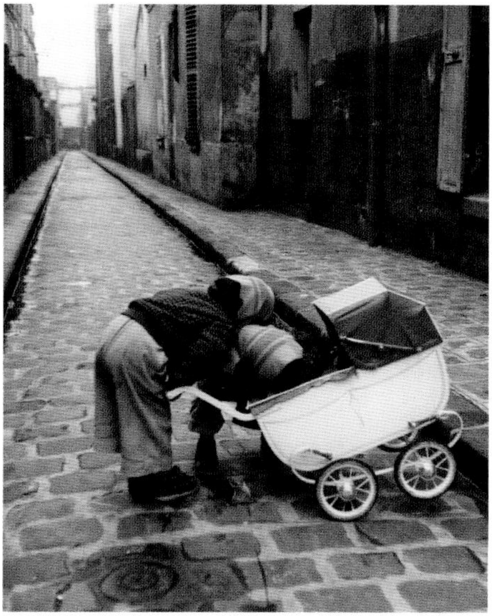

'I have tried to create order out of chaos, to find stability in flux and beauty in the most unlikely places.'

Dorothy Bohm has been producing photographs since the 1940s, and is widely regarded as one of the doyennes of British photography. She sees the secret to her longevity as persistence, remarking that the 'most important thing for a photographer is to get consistency of good work. . . . Anyone can take a good photograph – but doing it consistently is the problem.' This tenacity comes from a deep-seated desire to preserve traces of the world around her, as she feels that the 'photograph fulfils my deep need to stop things from disappearing. It makes transience less painful and retains some of the special magic, which I have looked for and found. I have tried to create order out of chaos, to find stability in flux and beauty in the most unlikely places.' Find something that motivates you to go out every day to make pictures: as in many things in life consistency is king.

Do your research to challenge your assumptions

Tomas Van Houtryve *Wedding Shot from a Drone*, 2013

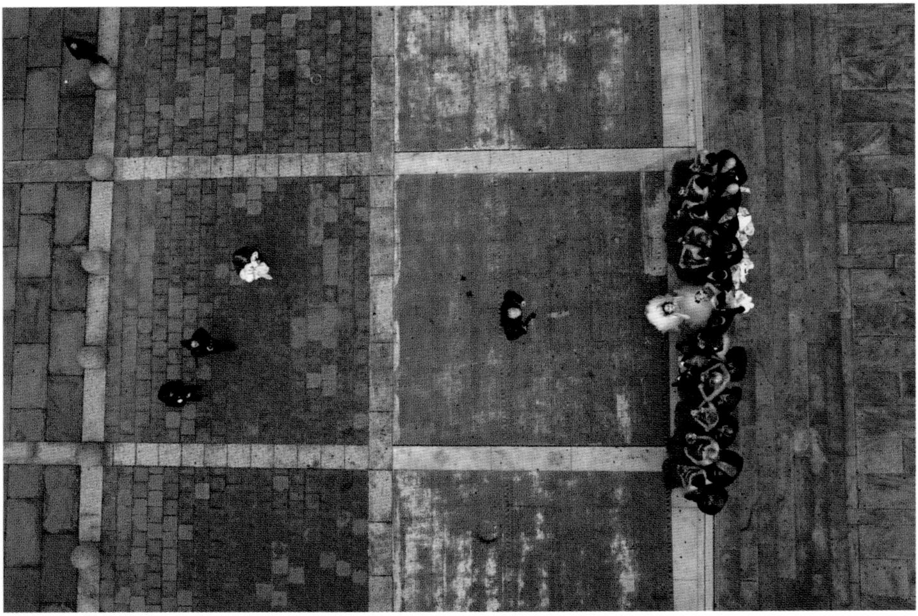

1. Find a subject that you are incredibly curious about – one that you makes you ask interesting questions.
2. Find out everything you can by research, interviews, observation and experience.
3. Take time to challenge any preconceptions you have on the subject or biases that appeared in the research. Do they hold up to scrutiny?
4. Choose a photographic approach that heightens your abilities to observe and honestly transmit those observations through your photographs.

Tomas Van Houtryve's work seeks to render visible certain subjects which are usually invisible to the eye, exploring themes including identity, ideology, memory, borders, surveillance and the relationship between the individual and the state. He comments that he begins many of his projects with a 'nagging curiosity about a subject, and occasionally I am seized by an obsession to understand, document and reveal that subject'. His playbook of rules to develop his ideas is given above.

Try everything

Alec Soth *Vasa, Minnesota*, 2002

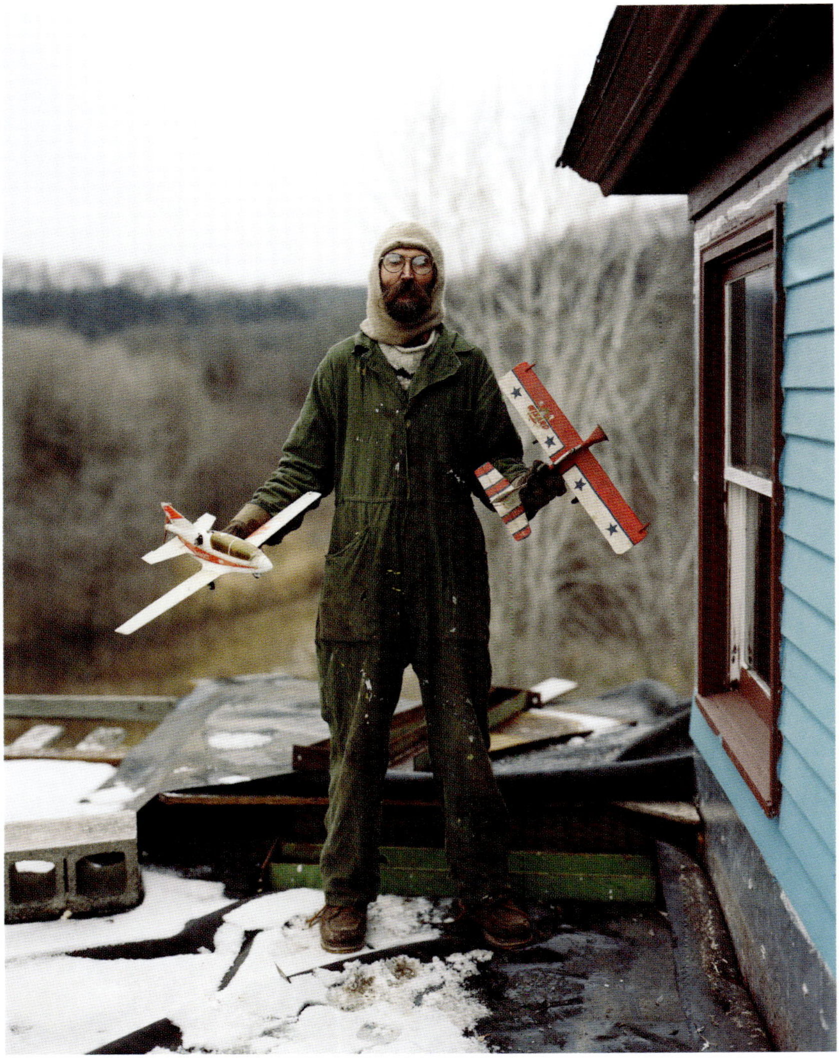

'Fun is important. You should like the process and the subject. If you are bored or unhappy with your subject it will show up in the pictures.'

It's very easy in photography to become stuck in a rut and set in your ways. Often, photographers confine themselves to a particular genre because they have not taken the time to explore other possibilities. To break out of a visual straightjacket, follow Alec Soth's advice to 'try everything. Photojournalism, fashion, portraiture, nudes, whatever. You won't know what kind of photographer you are until you try it.' In the early days of his career as an artist, Soth himself worked with sculpture, in a studio photographing tabletops, and for a suburban newspaper chain where he realized he actually liked and enjoyed assignment photography. He further stresses that 'fun is important. You should like the process and the subject. If you are bored or unhappy with your subject it will show up in the pictures.' Every now and then, take a moment to rethink your practice and deliberately push yourself into territory that you have not explored before; you might well discover a whole new way of making pictures that deeply resonates with you.

Acknowledge your own personality

Bruce Davidson *The Dwarf. Jimmy Armstrong. Palisades, New Jersey*, 1958

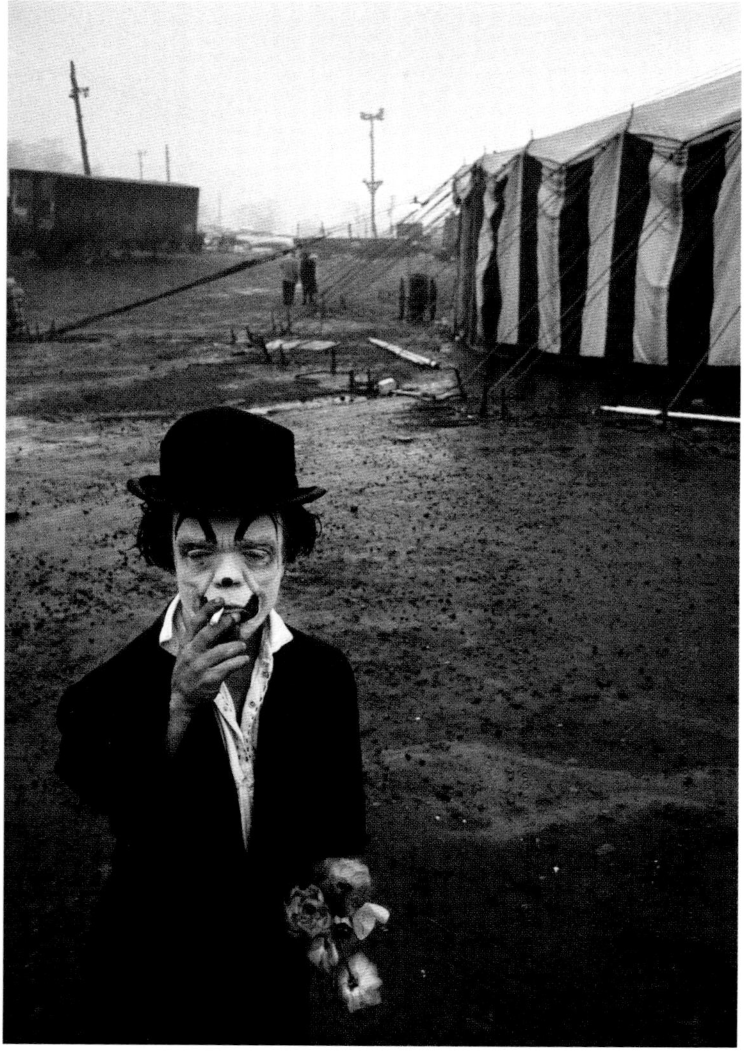

'All my photographs are portraits – self-portraits, because you can't photograph someone without reflecting/ echoing, like a bat sending out a signal that comes back to you. You get not only a picture of who you're photographing, but also a picture of yourself at the same time.'

Bruce Davidson has created an extensive body of work in successive long-term photographic projects, working with communities on the edges of society. He feels that he is drawn in some way to these subjects by an internal drive, explaining that he feels like an 'outsider on the inside. I am better seeing on the dark side of things than I am on the light.' He is very conscious that like any photographer, he brings his own set of concerns and viewpoints to his work, noting that 'all my photographs are portraits – self-portraits, because you can't photograph someone without reflecting/ echoing, like a bat sending out a signal that comes back to you. You get not only a picture of who you're photographing, but also a picture of yourself at the same time.' Acknowledge and be aware of your own personality and how that shapes your approach to your choice of subjects: we are not neutral observers.

Think like an amateur

Donald Weber *Omaha Beach, Dog Green – May 6, 2015, 9:57 am.*
14°C, 62% RELH, Wind WSW, 19 Knots, VIS: Good, Broken Clouds.

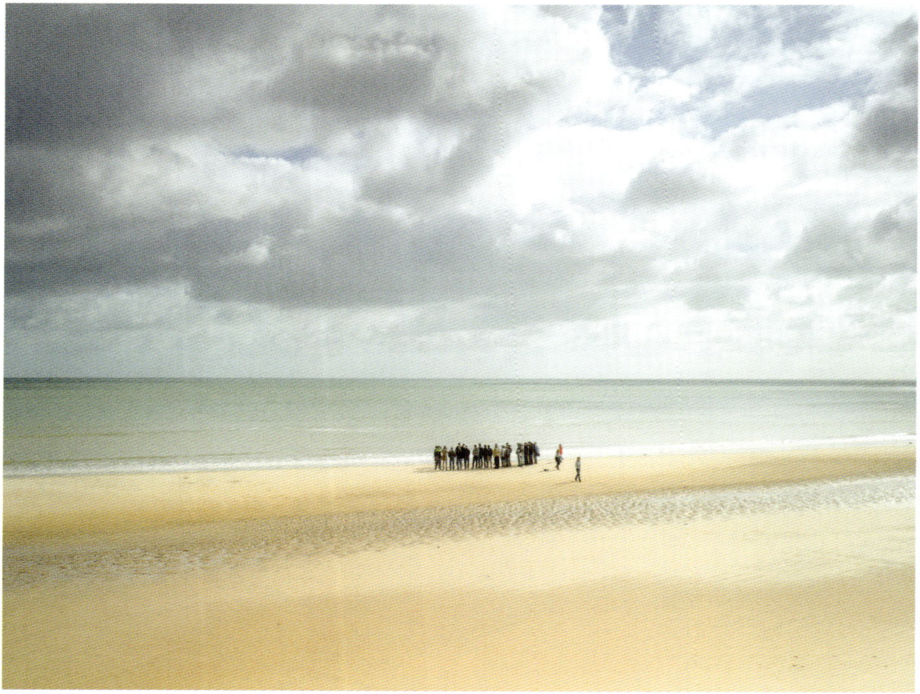

‘Think like an amateur, and make sorties into the terrain of the professional. Amateur means just that – doing something that you love. This needs to be front and centre over anything else. Discard the recognition the industry so badly needs you to conform to. Instead, carve out your own space in your own image. Let’s not confuse ‘amateur’ with someone who is a dilettante, unprofessional. No, an amateur is someone who finds joy – love – in what they do. Perhaps the best way to condition yourself as an amateur is to look at its etymology. *Amator* is the Latin for ‘lover’. Don’t you want to do something that you love, that fulfils you, that provides meaning? To me, the world of possibility is open. I can drift across disciplines and collaborate with others; I can engage with institutions and challenge their power; the freedom to work outside the constricted norms provides sudden portals for a future I could never imagine. Do what you love. Others will want to participate, opportunities emerge.’

Donald Weber is one of the most thoughtful and insightful documentary photographers working today. He encourages us to find the intrinsic value in what we do, and not be a slave to external validation.

Stay close to home

Annie Leibovitz Annie Leibovitz and Mick Jagger pose at Niagara Falls during the Rolling Stones Tour of the Americas, 1975 (photograph by Christopher Simon Sykes)

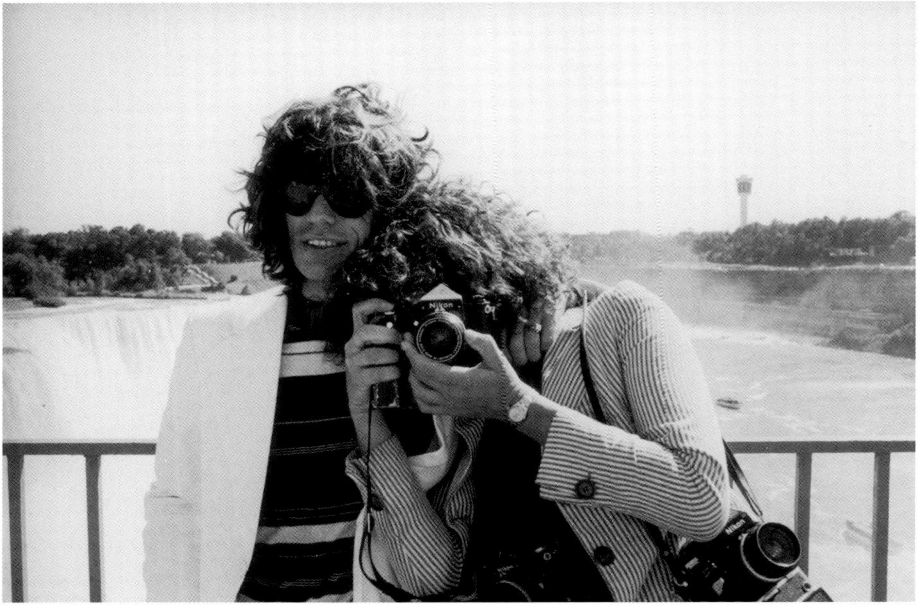

Annie Leibovitz has photographed hundreds of celebrities all over the world, yet feels strongly that photographing what you know best is an essential formative step for any photographer, as she explains: 'I've said about a million times that the best thing a young photographer can do is to stay close to home. Start with your friends and family, the people who will put up with you.' This proximity to your subject will allow you to explore how to work closely with people, and to 'discover what it means to be close to your work, to be intimate with a subject'. You can then calibrate this experience against that of working with strangers, and 'measure the difference between that and working with someone you don't know as much about'. Some of the strongest bodies of work have come from photographers documenting their own close relatives and friends, as such an intense level of intimacy and involvement is hard to obtain with strangers.

Find a connection

Martin Parr *Self-portrait*, 1997

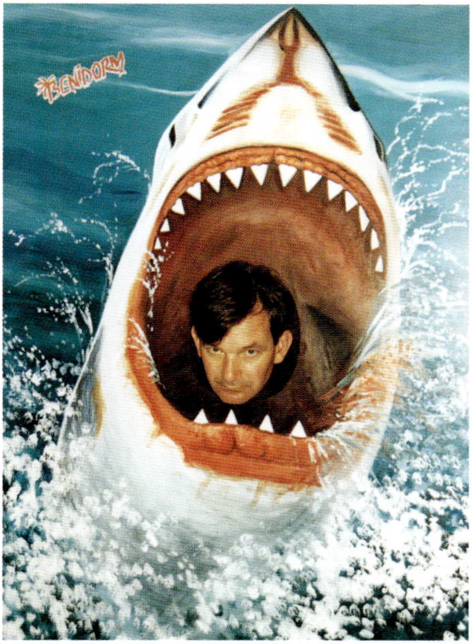

‘If you’re excited, then you’re going to be motivated to work and it will all pan out. That excitement will have the potential to be transmitted to the viewer.’

Martin Parr has been obsessively documenting and critiquing the colourful world of consumer culture for decades now, and has sustained his interest in it through a wide range of projects each with its own distinctive visual approach. Through all these bodies of work, he believes that ‘It’s the quality of the connection you make with the subject which is absolutely key. And there should always be some kind of story behind that, some kind of tension or vulnerability. That’s when good work emerges.’ Once you have found that point of contact, then your passion for depicting it has to come through, as he instructs us: ‘you’ve got to be excited by that. If you’re excited, then you’re going to be motivated to work and it will all pan out. That excitement will have the potential to be transmitted to the viewer.’ This combination of enthusiasm for your subject expressed in a deep connection with it is a formula for powerful work that an audience can connect to.

Fall in love

Ruth Bernhard *Receding Tide*, 1970

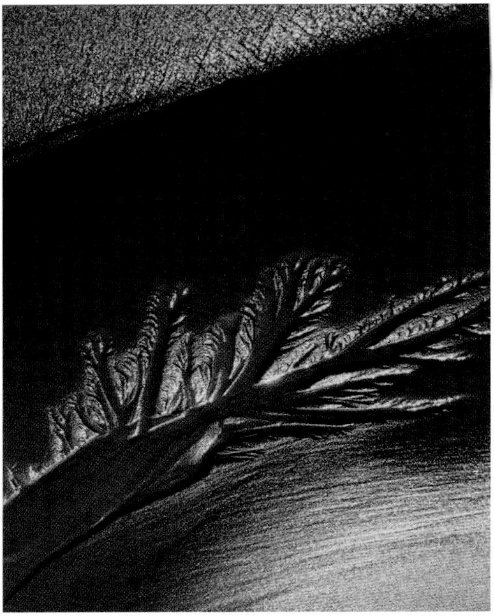

'Fall in love. Every day. With everything. With life. If you can fall in love, you can be a photographer. I think that is absolutely essential.'

For Ruth Bernhard the 'creation of a photograph is experienced as a heightened emotional response, most akin to poetry and music, each image the culmination of a compelling impulse I cannot deny'. Her images carry a strong psychological charge, heightened by a sense of spirituality and often surrealism. She regarded a strong personal connection to the subject as vital, exclaiming that we should 'Fall in love. Every day. With everything. With life. If you can fall in love, you can be a photographer. I think that is absolutely essential.' Find your passion and establish a deep connection with your subject to give your work a deeper emotional charge.

Play

Laura Pannack *Youth Without Age and Life Without Death*, 2018

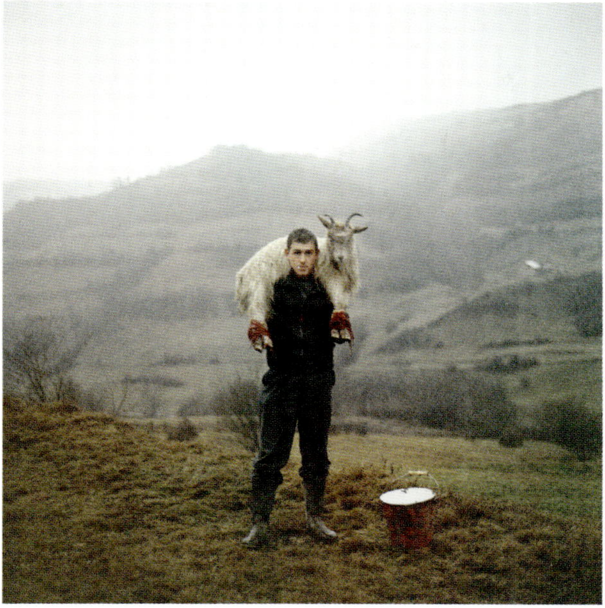

Laura Pannack is known for her emotionally and psychologically charged portraits, in which she demonstrates a powerful ability to connect deeply with her subjects. She defines a successful and compelling image as 'one that provokes emotion and encourages an attachment. I like the idea of a threaded connection from subject, to photographer, to viewer – one that flows effortlessly and connects all three.' Part of this connection comes from spending time with people but part also from the immediacy of the encounter with the subject, as she describes her approach: 'I like to spend a day with the subjects. I have ideas of how I want a shot to look but I don't like to plan. The spontaneity is crucial. This is what portraiture is about.' She sums up her philosophy in photography as 'Have fun, take your time, and play.' Follow her advice and give yourself the freedom of the space to experiment and explore your subject without constraints.

Slow down

Nolan Ryan Trowe *NYC Street*, 2017

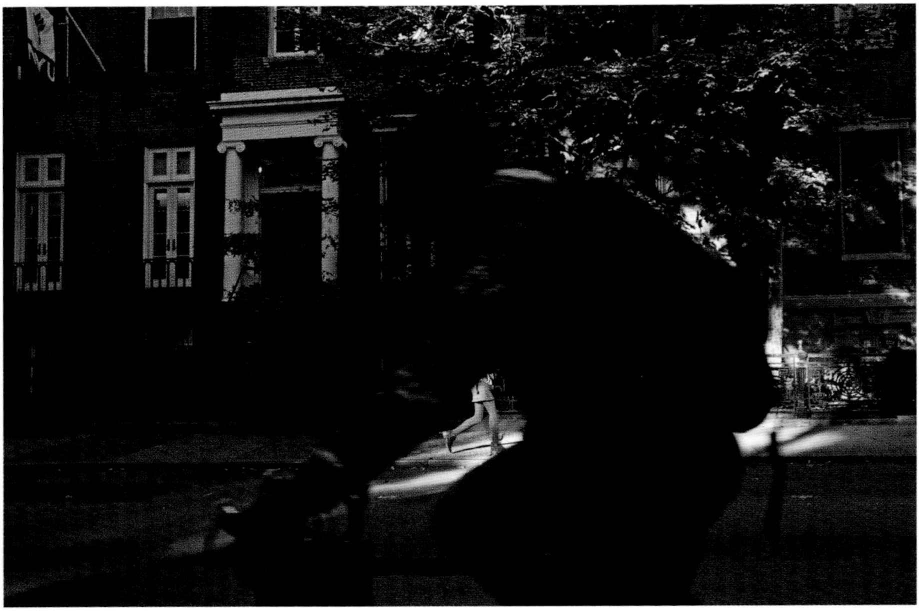

When things are moving fast around you, it can be easy to get carried away in the heat of the moment and rush into a situation. Nolan Ryan Trowe advises that slowing down mentally and becoming deliberate in your actions and thoughts is essential to get strong images. He explains that 'finding the right frame isn't always easy. When you do find the frame, be patient. It may take a while to get the shot you need. It's better to wait for that shot than to try a bunch of frames that aren't going to work. Sometimes it takes a few minutes for every piece to align in the frame.' Slowing down and taking a mental deep breath will help you to control your composition and timing, instead of rushing headlong into shooting and making a lot of mistakes. Ask yourself: Is it better to walk away with 5 good pictures or 500 bad ones?

Photography is not the same as video

Claudia Hinterseer

'Don't think you know it all when switching to video.'

Many photographers are moving into video and multimedia production, as the new generation of digital cameras can also shoot very high-quality moving images. However, this is not as easy a transition as it might appear at first sight. Adding sound and movement to still photography adds a whole new dimension to the narrative, demanding a whole new skillset.

Claudia Hinterseer made the transition into multimedia journalism and has this advice to those wanting to do the same: 'Don't think you know it all when switching to video. Although you know a lot, you have to learn about story arcs, writing, movement, film editing, audio and the possibilities of the equipment; you're a newbie!'

But photographers can bring a unique personal vision to video, and Hinterseer advises that you don't forget your background: 'Bring along your stories, your style and aesthetics.' Consider what it is that your experience can bring to the video to make it truly original.

Do your research, but then go with an open mind

Maggie Steber *A Young Haitian Man Writhes in Grief at the Funeral for his Mother*, 1987

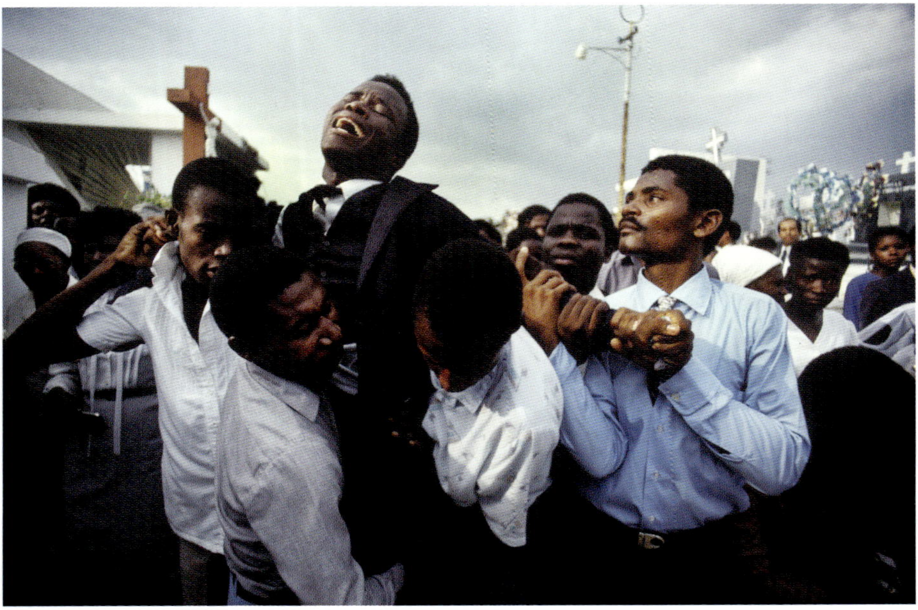

Maggie Steber has worked in more than sixty-seven countries, documenting communities under stress from conflict, social inequality and economic hardship. She has this advice on how to prepare for a story in advance but then to keep an open mind once you are in the field.

‘Do your research, especially when going into a culture or country that is not your own – and then go in like a baby, like you know nothing, and learn from the people whose stories you are trying to tell. Be the blank page and let them write their own story, not the assumptions we tend to form from mere research and word of mouth. And understand that ultimately you will never fully understand the cultures or people whose lives you enter. More important than anything else, however, is how you treat your subjects. Treat them with nothing but respect. Always keep your ego in your back pocket where you can sit on it. It’s not about us . . . ever! It’s about them . . . always!’

Think like a poet

Imogen Cunningham *Magnolia Blossom*, 1925

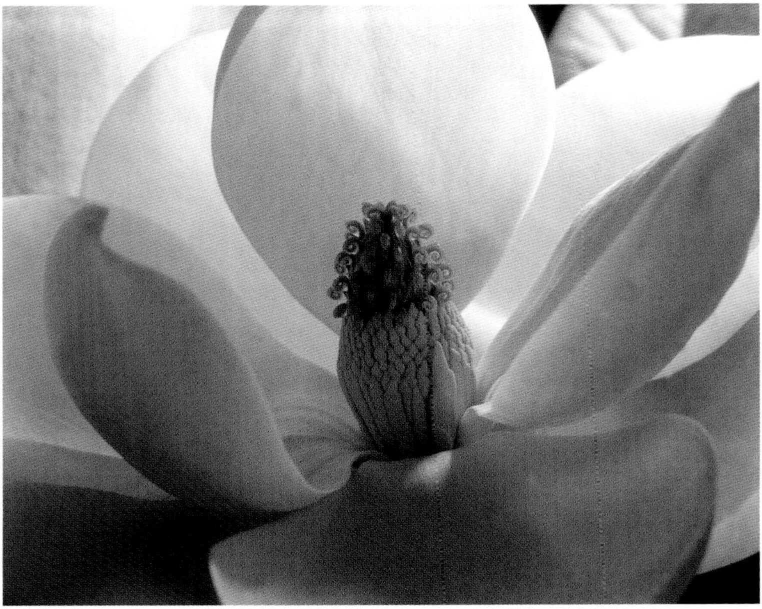

Over her seventy-five-year career, Imogen Cunningham explored how light could modulate shapes to produce expressive images, especially of nudes and of flowers and plants. Her modernist images are tangible and dense, distilling form via the play of sunlight and shadow, and rendering detail in exquisitely subtle shades of black, white and grey. She created photographs that had their own internal logic, each one a miniature haiku on the beauty of nature. This was a conscious attempt to tap into a more literary aspect of the medium, she insisted that the 'formula for doing a good job in photography is to think like a poet'. Her images also work in the realm of symbolism, and she claimed that 'the imaginative photographer is always dreaming and trying to record his dream'. Images do not have to be literal representations of the subject: they can retain a strong referential connection to the material world, yet still be full of mystery and metaphor.

Use the camera to learn

Larry Fink *Pat Sabatine's Eighth Birthday, Pennsylvania*, 1977

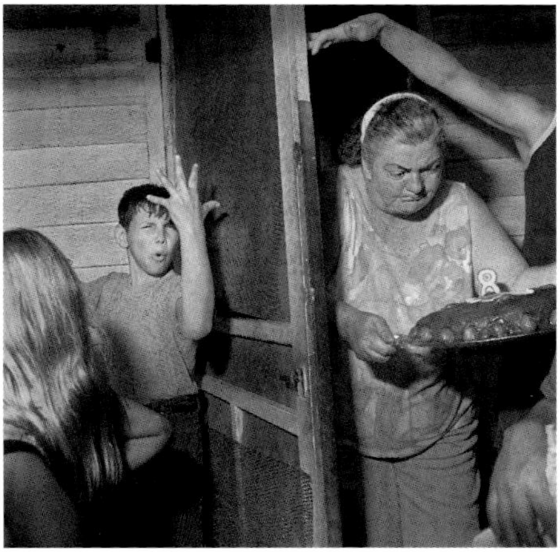

'Photographs are teaching too. You're opening up avenues for feeling, for storytelling, for human worth. Monumentalizing even the most mundane of things.'

Larry Fink impresses on the students he has taught over the last forty years that 'photography is a marvellous way to empower people's curiosity'. The camera can be a unique tool to learn about other people, but perhaps more importantly, about yourself. Fink sees the roots of originality in self-reflection, asking his students to consider 'who you are, what you need and what you mean. What are your hungers and your fears and your hopes?' He also regards the images themselves as pedagogic spaces, maintaining that 'photographs are teaching too. You're opening up avenues for feeling, for storytelling, for human worth. Monumentalizing even the most mundane of things, combining a sense of curiosity about the world with the curiosity to explore how the camera records it in its own unique way, lies at the heart of photographic practice.

Learn the grammar and vocabulary of photography

Alec Soth *Two Towels*, 2004

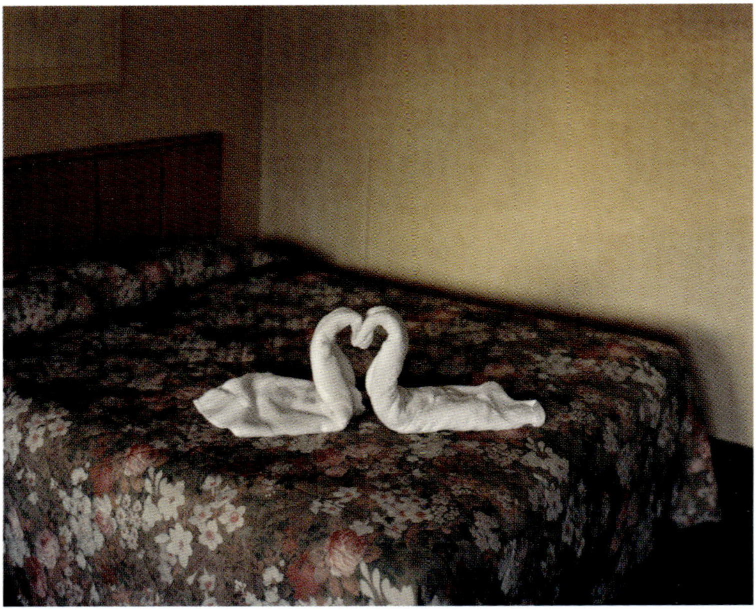

Magnum's Alec Soth is not only a highly accomplished image-maker, he also thinks and writes about photography in very profound ways. He maintains that photography is also a form of language, and that to communicate, you need to learn its grammar, syntax and structure. Through this process, you will understand where you fit into the story of the medium, observing that 'the history of photography is like the vocabulary and influence is like a dialect. One shouldn't be embarrassed about having an accent.' He continues his literary analogy by arguing that photography 'doesn't function as a narrative, but the photographer takes the place of the protagonist in the story, and you take the place of the photographer'. Conceptualizing learning to see photographically as like learning a language will make you more aware of just how much work and time you need to commit to becoming fluent.

Connect with your subject

Nadar *Alexandre Dumas*, 1855

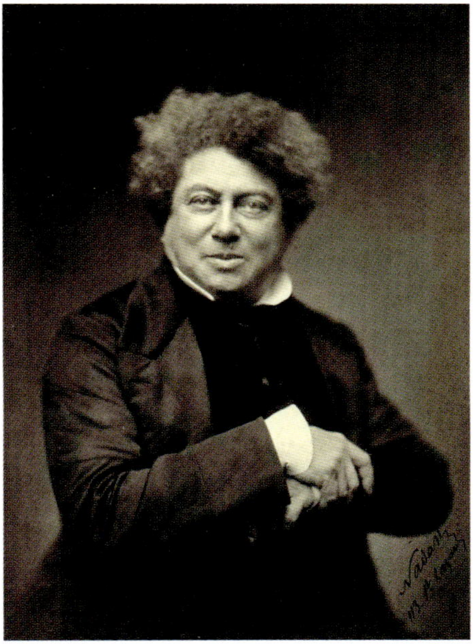

'The theory of photography can be taught in an hour; the technique in a day. What can't be taught is the feeling for light.'

Nadar (1820–1910) was one of the greatest portrait photographers, able to create images that seemed to connect deeply with the personality of his subjects. He advised that 'To produce an intimate likeness rather than a banal portrait, the result of mere chance, you must put yourself at once in communion with the sitter, size up his thoughts and his very character.' He was also a master of light, frequently using strong but soft directional light to give the faces of his subjects a sense of three dimensions. He identified the ability to use light as a key requisite: 'The theory of photography can be taught in an hour; the technique in a day. What can't be taught is the feeling for light; . . . it's the understanding of this effect which requires artistic perception. What is taught even less is the immediate understanding of your subject . . . that enables you to make not just a dreary cardboard copy typical of the merest hack in a darkroom, but a likeness of the most intimate and happy kind.'

Find your own voice

Shannon Ghannam

'The best photographic work feels like something we have not seen before, whether that is a story, a style or a feeling that it evokes. When conceiving a project, ask yourself the hard questions about why you have chosen this story: are you the best person to tell it? What are you adding to the genre, or the story, that has not been said or done before? Why do you care and how are you going to make an audience care? Give yourself a head start and choose the project or the approach that helps you answer these questions well. Every emerging photographer needs to have a personal project that shows what you are capable of, that expresses what you're about. This may take years to develop but it will be the launch pad for other commissions and will help cement your individual identity as a photographer.'

Shannon Ghannam has worked for Reuters and Magnum developing their education programs, and recommends finding a project that will allow you to express your own individual approach.

You have to feel it

Don McCullin British photojournalist Don McCullin in the walled city of Hue, 1968 (photograph by Nik Wheeler)

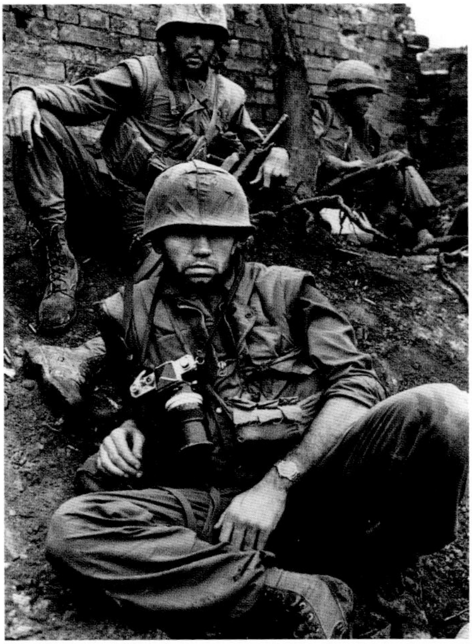

'Photography for me is not looking, it's feeling. If you can't feel what you're looking at, then you're never going to get others to feel anything when they look at your pictures.'

The epitome of the war photographer, the British photojournalist Don McCullin has covered conflicts from Northern Ireland to Vietnam to Lebanon to Biafra in a career spanning more than five decades. Witnessing this endless toll of human rights abuse has left its mark on him, as he admits: 'sometimes it felt like I was carrying pieces of human flesh back home with me, not negatives. It's as if you are carrying the suffering of the people you have photographed.' But he feels strongly that you have to use this anger to fuel your work, arguing that 'Photography for me is not looking, it's feeling. If you can't feel what you're looking at, then you're never going to get others to feel anything when they look at your pictures.' As a documenter of such difficult situations, you have to find ways to channel your emotions into your work.

Keep it simple

Alfred Eisenstaedt Alfred Eisenstaedt stands in a street, surrounded by children, 1960

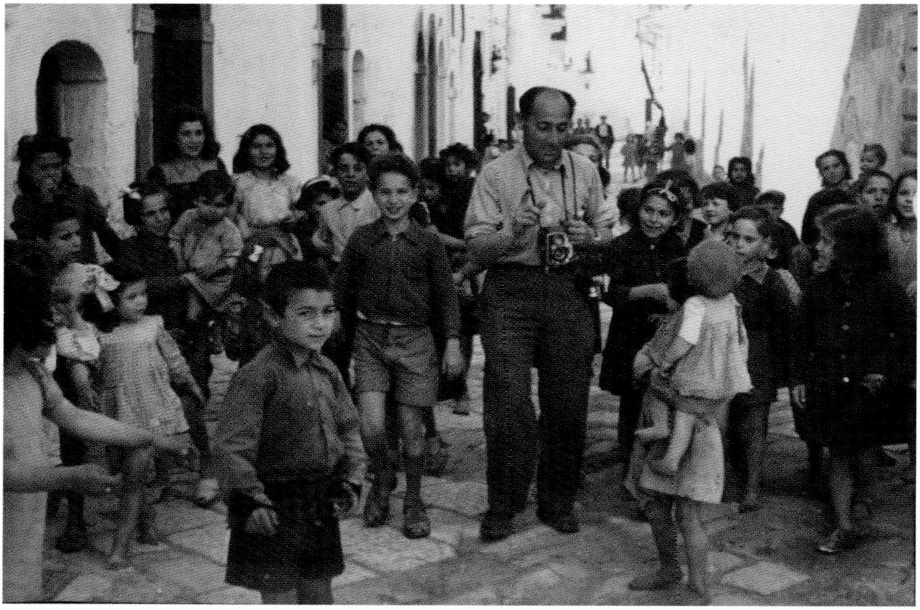

Eisenstaedt photographed the full range of humanity, from kings, dictators and film stars to ordinary people in everyday situations. His guiding principle was to work as directly and simply as he could, using natural light wherever possible.

‘My style hasn’t changed much in all these sixty years. I still use, most of the time, existing light and try not to push people around. I have to be as much a diplomat as a photographer. People don’t often take me seriously because I carry so little equipment and make so little fuss. . . . I never carried a lot of equipment. My motto has always been “Keep it simple.” I always prefer photographing in available light – Rembrandt-light, I like to call it – so you get the natural modulations of the face. It makes a more alive, real, and flattering portrait. I always remembered what Wilson Hicks, the picture editor of *LIFE*, said to me when I was on assignment photographing the most glamorous stars in Hollywood: “They may be queens in their profession,” he said, “but you are a king in yours.” This has helped me with anyone and everyone. Today’s photographers think differently. Many can’t see real light anymore. They think only in terms of strobe – sure, it all looks beautiful but it’s not really seeing. If you have the eyes to see it, the nuances of light are already there on the subject’s face. If your thinking is connected to strobe light sources, your palette becomes very mean – which is the reason I photograph only in available light.’

Be serious about not being serious

Elliott Erwitt *France, Cannes,* 1975

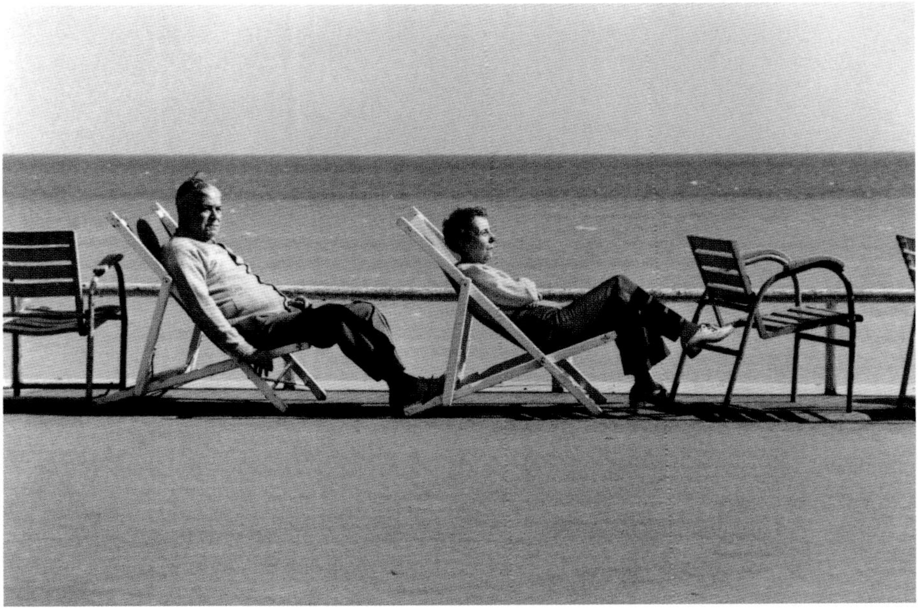

Elliott Erwitt is one of those very rare photographers able to make seriously funny photographs from the everyday world. He has applied his sense of humour and gentle wit to wry observations on the foibles and failures of humanity for more than fifty years. In his typically comic way, he quips 'it's about time we started to take photography seriously and treat it as a hobby'. But he is also the consummate professional, able to work to a tight brief for a demanding client across a wide range of photographic styles and situations. His advice on how to balance your own personal vison with making a living is valuable, as he tells photographers to 'learn the craft (which is not very hard). Carefully study past work of photographers and classic painters. Look and learn from movies. See where you can fit in as a "commercial" photographer – "commercial" meaning working for others and delivering a product on command. But most of all keep your personal photography as your separate hobby. If you are very good

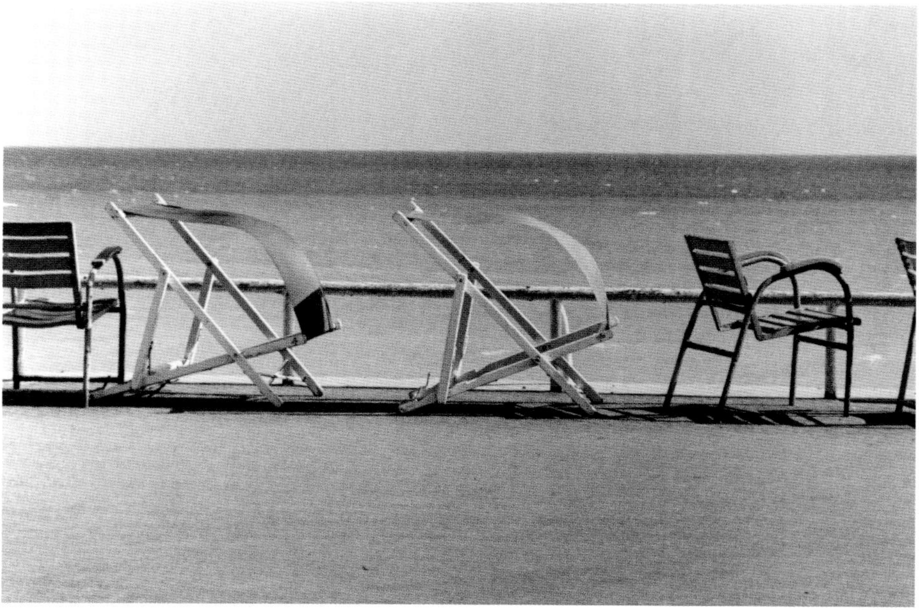

'Learn the craft (which is not very hard). Carefully study past work of photographers and classic painters. Look and learn from movies.'

and diligent it just may pay off.' This strategy of using commercial and assignment work to create a space where you can fully express your personal vision.

Look and think before opening the shutter

Yousuf Karsh *Winston Churchill*, 1941

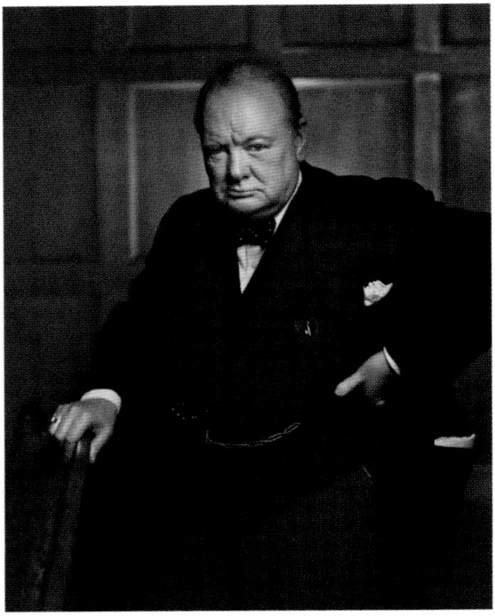

'Look and think before opening the shutter. The heart and mind are the true lens of the camera.'

The acclaimed portrait photographer Yousuf Karsh was known for his penetrating studies of human character, epitomized in his powerful study of Winston Churchill. He maintained that his task as a photographer was to portray the hidden secrets of his subject, and that this revelation was often the result of a 'small fraction of a second with an unconscious gesture, a gleam of the eye, a brief lifting of the mask that all humans wear to conceal their innermost selves from the world'. He also felt that technique, creativity and emotion were all fused together, such that the science and the art of photography are really one, and not opposed to each other. However, he also felt that observation was the key to portraiture, advising that one should 'look and think before opening the shutter. The heart and mind are the true lens of the camera.' In the end, it is the human connection between the photographer and their subject that creates the image, not the technology.

Question yourself

Robin Maddock *A Man in an England Shirt Eating a Kebab in front of Evening Prayers to Mark the End of Ramadan, Birmingham, 2017*

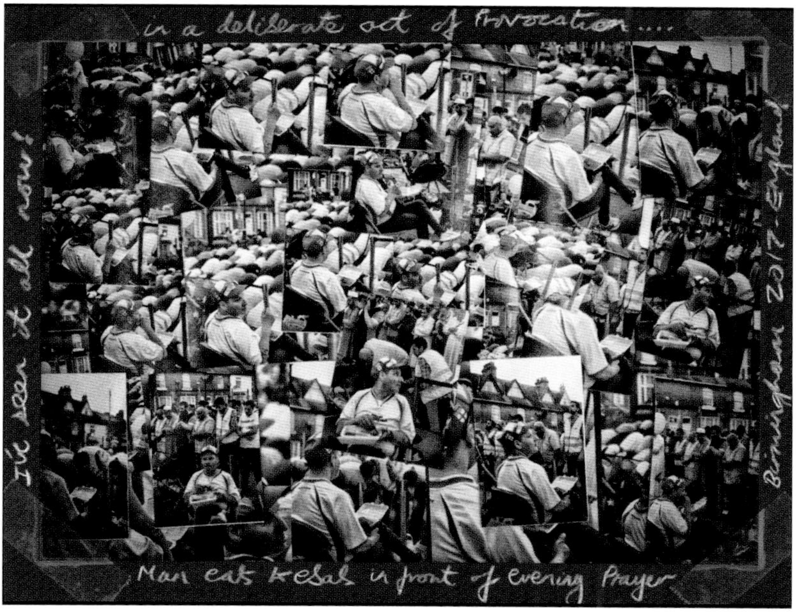

The British documentary photographer Robin Maddock believes that great work comes from a 'desire for showing how something is, not just what it looks like'. He argues that this 'takes a level of dedication and integrity I often wonder if I have' and that 'honesty has to be also applied to yourself. Who am I to speak? What are my fears and prejudices? How far am I prepared to risk my safety, health or sanity? To botch my personal life? To have no home, be in places I'd rather not be in at all?' Ultimately, he asks the question: 'Are we prepared going into something deeply enough to find out something about ourselves as well?'

Embrace ambivalence

Lisa Barnard *Canary and the Hammer*, circuit board photographed at an artisan electronic waste (e-waste) recycling factory in Shenzhen, China, 2016

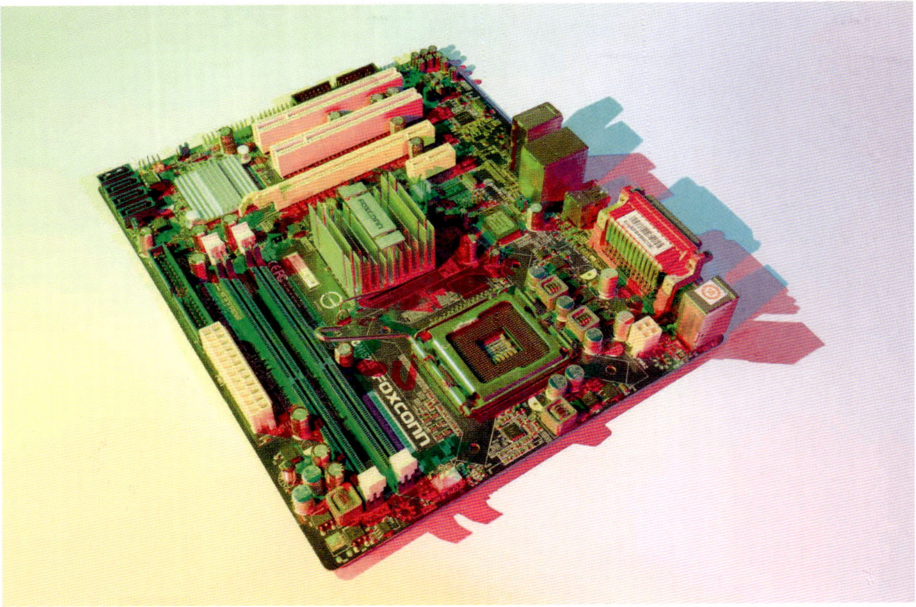

Lisa Barnard's photographic practice explores real events, embracing complex and innovative visual strategies that utilize both traditional documentary techniques with more contemporary and conceptually rigorous forms of representation. She explains how being open to uncertainty is a valuable asset.

'Being aware of inherent contradictions is an important and necessary aspect to the creation of my documentary projects. Having the courage to be ambivalent or have mixed feelings about things is normal and has a long history within psychological aesthetics. I have an innate curiosity about the world and being a photographer is a privilege and provides me with an excuse to explore all the contradictions that are inherent within it. For example, it is widely understood that gold is not only the disease but the cure of society's problems; I am fascinated by this example of contradiction in our capitalist framework. Good research opens up different perspectives, positions and uncertainties and what I am interested in is the ambiguity in the information that you garner through that process. If you listen to the confusion that will ensue and respond by embracing the conflicting dialogue within yourself, then you will be rewarded with energy and creativity. There are no simple answers – life is confusing – and a good documentary project addresses the complexities that are evidenced in notions of the real. To have courage in ambivalence could be the most rewarding and creative decision that you will ever make.'

Stick around

Bruce Davidson *East 100th Street*, 1966

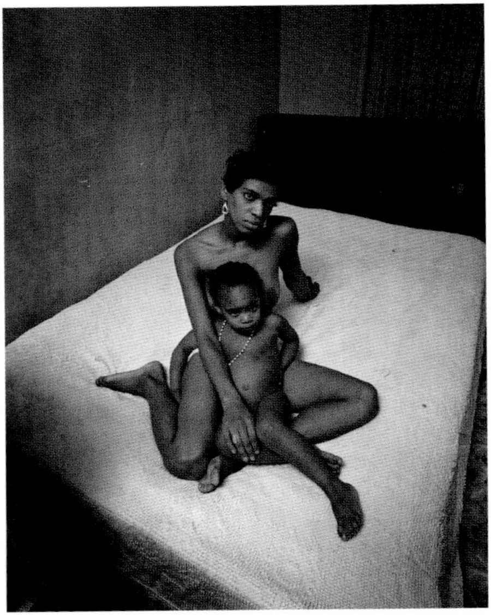

'You've got to stay around for a while; you've got to earn your dues.'

Magnum's Bruce Davidson has an exceptional ability to immerse himself into other people's lives. He believes that this takes patience and persistence, noting that 'you've got to stay around for a while; you've got to earn your dues'. To make his seminal book, *East 100th Street*, a series of large-format black-and-white portraits of the residents of one city block in Harlem, New York, Davidson spent two years knocking on doors and following up on contacts to gain the confidence and trust of his subjects.

He finds that too many photographers expect quick results, they 'tend to stop too soon. They mimic something they've seen, but they don't stay long enough.' Instead, he recommends that a photographer should 'spend a long time with it so your subconscious has a chance to bubble to the surface'. Take the time to really get to know the people you are photographing, so that they trust you and will open up to you.

Five rules

Gary Knight

Gary is an award-winning photographer and a co-founder and director of the VII Photo Agency. His rules offer a survey of the key guidelines for documentary photography.

1. Put what matters before aesthetics.
2. Allow the issue to drive the evolution of the story, not trivial photographic concerns like dogmatic aesthetic conventions and photographic style.
3. Accept and embrace your own prejudice and ignorance, then try to overcome it. We are all prejudiced and our experience and knowledge is severely limited whether we think so or not. Often, the more experienced we are the better informed we think we are, when in fact the opposite may be true. Try to understand better what it is you are looking at, talk to informed local people who have a different perspective, read and immerse yourself as much as possible in the lives around you. Then try to reimagine what you see and photograph it with as much empathy and nuance as you can.
4. Don't try to be someone you are not, it will be evident in your work.
5. Learn to see the magic in the ordinary. The world cannot be understood by the photography of spectacular events and freak shows.

If you don't feel it, no one will

Line Ørnes Søndergaard *Time to Rest*, 2018

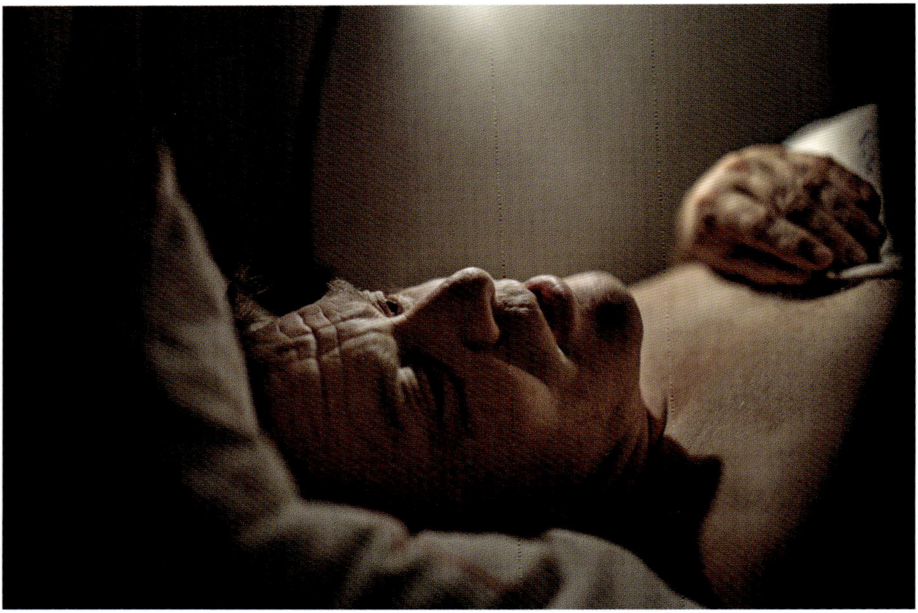

‘A lot of my work tries to tackle larger subjects through close and personal encounters where I move into people’s personal sphere and try to translate their world in that moment of shared time. So to me photography is – as with all encounters that involve others – a process of daring to be emotionally close to someone. It’s about finding a way to be together that is genuine, also when things are sensitive. It’s about remembering that the person across from me is always the wiser one in the story about their life. And that I also have to have something at stake in my encounters. Because if I don’t feel it, surely the viewer won’t.’

The Norwegian documentary photographer Line Ørnes Søndergaard explores social and political issues using intimate encounters as the framework for her projects. She tries to connect to the emotional aspect of the situation people find themselves in, looking for points of connection to her audience.

Professional Practice

Don't rush

Taha Ahmad *Swan Song of the Badlas*, 2016

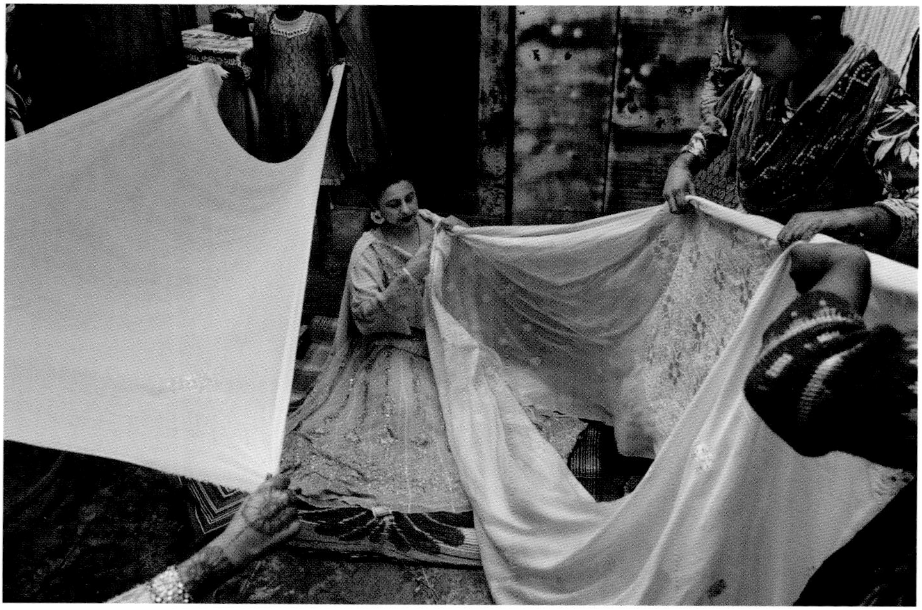

The Indian photographer Taha Ahmad works on long-term documentary projects, and argues that taking your time is a key virtue:

'Patience is a virtue. It serves as the most important tool for research, making decisions, analysis of the visual narrative and the future approach towards the desired project. Today, in this digital era where millions of photos are clicked and uploaded every minute, we see a lot of image-makers hungry for instant gratification including their desperate rush for winning competitions and grants. This attitude becomes problematic especially with long-term projects. Spending time with maturing one's work and approach with such long-term projects has its merits and shortcuts can negatively impact the output. Sometimes even taking a break is important. Photography projects can become obfuscating, tedious and perplexing for a photographer. Thus, taking a break can be one of the most fruitful things for the body of work. It helps to revitalize the interest, giving the photographer the power to replan or rethink the artistic approach. Taking a short sabbatical from a project to return later with fresh vigour and ideas can help break through impasses and develop a cohesive body of work.'

Avoid these mistakes when applying to a photography grant

PHmuseum

The PHmuseum is a curated platform dedicated to contemporary photography, and has organized grants since 2013. Based on their experience, they highlight several recurring mistakes that can make or break an application for funding.

1. **Select a strong cover picture:** What gives a first impression of your work is the cover image. So think about something that catches the judges' attention and will help them remember your project among the many submissions they have to go through.
2. **Less is (often) more:** A grant is not the right place to improvise and submit pictures that you consider a maybe. If you are sure about your core edit, go for it. Don't undervalue your edit by inserting more 'filler' images.
3. **A good contextual statement:** Even if we are visual people, we must accept that text is a very important element of a submission. It helps judges to get into your work. Stay within the word count, divide the text into clear paragraphs, and start with a strong intro.
4. **The right sequence:** Think of your project as a movie. The right sequence might make the difference and really get the judges into your project.
5. **The right title:** Present your work and make it stand out among the others. Spend some time thinking of a good title, coherent with your work. Be bold but not pretentious, think simple but don't be banal.
6. **Do not wait for the deadline:** There are many reasons to prepare your application in advance, so do not wait until the very last moment. It might impact the quality of your submission.
7. **Details, details, details:** Make a list of all the points above and ask yourself if everything is in order. Details always make the difference, especially if the judges have to pick a work among others that are on the same level. Before clicking submit, take a few minutes to double check everything again.

Think laterally

Aidan Sullivan

'Think laterally – look at as many options as possible to help you get that funding and recognition. There are myriad grants, awards and scholarships – seek them out.'

Aidan Sullivan is the Chairman and Founder of the Ian Parry Scholarship, awarded annually to photojournalists in memory of the photographer who was tragically killed aged just twenty-four in December 1989, covering the downfall of the Romanian dictator Nicolae Ceausescu. As the mainstream media has contracted, and assignments have reduced drastically, he advises that you have to be creative and energetic in finding the backing for your ambitions, acknowledging that 'in today's environment with our industry facing tectonic shifts that have seen the massive reduction in funding for projects, you need to think smart'. He recommends spending time researching where to find support, and that you should 'think laterally – look at as many options as possible to help you get that funding and recognition. There are myriad grants, awards and scholarships – seek them out'. Going beyond the 'photographic ghetto' is important too: there are many sources of funding from organizations interested in the same issues and themes as you, beyond the world of the media.

Trust is paramount

Damir Šagolj *A Detained Iraqi Man with a Plastic Bag Covering His Head Sits in Garden of a House Searched by US Soldiers during a Night Raid in Tikrit*, 2003

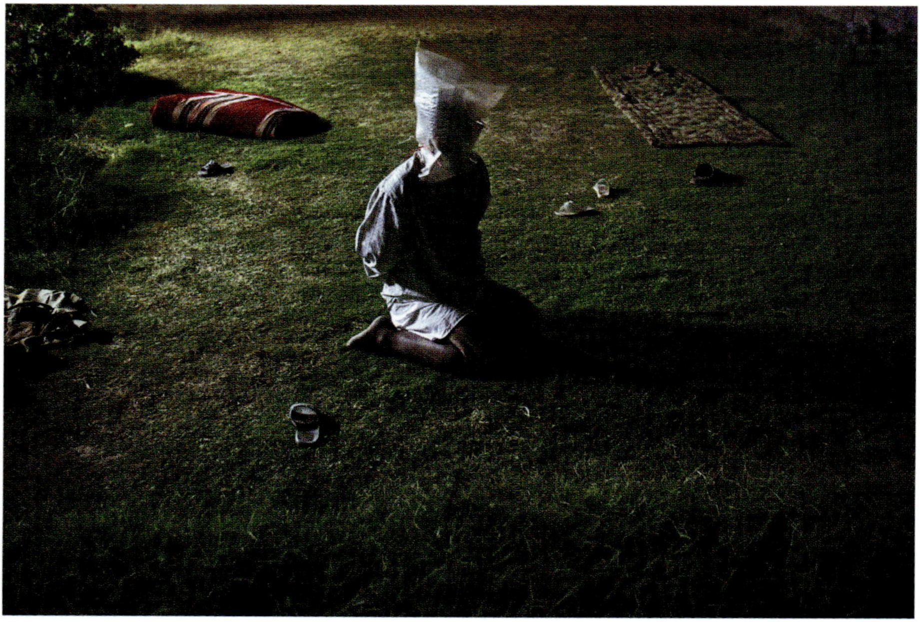

Former photojournalist Damir Šagolj covered major news all over the world for over twenty years. He is a reporter and documentarist whose main tool is a camera, and a teacher of photography and contemporary documentary approaches in Sarajevo.

'The picture "works" if the scene a photographer witnessed is transported to the viewer in such a way that they are informed, intrigued or moved by the subject.

'If we are aiming for more than just the "beauty of it", then the aesthetics of the image serves purely as a vehicle that carries and delivers the main subject – the information, emotion and feeling. Equally, or even more importantly if we are talking journalism or documentary work, is the other part of the equation – the trust in the author. Who is the person taking and delivering that picture to us? What do we know about him or her? And ultimately how much we can trust them?

'A very simplified equation would be: "How much we trust the picture equals how much we trust the photographer, multiplied by the aesthetics of the image."

'Unfortunately, in reality, the equation is more complex and dynamic as a picture often gets distorted, taken out of context and otherwise misused between being taken and being presented to the audience.

'What makes a good picture therefore goes well beyond the picture itself and depends heavily on the integrity of the author, something that builds over time, and the trust we have in the whole process the picture goes through before being presented.'

Support others

Laura Noble

Laura Noble is a renowned gallerist, curator, writer and artist, and she advises to take care of your friends.

'Support your peers: go to their exhibitions, talks and events. Be sure to support others' crowdfunding efforts, for example. Turning up and being seen on the scene is everything in this industry. Don't contact people only when you want something, as this wears thin very quickly. It doesn't take long to gain a reputation for self-absorbed behaviour. People want to work with those whose intentions are good. Positivity rubs off and in the end will benefit everyone you connect with. Don't just share your own work on social media, share others that you like and support too. If you are represented by a gallery, share your fellow artists' and gallerists' endeavours by showing up and promoting both – it will pay dividends in the future for all of you. People work harder for those who are nice to work with. Be present and whenever possible discuss things in person. The human touch goes a long way.'

Mine your archive

Paul Lowe

'Often with hindsight photographs that appeared unimportant in the past can take on new significance because of their content, or because your sense of aesthetics and what makes a good picture has changed.'

Assuming you have followed the rule of organizing your analogue negatives and digital files, you should have a searchable archive of your work from the whole of your career. Periodically, it is a hugely worthwhile exercise to go over old work with a fresh eye to see if there are images that you missed in the editing process the first time round. Often with hindsight photographs that appeared unimportant in the past can take on new significance because of their content, or because your sense of aesthetics and what makes a good picture has changed. This is particularly true of images made on assignment, as it is likely that the selection made at the time was based on their editorial or commercial value, not on other considerations. Mining your archive can produce exciting and valuable new interpretations of your work, especially once the images have taken on a historical context.

Don't bulk out your submissions

Emma Bowkett *Two Young Women Enjoy a Summer Day on Blackpool Promenade*, 1951 (photograph by Bert Hardy)

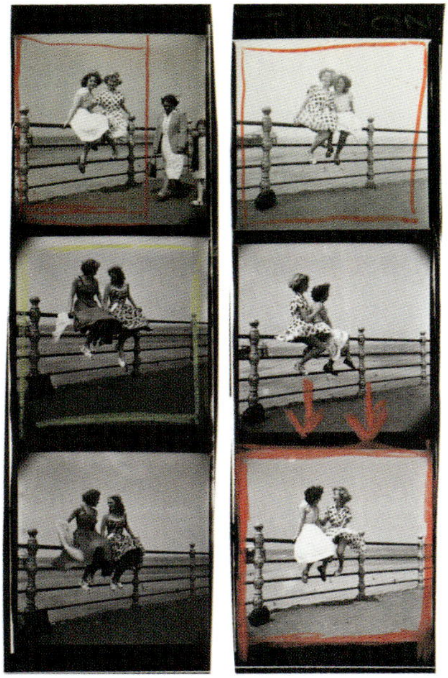

'[Be] confident to send only the pictures that you are comfortable with.'

Emma Bowkett is the picture editor of the *Financial Times* magazine, and offers this simple but sensible advice: 'Only send work that you are happy seeing published.' She says she often gets feedback from photographers that the magazine didn't publish their best pictures, and although she accepts that deciding which the 'best picture' is will be subjective, she advises photographers to be 'confident to send only the pictures that you are comfortable with'. Be ruthless with your editing when submitting work to a client; don't send extra images to bulk out your selection to make it look like you have worked harder, and ask yourself if you would be happy if they used every photograph you send.

Dig deep into your subject

Gaia Tripoli

'You want to take on the story as prepared as possible and then be completely open at the same time. Knowing your subject does not mean having preconceived ideas.'

As a photo editor for the *New York Times*, Gaia Tripoli has worked with hundreds of photographers on their assignments. She emphasizes how important it is to know your subject in detail when pitching a story to a publication or working on a project, noting how 'nuances are important [and] understanding the environment you will be working in will help you produce more solid and layered work'. This depth of knowledge will also help you to be more respectful of the people you are depicting. She also argues that research will help you to see all the different angles you can potentially explore. This does not mean that you should set your ideas in stone before the shoot, however, as Tripoli maintains that 'you want to take on the story as prepared as possible and then be completely open at the same time. Knowing your subject does not mean having preconceived ideas.' And her final take-away is 'go the extra mile.'

Do what you want to do, not what you think everyone wants you to do

Jess Crombie

'As an editor I don't know how many times people approached me with examples of the work they think I want them to do, not what they actually like doing.'

Jess Crombie worked as the Global Editor for media for the NGO Save the Children, and has looked at hundreds of photographers' works for potential assignments. In a portfolio review, she feels that you should only show work you truly believe in yourself, noting that 'as an editor I don't know how many times people approached me with examples of the work they think I want them to do, not what they actually like doing'. Instead of trying to second guess an editor's needs and what they want, she recommends showing projects you are passionate about and that you like doing. Establishing in an editor's mind that you have your own distinctive vision and identity is vital in standing out from the crowd.

Have faith in your ideas

Ilvy Njiokiktjien *The Michaelhouse Swim Team, South Africa*, 2019

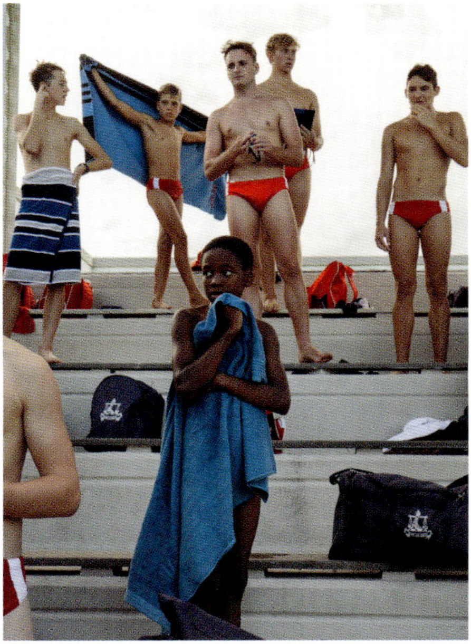

'The photos I got were not "newsy", "not shockingly interesting" and so on. It was difficult to get published during the early years.'

Ilvy Njiokiktjien worked on her project documenting the changing lives of young South Africans for more than a decade, finally publishing it as a book entitled *Born Free* in 2019. She reflects on how losing faith during a long-term project is easy – keeping the faith is more difficult. Her key advice is to listen to your heart and follow it. She explains how at the start of her project she was told by editors the 'photos I got were not "newsy", "not shockingly interesting" and so on. It was difficult to get published during the early years.' But even though she was convinced that the twenty-fifth anniversary of the end of apartheid in 2019 would be a moment that editors recognized as key, she began to falter between 2015 and 2017 because the project was getting so little support. However, she returned to shooting it and the *Born Free* story has now been published and exhibited worldwide to great success. In the end it was all about timing, and self-belief in her own vision, because she felt that the story was important.

Know why you are doing the work

Shahidul Alam *Mizan Watching TV, Dhanmondi, Dhaka*, 1995

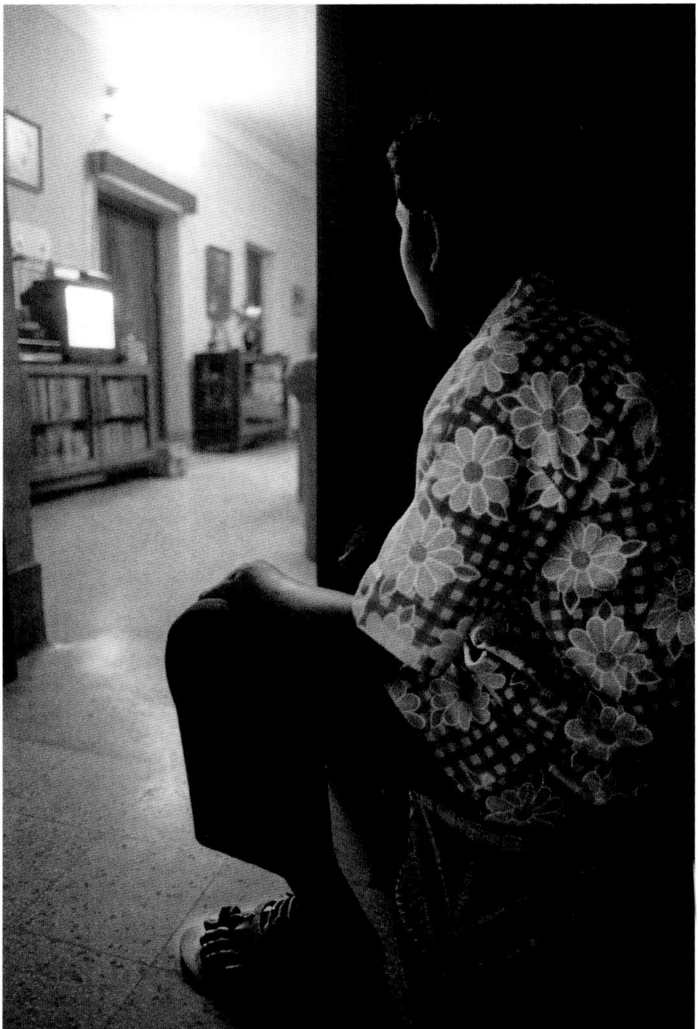

'It was a small thing in some ways, but it changed Mizan's life and my mother's and certainly changed mine.'

Shahidul Alam tells the story behind this photograph: 'Mizan used to work at my mother's. His jobs included cleaning the room where we watched television. But he wasn't allowed to watch TV with the rest of us. He would watch his favourite programme *Alif Laila*, sitting in the veranda outside the TV room, through the open doorway. After taking this photograph, I published it in the Drik calendar and gave a copy to Mizan and one to my mother. The next day, Mizan sat inside to watch TV with the rest of us. It was a small thing in some ways, but it changed Mizan's life and my mother's and certainly changed mine.'

The Bangladeshi photographer is one of the most important voices in contemporary documentary photography, and is celebrated for his strong ethical stance on human rights issues. His advice is to be clear of your motivations for making work.

You should know why you are doing the work. Is it the client? Is it yourself? Is it the public? As a photojournalist, make sure what you do is in the public interest. Otherwise you are doing it for the wrong reasons. One can have personal reasons for doing work, and projects you really believe in will generally be the ones you'll do best. If you can survive doing work you love doing, then you are exactly where you belong. We all need to survive, and there are times when we do things for survival alone, but that cannot be the sole reason for doing photography. You'd make more money as a used car salesperson anyway. If it's a photojournalist you want to be, public interest must come before your own. It can be a lonely, scary and often difficult journey. While it can be fraught with danger, it can also be immensely gratifying. But you make that choice before you pick up a camera. Being rich, or famous, or popular is not part of your job description.

The rules of doing a photobook kickstarter

Tom Broadbent *At Home with the Furries* (photobook, 2018)

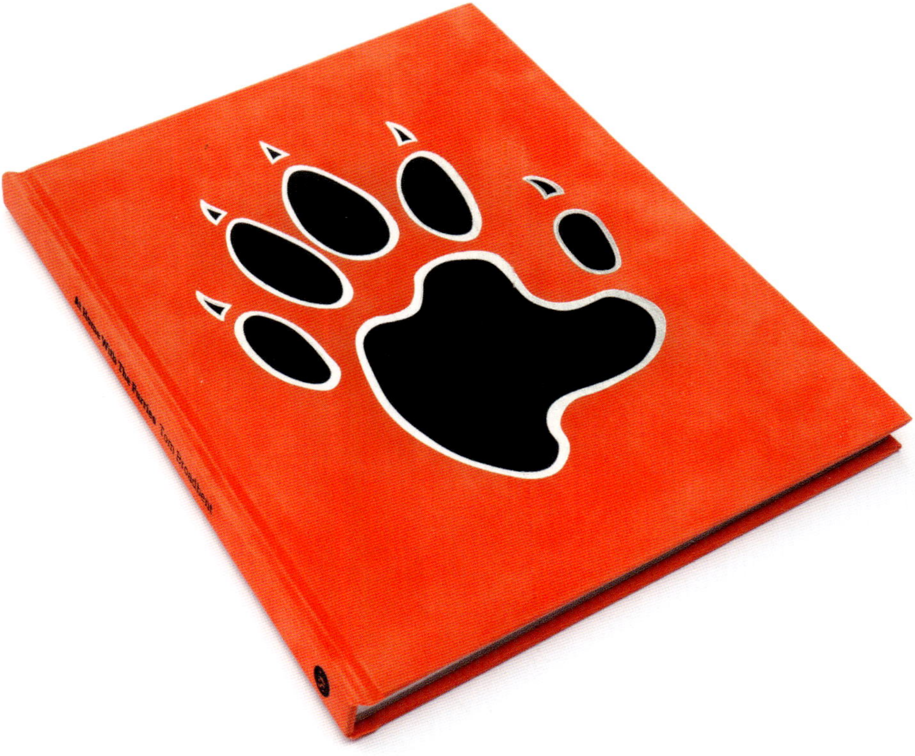

Tom Broadbent successfully funded his photobook *At Home With The Furries* using the Kickstarter platform and offers these rules for a successful fundraising campaign.

1. **Don't do a Kickstarter**
   Honestly, if you have any other way of funding your book, exploit it. The crowdfunding process is without doubt the most challenging and emotionally draining experience you'll have.
2. **Timing is everything**
   Launch in spring or autumn – it's the prime time to get people's attention.
3. **Ask for what you need, not what you want**
   Always ask for less than £10,000 – it has to be a manageable amount and something that is achievable over the campaign.
4. **Limit the campaign length**
   After you launch it's a full-time job and there's no way around that. It will suck up all of your time. I recommend 30–35 days.
5. **Set the level of rewards right**
   As the price goes up, it's a good idea to offer the backers more and more bang for their buck – postcards, signed books, signed prints, a day with the photographer for example.
6. **Get all your ducks (or wolves) in a row**
   Plan the social campaign so you have about ten social media posts ready to launch – video clips, promos, interviews, at least one per day. You cannot stop talking about it: hammer social media to pieces, do not stop. It's relentless. Be creative, don't beg, just be really interesting and make it look like a lot of fun because it is.
7. **The beginning and the end of the campaign is where all the action is**
   Once you launch, expect a flurry of activity. The first three days are key – good campaigns get 30 per cent funded after three days. After that expect a plateau, then a rush at the end.
8. **Deliver on your promise**
   Once you've reached the finishing line, the real work begins as you've got to produce it to the ridiculously high standards you've set in your campaign. Enjoy this moment though, it's an amazing achievement.

Don't rush it

Kate Peters *Do You Want to Know a Secret?*, 2010

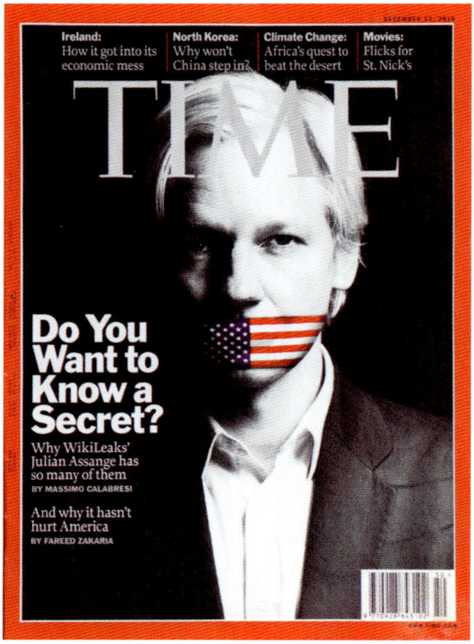

'Be in it for the long haul: you don't want to burn out quickly and you also don't want to release work before it's ready to be seen.'

The British portrait photographer Kate Peters has built a successful career blending long-term projects with commissioned portraits for clients like the *Guardian* and *Time* magazine, which used her photograph of Julian Assange on its cover. She feels that taking a long-term view of your career is vital, and that the temptation to expect success too soon can be dangerous.

'Don't be in a rush to be an overnight success. There seems to be so much pressure for people to "make it"' really quickly and in a way it may seem like everyone else is. Social media has warped our sense of what's really going on for people and that has a tendency to make us feel anxious and rush to get things out there. Be in it for the long haul: you don't want to burn out quickly and you also don't want to release work before it's ready to be seen.'

Get consent

Paul Lowe

'Whenever possible, explain carefully to the people you are photographing before you start shooting why you are doing it, and where the photographs will be used.'

Getting the informed consent of your subject is very important, especially in documentary work and is increasingly being required when working with NGOs. It's important to distinguish between a model release form, which is a commercial contract between you and a paid model, and a consent form, which exists to protect the rights of the subject, not you. Whenever possible, explain carefully to the people you are photographing before you start shooting why you are doing it, and where the photographs will be used. Use a translator if you don't speak their language. You should get their contact details whenever possible. Ideally get written consent: prepare a consent form that has an information sheet about your project and clear yes/no questions for them to agree to or not. If written consent is not possible, then try to record their agreement on audio or video. Remember that consent is a dynamic process: if you change the way the images will be used in the future, you should go back to the subject to ask them for permission for the new usage.

Have a three-year plan

Rebecca McClelland

'Start with where you want to be in three years' time, and then work backwards from there.'

The photo editor and educator Rebecca McClelland says you have to take a long-term view of your plans for success. She recommends working towards a specific goal in the future and then thinking about the steps you need to achieve to get there. She advises to 'start with where you want to be in three years' time, and then work backwards from there'. So, for example, you might want to have a show at a major gallery, so you have to think about what you need to do to achieve that – you have to meet the director for example; how do you do that? At a private view, at a photo festival, in a portfolio review? You need to identify the 'blockers' – the things that are preventing you from achieving your goal – if you lack confidence for example, then work on talking to people in professional settings; if you are lacking money, think of creative ways to fundraise like Kickstarter. Ultimately, Rebecca feels that to succeed you have to be 'completely honest with what your dreams are and how you make them happen'.

Don't shoot for free

Paul Lowe

'Unfortunately, freelance photographers are in a weak negotiating position with clients, but you have to fight for your work to be properly valued and regarded professionally.'

One of the biggest dilemmas when starting out on a career and even for established shooters, is whether or not to shoot for free in the hope of getting some exposure for their work. However, this can be a recipe for disaster, as 90 per cent of small businesses fail within the first two years, and working for free is one of the fastest ways for freelance photographers to become part of this depressing statistic. Imagine asking any other professional to do a job for you and then not paying them. Try asking your plumber to fix your boiler for nothing. Don't forget that as well as not getting a fee for your time for the shoot, you are also not being paid for having all your equipment, and likely for the time you spend in post-production, so effectively you are not working for free, instead you are effectively paying the client and making a loss! Unfortunately, freelance photographers are in a weak negotiating position with clients, but you have to fight for your work to be properly valued and regarded professionally. Spend the time you could be working for 'free' on developing your own photography instead.

Develop good business sense

Neil Turner *Ian Smith, Chief Executive Officer of Oracle*, 2006

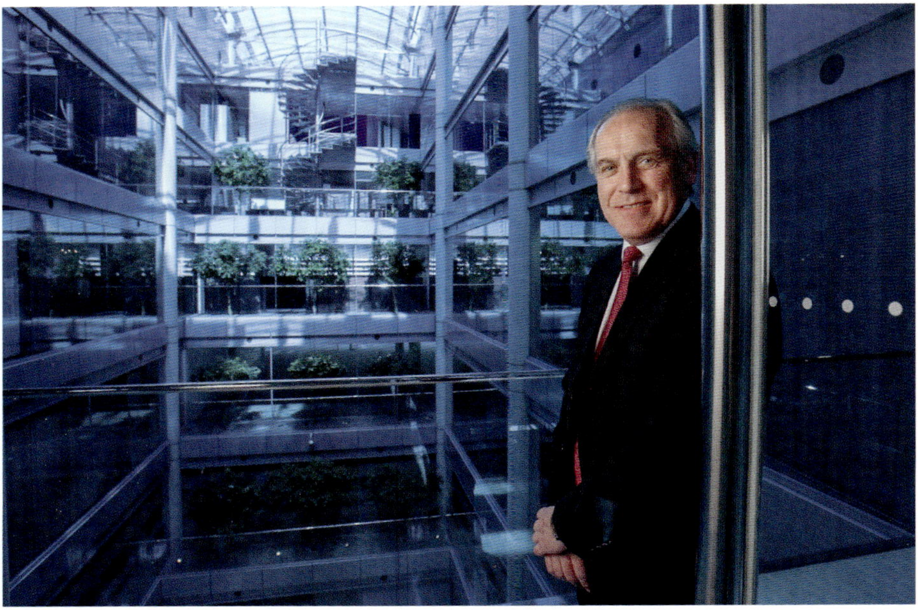

Neil Turner has worked as both a photographer and a picture editor, and has a shrewd and businesslike understanding of the industry. His top tips for a sustainable career are:

1. Whilst it might seem a privilege to make your living in such a wonderful job, you still have to pay the bills.
2. Keep every receipt. Claim everything against tax and make sure you get paid.
3. Only buy equipment to do the bread and butter jobs. Renting makes sense.
4. Spend as much time looking at other people's work as you do fretting about your own.
5. It's good to know how to make beautiful prints, but only so you can tell your printer where they are going wrong.
6. Get a great portfolio, keep it up to date and never let it gather dust.
7. Never take advice on photography from someone who tells you that there is only one way to do something!

Kill your darlings!

Shannon Ghannam

'[If] you can't be brutal with your own images, find someone you trust who can.'

Magnum's Global Education Director, Shannon Ghannam, works closely with the agency's photographers and offers sound advice on the value of being ruthless with your selection of images. She says that 'editing is crucial' and you have to be able to distance your emotions from your work, recommending that if 'you can't be brutal with your own images, find someone you trust who can'. As Ghannam observes, if you are working on a project over a long period of time, 'you will edit out many "good pictures", but the overall work will become better for it'. Killing your darlings means asking yourself the hard question if every image is really contributing to the story. If it is not then edit it out, even if it is a strong photograph visually.

Don't try too hard to be too successful straight away

Juno Calypso *A Dream in Green*, 2015

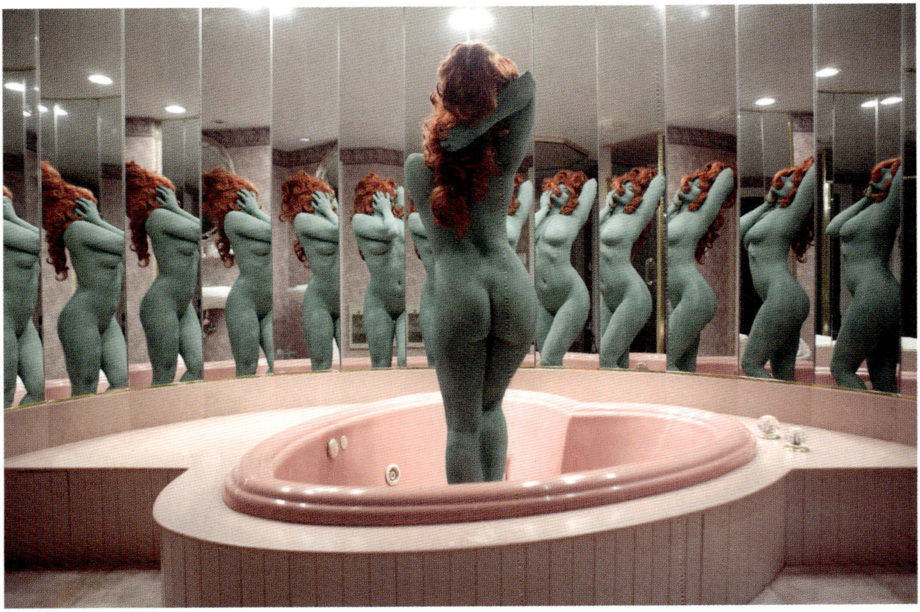

Juno Calypso broke into the photography scene in spectacular fashion as her alter ego, Joyce, whom she took to a romantic themed hotel in America where she created a surreal series of self-portraits entitled *The Honeymoon*. Despite her rapid success, however, Juno cautions against getting too carried away too early, as you have to think about the long haul of a sustainable career. She advises that photographers should not 'try too hard to be extremely successful and reach the peak of your career while you are still young. Artists never retire, and you can carry on working until you die.' Her advice to pace yourself is very astute given her relative youth, as she cautions photographers to 'take a break now and look after yourself, and do not burn out too early'. Thinking about your career as a marathon rather than a sprint is sound advice.

Hook documentary captions on quotes

Nicola Moyne

Nicola Moyne is an editor, writer and photographer, and explains how a strong text can support your photographs for publication.

'Nothing engages the reader more than hearing how your subject felt when the photograph was taken. Simply listing a date, location and description of the scene doesn't encapsulate the mood or provide an emotional narrative, so when researching reportage features to run in the magazine or shooting stories myself out in the field, I always try to obtain a quote from the subject that explains why they're there – and, more importantly, how they feel about it. A few powerful words can instantly lift a piece, and help to create a more meaningful dialogue between the copy and image(s).'

Don't wait for inspiration

Chuck Close Chuck Close sits in front of one of his paintings, a self-portrait, 2007 (photograph by Henning Kaiser)

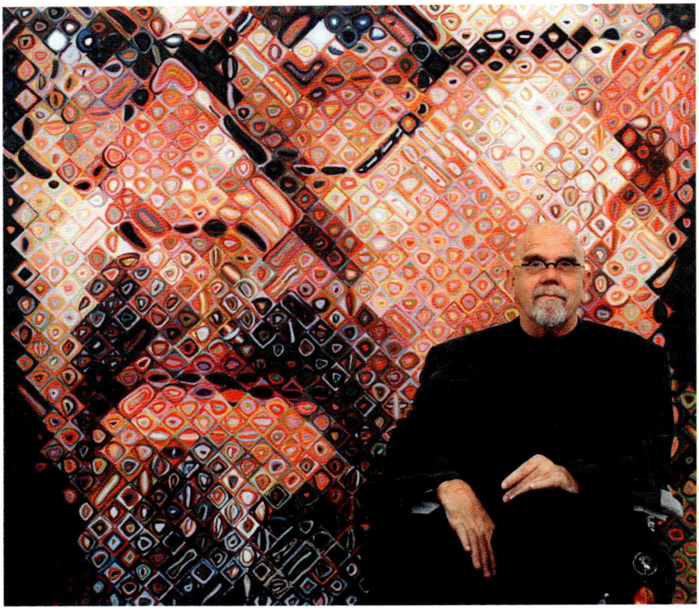

The American artist Chuck Close is a believer in process and that hard graft and consistency of application to the medium is what marks out the successful practitioner; he argues that 'inspiration is for amateurs; the rest of us just show up and get to work'. This may seem deceptively simplistic, but he emphasizes that only by actually making work can you discover the connections and pathways that can lead to new ideas, maintaining that 'things will grow out of the activity itself and that you will – through work – bump into other possibilities and kick open other doors that you would never have dreamt of if you were just sitting around looking for a great 'art [idea]'. Accept that premise, and immerse yourself in the process of making work, and the connections, breakthroughs and new insights will come if you give them enough time.

Go for the wow factor

Aidan Sullivan

'When putting together a portfolio for presentation, only include stand-out images – if there are any that don't have a "wow" factor or work in a narrative, don't show them.'

Aidan Sullivan is the director of Verbatim Photo and represents some of the world's most respected film-makers and photojournalists, and was the former picture editor of the *Sunday Times Magazine*. He has reviewed hundreds of photographers' portfolios, and is always impressed by a careful edit that showcases your best work, recommending that 'when putting together a portfolio for presentation, only include stand-out images – if there are any that don't have a "wow" factor or work in a narrative, don't show them'. He also feels that you have to get your personality across to the reviewer, and advises that 'during a meeting with potential clients and when showing your work, don't just stand there hoping they will be blown away by your work, this is your chance to shine. Show your passion.' Finally, he concludes that the most important element is to build a personal connection with the client, as 'relationships can be as important as your work. There are many people trying to find their place in our industry, and to stand out you need more than a good portfolio, you need to connect with anyone who might consider commissioning you.'

Never assume

Laura Noble

'Assumption is the basis of most mistakes in this industry. The photography world can be very small, with far less than six degrees of separation from one person to another. If you must assume, assume that the person you meet knows someone else that you also know or want to know, and behave accordingly. People have longer memories than you think and if your first impression is a bad one it stays that way for them and perhaps others that they cross paths with. It costs nothing to be polite, interested and engaged. Assume that the other person is more interesting than yourself and keep your ego in check. Even the most influential person is human too. Be polite and learn from them. Everyone has something to offer, often when you least expect it.'

Laura Noble gives some sanguine advice on the value of personal connections and respecting the perspectives of people you want to work with in the industry.

Throw out the trash

Eric Bouvet *Refugees in Somalia in July*, 1992

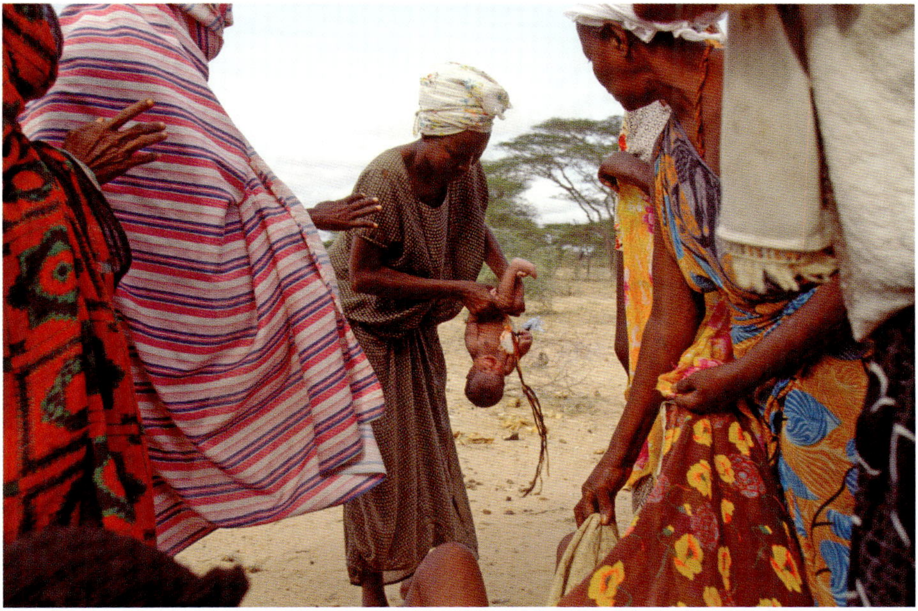

Some photographers recommend shooting a lot of frames and archiving everything, arguing that you never know what you might miss and what might be valuable in the future. However, photojournalist Eric Bouvet is a great believer in 'la poubelle', French for the rubbish bin. He says that you should be disciplined and selective in taking pictures, urging photographers to shoot as little as possible, so that 'one shot is the nirvana'. He applies this rule to his editing too, recommending to 'keep as few pictures as possible and put everything you don't need in the trash. You have to be strict and hard with yourself.' He feels that this ruthless attitude is a useful way to push yourself to improve, maintaining that 'if you keep the not so good pictures you will be always be a not so good photographer, and you will ask you never the best of yourself'.

Encourage others

Maggie Steber *Katie Stubblefield Is a Patient in Cleveland Where a Surgical Team Has Performed Multiple Surgeries to Prepare Her Face for a Transplant*, 2016

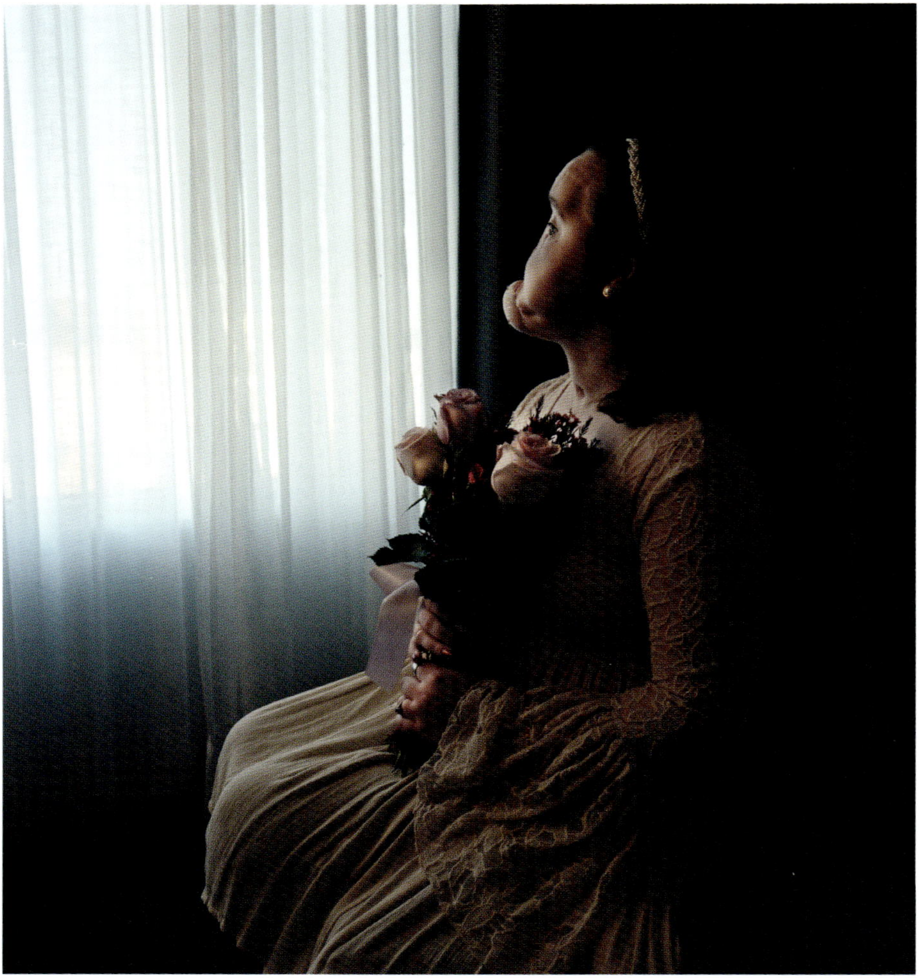

‘I have found that being kind and encouraging to other photographers and editors has kept me in this business for a long time. I realized long ago that being generous rather than feeling competitive with other photographers was healthier and easier; I congratulate colleagues on their successes and am excited for them. This not only made me feel better but it helped keep me focused on my own work. Selfish people who have big egos don’t last in this business. Something always brings them down. Part of the aim is to remain standing in this business with dignity and respect, and you do this with ideas and an open mind. Never let anyone make you feel lesser than them. Listen to the opinions of editors, even if you don’t agree with them. Listen, take things in, weigh them and then decide.’

Maggie Steber is an inspirational teacher, holding workshops all over the globe that help photographers break through barriers in their practice. She emphasizes giving back to your community by supporting others in their work.

Don't delete

Dirck Halstead *Monica Lewinsky Embraces President Bill Clinton at a Democratic Fundraiser*, 1996

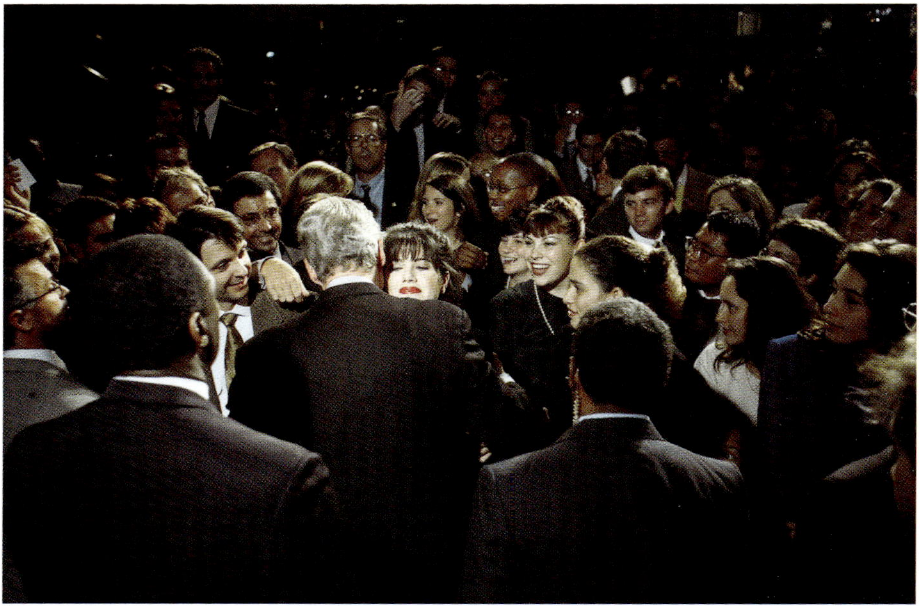

As camera sensors become larger, if you follow the rule of shooting in RAW, the amount of data you generate is becoming enormous. However, resist the temptation to delete files, especially in camera, unless they are technically unusable. You never know when an image that seemed unimportant today might be very relevant in the future. A great example of this is the experience of Dirck Halstead, who found an in his archives an image of Monica Lewinsky embracing Bill Clinton he had taken one year before the scandal about their relationship appeared in the news. When the story broke, he was convinced he had seen her face before, and hired a researcher to go through thousands of his slides in his archive until they found one frame taken at a political rally in 1996. *Time* magazine published the exclusive image on their cover, and when the rival photo agencies searched their digital archives they couldn't find the same image as it had likely been deleted as unimportant at the time.

Brian Griffin's rules

Brian Griffin *Margaret Thatcher at 10 Downing Street*, 1986

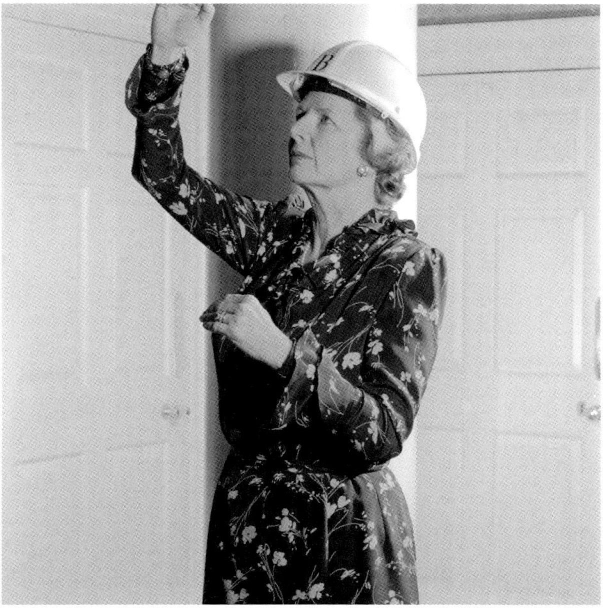

Teeth

Because portrait photography necessitates close contact with the sitter, it is important to ensure you have a broad smile and clean white front teeth. If the subject can experience your smile behind the camera, all the better.

Toilet

I have found over the years that wanting to visit the toilet during a photography session can be advantageous. Many of my best photographs have come about when withholding that toilet visit.

Brian Griffin's work is suffused with a surreal and witty sense of humour and satire, which he uses to great effect to create portraits that subvert the world of business and politics. His rules are typically amusing.

Learn the four Cs of captioning

Neil Turner and Andrew Wiard The Beatles during the filming of *A Hard Day's Night* (back of print), 1964 (photograph by David Hurn)

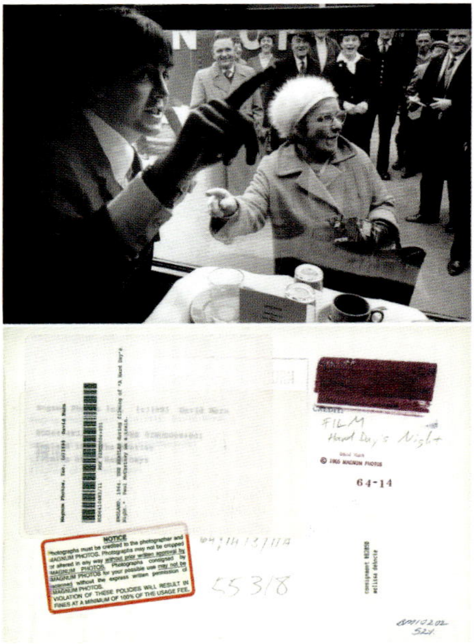

Neil and Andrew drew up these rules for captioning for the British Press Photographers Association (BPPA) to advise on how to make sure that your images contain all the metadata needed to protect copyright. Make sure you include all of the Four Cs in the IPTC data of your digital files.

1 **Creator/photographer or author**
If you do not identify yourself, no one will know who to contact for permission to publish them or pay you. Worse, your work may then be considered an 'orphan' and in certain circumstances used without either permission or payment.
2 **Caption or description/caption**
That's the five 'W's: who, what, when, where and why. Without this information a picture is useless for editorial purposes. There is no limit to additional details but these five are mandatory.
3 **Copyright or copyright notice**
You are the owner of your intellectual property. In three parts, the symbol © and/or the word 'copyright', your name and the year of first publication. Omitting this does not restrict your rights but can make it more difficult to enforce them.
4 **Contact details**
That's so you can be found. To be clear, that is a minimum of your telephone number with the international dialling code and a valid email address. Adding a URL with your copyright statement is also strongly advised.

All that leaves is the single A: **always**. Always add these basics of metadata to every single picture that you deliver to clients, place on the web or in any other way make available in a form that is accessible by those who may seek permission to use your work.

Find safety in numbers

Fiona Rogers Magnum photographers during the annual meeting, 1988 (photograph by Elliott Erwitt)

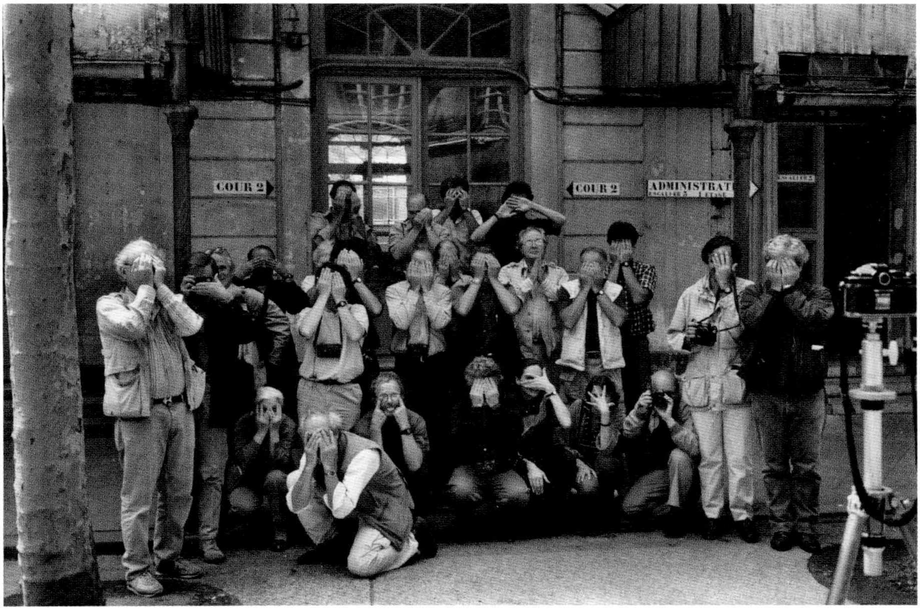

Fiona Rogers is the chief operating officer for the cooperative photo agency Magnum, and she recommends emerging photographers should follow the co-operative model and team up with friends to create alliances to support each other, arguing that there is 'safety in numbers'. She says she sees a 'lot of students coming out of graduating all doing the same thing, all trying to network and to break into different industries'. This is difficult on your own, especially after leaving the support system of college or university. Finding colleagues to form small cooperatives or agencies is a 'really smart way of getting more visibility, co-funding projects together and networking'. Having a group of supportive peers to act as 'critical friends' to bounce ideas off in a safe environment is really useful in developing your projects.

Use Instagram as your playground

Ed Kashi *Rodeo, Colorado*, 2012

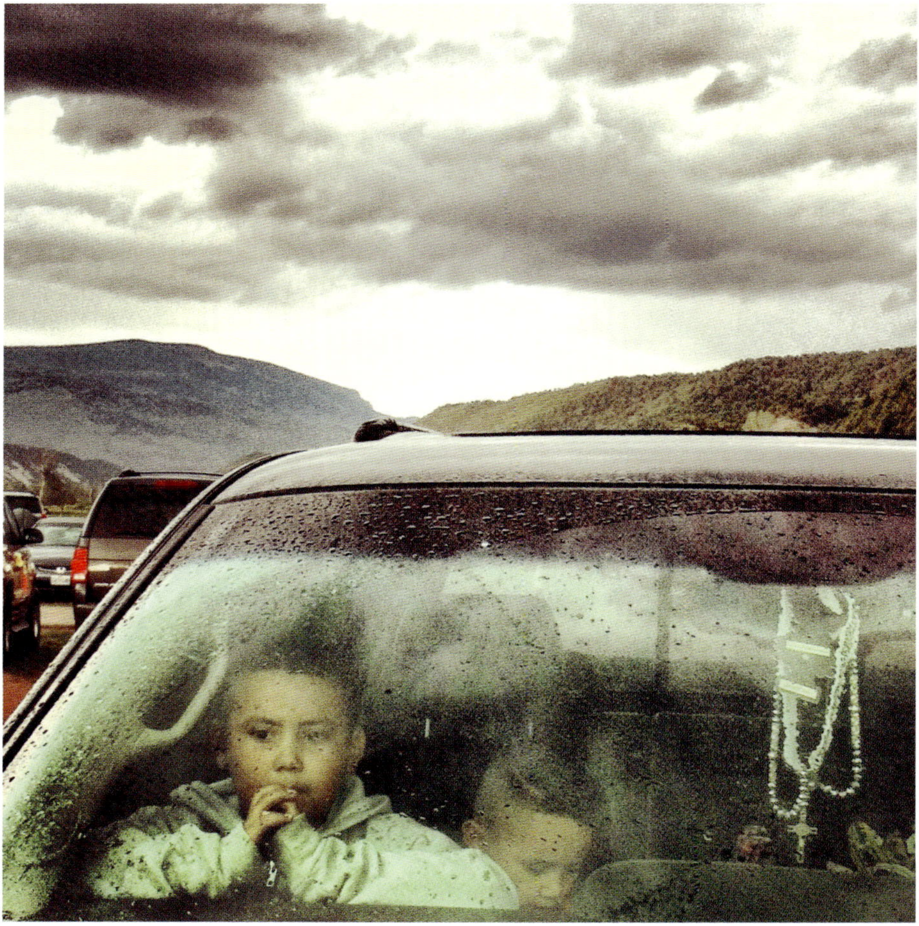

'Authorship and control of my work makes Instagram the only channel that exists today where I am a photo publisher and can reach a growing audience without any filters or gatekeepers. Simply put, it's a space that does not exist anywhere else in photography today.'

The VII photographer Ed Kashi uses Instagram as an alternative platform for publishing his photos and stories, bypassing traditional media to reach out to an audience directly. He sees it as a 'special space for visual artists and storytellers, a place where I can play with imagery like never before, experimenting with making double exposures, working with post-production/darkroom tools I would never use in my 35mm work, and capturing pure moments in my daily life'. But he also regards it as more than a place to be playful, recognizing that it can provide a powerful platform for advocacy too. Above all, it is the control over what he can publish there that is paramount, as he maintains that 'authorship and control of my work makes Instagram the only channel that exists today where I am a photo publisher and can reach a growing audience without any filters or gatekeepers. Simply put, it's a space that does not exist anywhere else in photography today.'

Editing is where the real narrative is made

Taha Ahmad

'Editing is the backbone of any solid body of work of narrative storytelling. The photographer has to choose from thousands of images shot over a couple of years to build a tight and powerful sequence. Though editing totally depends upon storytelling, there are a few things which may be looked upon while making an edit of a particular body of work: story, consistent images similar in narrative, removal of repetitive images or images depicting the same event, rhythm and feelings, similarity in tonal values, intuition, etc. An edit should also always be accompanied with accurate captions. A good edit does not happen overnight and takes time to develop. It requires a constant state of mind where the photographer reworks the story again and again, adding pieces to the narrative like a puzzle.'

Taha Ahmad is an Indian documentary photographer based in Delhi who works on themes related to the traumatic past and the culture threatened by religious conflicts, social injustice, politics, and the times we live in. He explains how the editing process is fundamental to any photographic project.

Keep your editor in the loop

Sarah Rumens Pupils at John Hampden School working on their own newspaper in the classroom, High Wycombe, Buckinghamshire, 24 May 1967 (photograph by Michael Stroud)

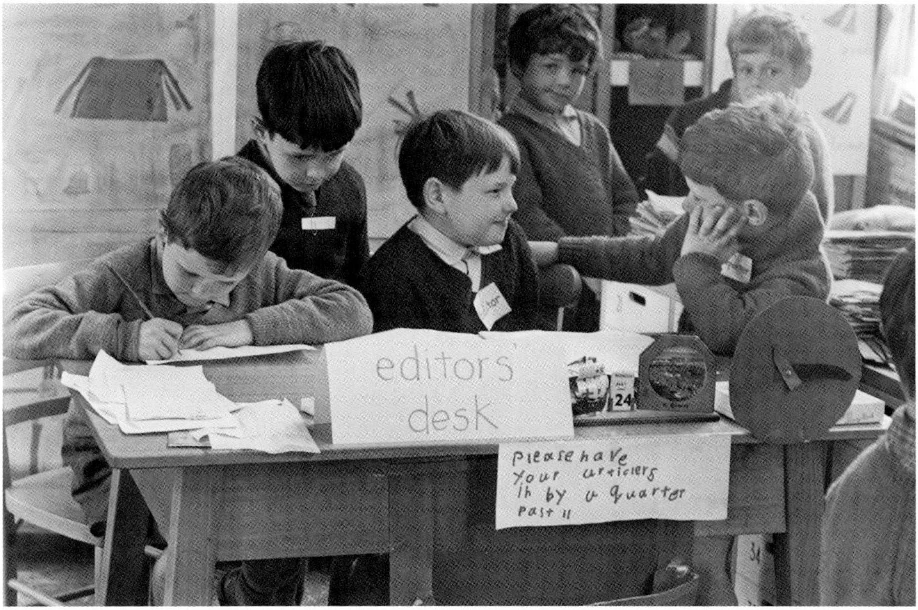

Sarah Rumens is a picture editor for *The Times*, and her strict advice is to stay in contact with the editor who has commissioned you. She cautions, 'I don't like surprises. If we have discussed the concept and set up for the assignment beforehand and you arrive on the day to find things are not as we'd understood, please call me. Every time.' Commissioned photography is often about problem solving, and stories don't always play out as planned. Keeping your editor in the loop if anything changes or goes wrong with the assignment ensures that you can resolve the situation collaboratively. Don't be afraid to reach out for help if things don't pan out as originally expected: editors will trust you more if you are honest and open with them.

The golden rules of self-publishing

Graeme Oxby *The Kings of England*, 2018

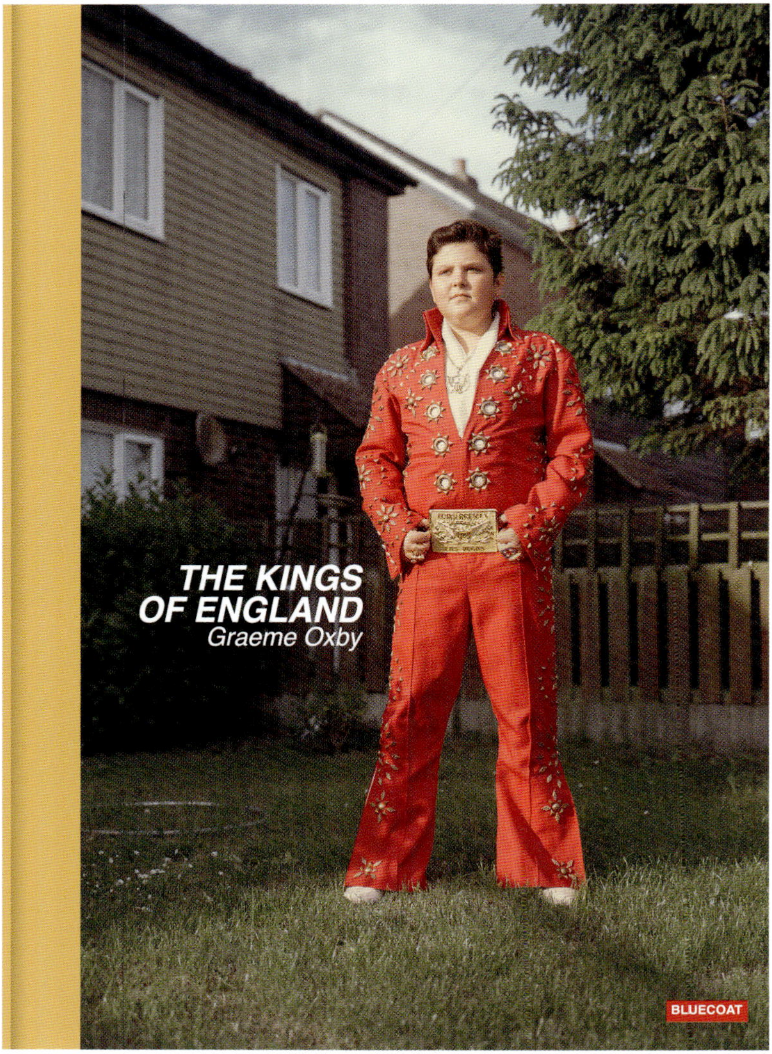

Graeme Oxby's five-year project on Elvis impersonators entitled *The Kings of England* was published by Bluecoat Press, and here he shares his insights into a successful self-publishing project.

1 Work with others wherever possible; ideally find a publisher who has extensive experience in crowdfunding photography books.

2 Be prepared. It takes a lot of work to prepare for crowdfunding and perhaps the most important piece of preparation is to build your networks, both online and in the real world.

3 Make a video which clearly communicates the personality of you and your project. Even if the presentation is simple, make sure the pictures and audio are good quality and keep it short, no more than two minutes.

4 Come up with a wide range of rewards which encourage people to invest in your project. As well as the actual book you can offer prints and other printed items. You can even offer experiences but a good selection of the key images from your project will often prove the most popular.

5 You might have arranged some publicity around the launch of your project but be careful that you don't overdo it so that when your book is printed, everyone has already heard about it.

6 Promote your book once it's printed – getting your book in print is an uphill battle but it's only the start. The really hard work comes once the book is off the press. Success breeds success.

7 Never give up. Believe in yourself and your project. Do whatever you can to make it happen. Work hard and work smart and it will pay off. Seeing your book for the first time is an emotional experience like no other but it wears off quickly. Then it's time to start the next one.

Give the editing process time and space

Anna Fox

'Ideally I would leave time between shooting and editing to create some kind of personal distance from the actual moment the photograph was shot.'

The British documentary photographer Anna Fox stresses how important it is to be totally involved in the editing of the body of work, allowing it all the time it needs, arguing that 'much of the meaning is created in the editing'. She recommends creating a space between making the work and reviewing it, stating that 'ideally I would leave time between shooting and editing to create some kind of personal distance from the actual moment the photograph was shot – I need to be able to understand it as an image rather than be able to relate it to something I was involved in'. Too often photographers choose images because of how hard it was to get them, or how difficult the access was, not how good the image actually is, and creating a certain distance from the work can help you judge and edit it more dispassionately.

Back up

Paul Lowe Computer hard disks, electronic scrap, collected, 2014 (photograph by Manfred Rutz)

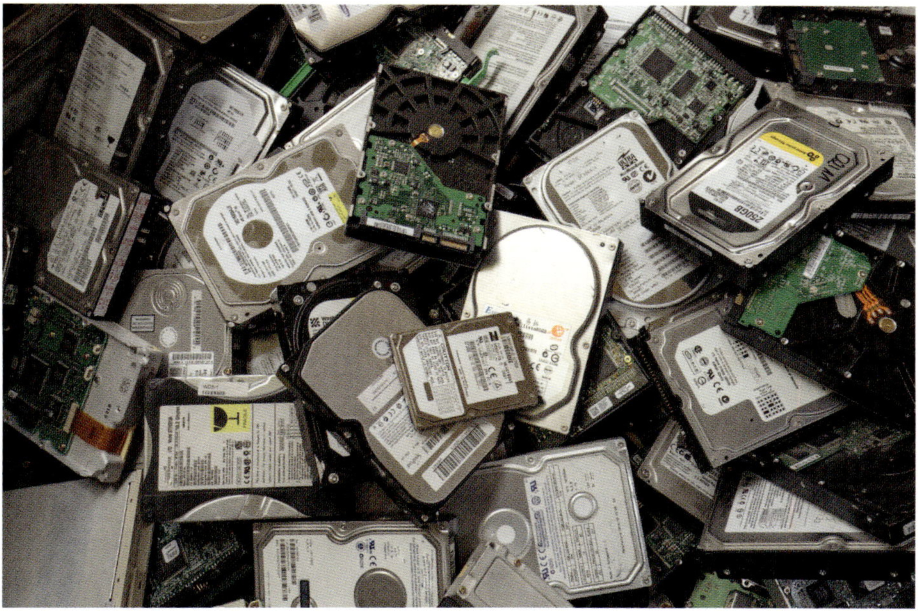

Storage of your data in an organized and secure way is essential if you want to ensure that your digital files are safe and accessible one, five, ten or even hundreds of years from now. Hard drives will fail, and hardware and software will become obsolete. Having a managed plan for backing up your data is essential. The 3-2-1 strategy is a good place to start:

3 Have three copies of your data
2 Keep them in two separate places
1 At least one must be offsite. You can use external hard drives, the cloud or DVDs, or ideally a combination of all of them.

Establish a workflow that becomes a habit to automatically store your valuable files in multiple locations, one you can access quickly and at least one that is located somewhere secure. And ensure that you periodically check that the data storage system you are using is still readable by your current computer.

Work without deadlines

Diána Markosian *Arrival to America*, from the series *Santa Barbara*, 2018

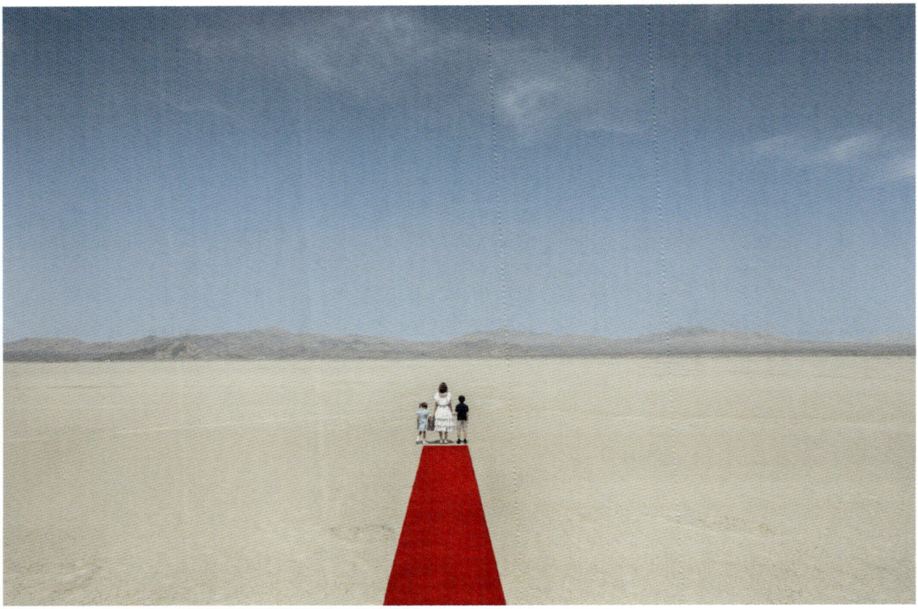

The Armenian-American artist Diána Markosian is fundamentally concerned with the relationship between memory and place, notably seen in *Inventing My Father*, an incredibly personal work about her connection with a man she hardly knew. She feels that spending time with a subject without the pressures of deadlines and assignments is central to creating work with meaning, explaining that 'there's so much pressure to create. To do the next thing. I am really not interested in that. I think art needs to come from within – and that's not something you can manufacture.' She feels that a deep commitment to a subject is absolutely vital, and cannot be forced, arguing strongly that 'if it's just one thing that you make in life, perhaps it is enough. You are not a conveyer belt.'

Be flexible when you are young and stubborn when you are old

Shoair Mavlian

'Be willing to compromise when you are young to get your work shown, and then when you get old you can be stubborn and stick to your principles.'

Shoair Mavlian is the director of Photoworks, an independent platform for contemporary photography whose programme includes commissions, exhibitions, publishing, learning and large-scale public events. She has curated many major exhibitions with established photographers, but also works with emerging talent at the start of their careers. Her advice for a sustainable long-term career is to 'be willing to compromise when you are young to get your work shown, and then when you get old you can be stubborn and stick to your principles'. Think about being as flexible as possible when you are starting out, as at that point you have to take any opportunities you can, and it's worth adapting your vison to an extent to fit with that of others. Later on, once you are well established and have a distinctive personal vision, you can be stricter about how you and your work are presented.

Chase every single opportunity

Briony Campbell

Briony Campbell is known for her sensitive work in photography and film documenting the intimate moments of people's lives. She has this advice on how to build your career:

Chase every single opportunity as long as it does at least one of the following:

1 Enhances your portfolio
2 Builds your skills
3 Lines your pockets
4 Contributes to a valuable cause
5 Is fun!

And none of the following:

1 Compromises your ethics
2 Exploits you financially (that doesn't mean don't do work for free)
3 Exploits you personally.

Know why you're making the work

Martin Parr *Bedminster, British Food*, 1995

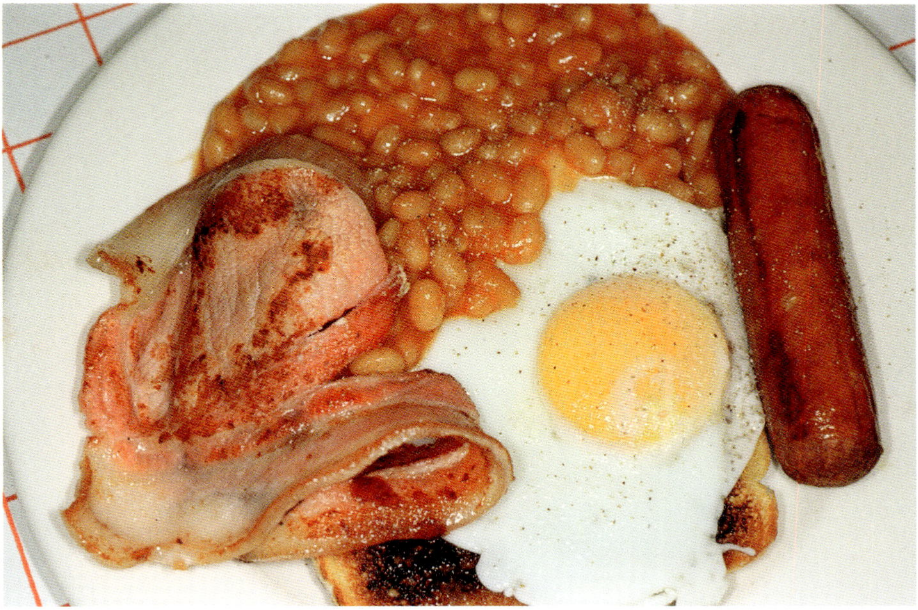

Martin Parr is one of the greatest supporters of emerging photographic talent, with his Foundation championing British documentary photography. From his experience of looking at the work of thousands of photographers, he argues that having a sharply focused coherent project is vital.

'Most of the work we look at is confused, because the photographers themselves don't know what it's about. And that's one of the things that can be taught to a certain extent, and encouraged, and facilitated with people, in order for them to be clear about what they are saying. The big mistake people make is trying to say too much. They want to change the whole world with one project. They don't realize that dealing with one small thing well, and very meaningfully, is much more effective than trying to cover too many aspects of the world at once. If you can't explain what you're doing in one sentence, it's hardly worth doing.'

Always try to be a decent human being

Stuart Freedman *Mentally Ill Man in a Secure Ward, Delhi*, 2010

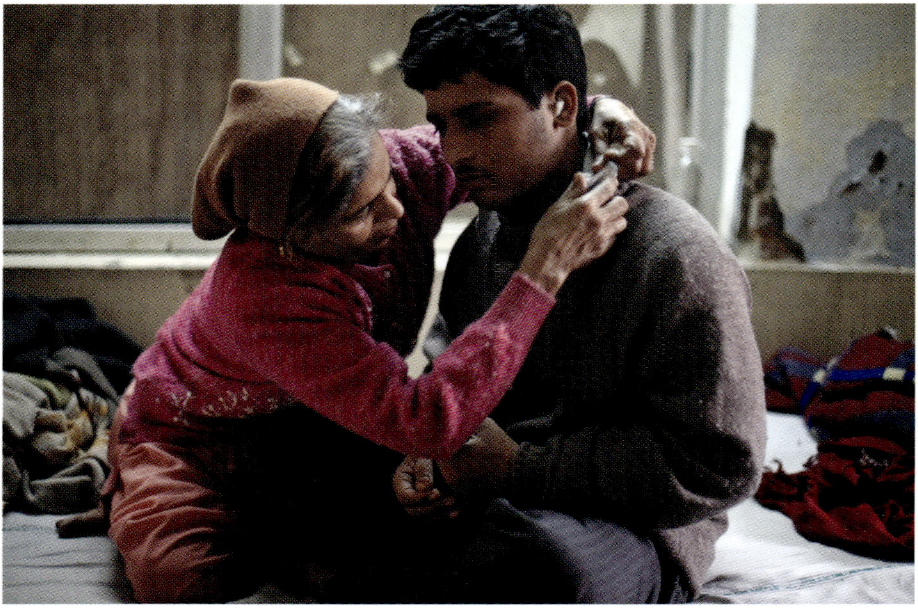

For British photojournalist Stuart Freedman, being respectful to the people you are working with is paramount. Sadly, he observes that 'so many photographers, especially those working in sensitive areas, assume that they have a God-given right to invade others' lives'. Indeed, he is confident that 'being respectful and courteous even in difficult situations often yields better results'. He is also mindful that others have to work in these areas in the future, so acting ethically and honestly is vital, as 'we often step into the footprints of others, so it makes life easier for everyone'. This is especially true of the people who work for the photographer in the field, the local fixers. Stuart is always aware that they 'live in the place that you're working in and will have to suffer the consequences of your actions long after you've left'. His advice is therefore to 'make sure that they're safe; make sure they eat and drink before you do; make sure that you pay them well and try and make them your friends'.

The 'rules' of participatory photography

Tiffany Fairey

Tiffany Fairey was one of the founders of Photovoice, the leading force in the development of methodologies for participatory photography projects empowering communities to tell their own stories. Although she stresses that there are no fixed ways of working in this way, there are certain guiding dos and don'ts for participatory photography practitioners.

1 **Don't assume** a) that people will want to participate; b) that the project will be relevant or have value to the community you are working with; c) that the pictures you think are interesting are the ones that participants will want to take or talk about; d) that participants will understand the implications of having their pictures out in the world.
2 **Do listen carefully** to what people say about their lives and their aspirations for what they want to say and do with their photography. Your role is not to impose your own thinking but to facilitate others.
3 **Do ensure** there is enough time and space for the process to evolve at its own pace. Be concerned not only with the quality of the pictures but with the quality of the process.
4 **Do be mindful** of ethics, of your own agenda and position, and of how power operates through the project.
5 **Do have fun.** Participatory photography projects are about building connections and dialogue with others. That won't happen if people do not enjoy themselves or feel comfortable and safe.
6 **Do build a network** around the project, to support participants to develop their photography and to get it seen, and to support yourself to navigate issues and tensions that arise.

Be honest

W. Eugene Smith *Dr Albert Schweitzer at his African Hospital*, 1954

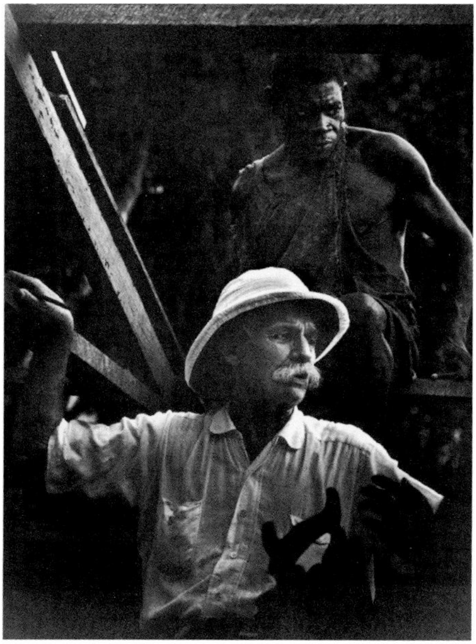

'[The] journalistic photographer can have no other than a personal approach; and it is impossible for him to be completely objective. Honest – yes. Objective – no.'

W. Eugene Smith was a passionate and committed photojournalist, who believed in authenticity and honesty to what he believed to be the core issues of the story he was telling, proclaiming that he wanted 'truth be the prejudice'. However, this did not mean that he wanted to remain neutral in the face of what he considered to be moral wrongs, instead arguing that the 'journalistic photographer can have no other than a personal approach; and it is impossible for him to be completely objective. Honest – yes. Objective – no.' He pointed out that 'up to and including the moment of exposure, the photographer is working in an undeniably subjective way. By his choice of technical approach, by the selection of the subject matter . . . and by his decision as to the exact cinematic instant of exposure, he is blending the variables of interpretation into an emotional whole.' It's important to acknowledge your own subjectivity, but also to remain honest and authentic to your ethical stance.

An advertising portfolio should be creative

John Wyatt-Clarke

'My heart sinks when a photographer brings in their portfolio and says they've made this folio specially out of the work that looks most commercial.'

John Wyatt-Clarke is one of the leading commercial agents, who expresses how he is often disappointed when photographers show him their work, saying 'my heart sinks when a photographer brings in their portfolio and says they've made this folio specially out of the work that looks most commercial'. He feels that they are mistaken about what advertising photography should look like, arguing that 'maybe twenty years ago it wasn't very varied, but it's hard to think of any visual style that's been out of bounds this century'. Wyatt-Clarke points out that people in the creative departments of ad agencies are highly visually literate, and that 'their raw material is your individuality. Don't insult them with second-best work that looks like an ad you saw once shot by someone else.' What they are looking for is your unique personal vision and aesthetic, and they are smart enough to see how they can translate that into the world of advertising.

Find your spot of beauty

Maria Teresa Salvati

'One golden rule, now more than ever, is to find your unique point of view and position your work clearly and directly, what I call finding your "spot of beauty". In parallel, you need to gain trust as author in terms of ethics, principles and values – either in the way you approach and relate with subjects or the way the story is contextualized and consumed. With the growing popularity of photography, being able to stand out from the crowd and communicate via the most appropriate channels (especially Instagram) is paramount to making a career in the various fields of contemporary photography.'

Maria Teresa Salvati is a personal branding consultant and educator and the editor-in-chief and founder of Slideluck Editorial. She has a monthly column for *C41* magazine called 'My Spot Of Beauty', where she presents established and emerging photographers seen through their personal and intimate motivation.

Don't touch the model

Paul Lowe Richard Avedon photographing model Jean Shrimpton, 1965 (Hulton Archive)

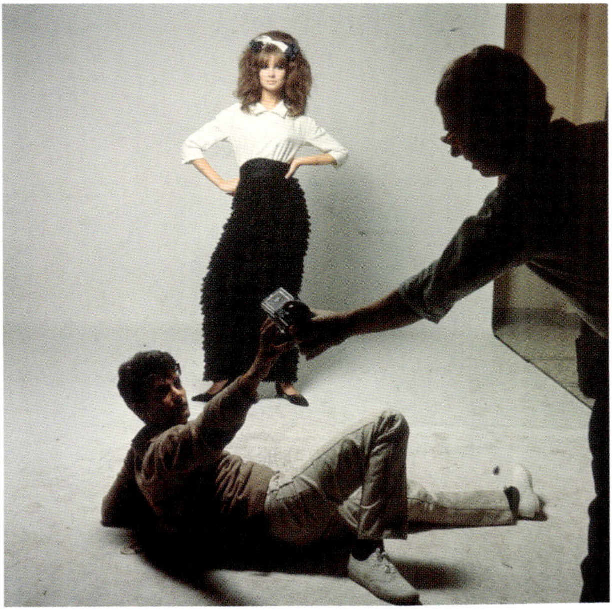

When you are shooting someone's portrait, or working with a model on a fashion or commercial shoot, as a general rule avoid any physical contact. If you want them to move in a certain way, or hold a pose, then give them clear verbal directions, point with your hand, or demonstrate the position yourself. Touching them directly is unacceptable unless you ask in advance, and even then, keep any contact to a minimum, perhaps moving a lock of hair or adjusting the position of a shoulder slightly. Even then, if you have a make-up artist, hairdresser or assistant on the shoot, ask them to do it for you.

Decide why – then what – then how

Dewi Lewis

'Do I really have something to say? Is there something fresh and unique about my project? If so is there a way of bringing the work together in a coherent sequence that adds a synergy to the individual images?'

Dewi Lewis is one of the most successful independent photography book publishers, who always asks the obvious question of potential authors 'Why do you want a book? Is it the best way to take things forward for you?' He advises photographers thinking of trying to publish to ask themselves hard questions like 'do I really have something to say? Is there something fresh and unique about my project? If so is there a way of bringing the work together in a coherent sequence that adds a synergy to the individual images?' A successful book project takes a huge amount of work and dedication, and you have to ask yourself if you have the skills to self-publish, including all the tasks involved in publishing – the edit, design, production, financing and marketing. Perhaps most importantly, the crucial issue is if you really want to give up your life for several months or more to just focus on the book. If at the end at the end of all that you are still 100 per cent convinced, his advice is 'then go for it'.

Don't seek external validation

Ed Kashi *People Bathe and Take Care of Their Ablutions, Hooghli River in Kolkata, India*, 2015

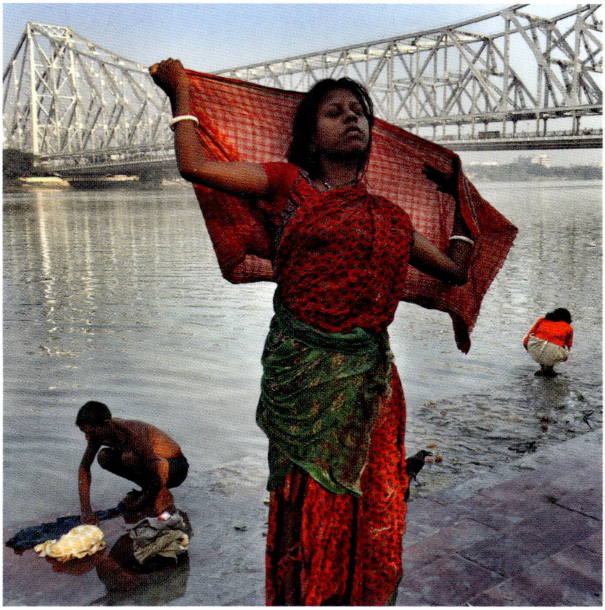

The veteran documentary photographer Ed Kashi has sustained a long career working on sustained projects, and he feels that self-belief is essential, arguing that the 'only way you can sustain the passion, drive and commitment necessary to accomplishing a long-term project is to truly care for and believe in your idea'. He also cautions against relying on other people's opinions to validate your work, and urges photographers, 'Don't let editors, art directors, curators, etc. stop you! Too often we hope for or wait for these external actors to affirm our ideas and work. That is a recipe for failure, disappointment and disaster.' Instead, he recommends that you 'must know why you do this work, what you want to do and pursue it with a single-mindedness that I often consider maniacal'. Kashi offers this encouragement: 'greatness starts with you and your unquenchable desire to create work'; if you have strong ideas, do your research, and work hard, then success will come.

Produce stories you would want to watch yourself

D.J. Clark

'Write down all the stories you remember watching over the last week and then try to work out how they were structured and what were the key elements you liked about them.'

The photographer and educator D.J. Clark has specialized in multimedia and video storytelling, and his rule is that if 'you would not watch it, don't expect your audience to'. He is critical of how often this rule is broken, arguing that 'you would be surprised how many young journalists working for media organizations produce content they would never watch'. His starting point for producing stories for online publications is to 'write down all the stories you remember watching over the last week and then try to work out how they were structured and what were the key elements you liked about them'. He recommends a careful analysis of what works and what doesn't, advising photographers to 'break down content on your favourite Instagram accounts, YouTube subscriptions and Facebook pages and try and figure out what makes you click on these stories'.

Be nice

Max Leonard

'There are so many people out there who are not nice and in this very small industry they really stick out.'

The picture editor Max Leonard has a simple maxim: be nice to people.

He recounts how many people there are in the industry who aren't nice and, in such a small world, news of their difficult nature travels fast. When choosing who to work with Leonard even stays clear of those who are 'much bigger and more important' than him to avoid working with people who have been rude to him in the past.

The industry is built on personal relationships, and editors often move around from publication to publication, asking each other for recommendations for photographers to commission. So if you are unpleasant to one editor the consequences may follow you around for a long time.

Research, research, then do more research

Natasha Caruana *Still Waiting I*, 2019

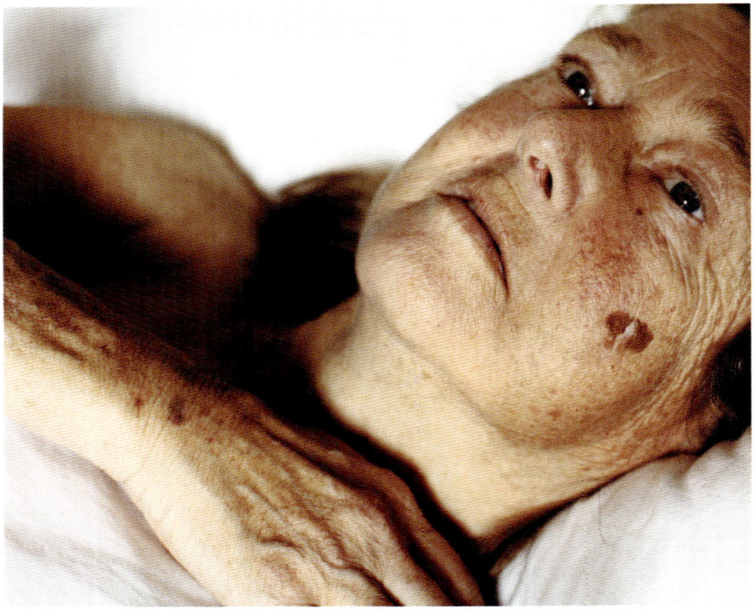

Natasha Caruana explores themes related to love, betrayal and fantasy, often drawing on archives, the Internet and personal accounts of loss and longing. Her work is underpinned by an iterative engagement with her sources, as she explains: 'I don't wake up in the morning and visualize the final images. The final work evolves over a period of time as I slowly work out where the idea is going and how to communicate it.' She sees research and practice as 'intrinsically linked, forming a continuous working process, sparking new ideas and innovative ways of working'. Research does not just happen at the start of a project, but informs the whole process, and can take on many forms, from interviews with your subjects to web-based research, collating data or looking at other artists' work for inspiration.

Work backwards from your goal

Simon Norfolk

'People pour their heart and soul into work and yet the biggest waste to my ears is when they say they're not sure what they expected the work to achieve.'

The documentary photographer Simon Norfolk works on long-term, meticulously researched projects that combine history, geography and memory to explore how the landscape can contain traces of its past. His golden rule is borrowed from the playwright Lucy Prebble, who says you should always think your project backwards. Start by asking 'what is the feeling I want to leave behind in the viewer as they walk out of the gallery having seen my work?' Then work out how you would go about creating that feeling. And then keep asking 'how does this contribute to the creation of that feeling?' all the way through the making of the work, until you get to the beginning. A fault he sees in a lot of work is that 'most of us fall into projects because we're commissioned to do it, or it carries on from the last thing I did or it was the least bad of all the ideas I had, etc.' By questioning the ultimate impact of the work, it should have a greater relevance to the intended audience. Norfolk cautions that without this foresight, the project risks failure, as 'people pour their heart and soul into work and yet the biggest waste to my ears is when they say they're not sure what they expected the work to achieve. The Prebble Test is the best fix for this.'

Understand the numbers

Paul McDonald

'Whenever you have an idea for a project, the numbers have to make sense. Do the boring part first: the Excel spreadsheet.'

Paul McDonald takes an entrepreneurial approach to his work, recognizing that 'as a creative you are being engaged to solve problems for your clients in a creative way', and that this is a valuable asset to sell. He argues that 'you develop and inform your creativity through research, study, personal practice, taking risks and your lived experiences. This all has a monetary value and needs to be factored into and considered in your pricing.' He feels that this is a resource that can be exploited to the full, and that 'there is a reason why your clients want to engage with you: they see the value in your creativity and ultimately it makes them money. So value it and own it.' But this creativity has to be tempered by the realities of the cost of doing business, and his advice is to be in control of the financial aspects of the job, because if the numbers don't work, you are running at a loss before you even start. He recommends that 'whenever you have an idea for a project, the numbers have to make sense. Do the boring part first: the Excel spreadsheet. Once the numbers balance, then move onto the fun part, the creativity. If you don't like, enjoy or understand crunching the numbers, learn how to do it or pay someone to do it for you.' If you ignore his rules of doing business, you risk financial failure, or as he puts it, 'you've heard of the line of the poor starving artist. It's your choice. Be this; or be a sustainable creative business. Your choice!'

Don't set things up

Antonio Zazueta Olmos

'In the digital age, when the veracity of photographs has never been more challenged, it is important that as photojournalists and documentarians we don't stage-manage situations just for the benefit of getting a better photograph. When a photographer loses the ability to be patient and to truly record the story in front of him, he transitions from a journalist and a documentarian into an illustrator. Photography is, from the start, a deeply subjective form of recording facts and relaying information. Our choice of lenses, exposure, vantage point and framing alone leads us to record things differently from what one sees with the human eye. To add an element of stage direction into the mix tips the photographer into the realm of fiction. Once you start setting things up for the benefit of a better photo, it won't be long before you start making bad ethical choices when working on your photographs in Photoshop as well.'

Antonio Zazueta Olmos is a photojournalist and editorial portrait photographer who has worked covering issues concerning human rights, the environment and conflict. He has worked extensively in the Americas, the Middle East and Africa for newspapers and magazines around the world, as well as leading NGOs.

Rules for working in traumatic situations

Poynter Institute for Media Studies Photographers take pictures of a starving child during the 1992 famine caused by the civil war in Somalia, 1992 (photograph by Paul Lowe)

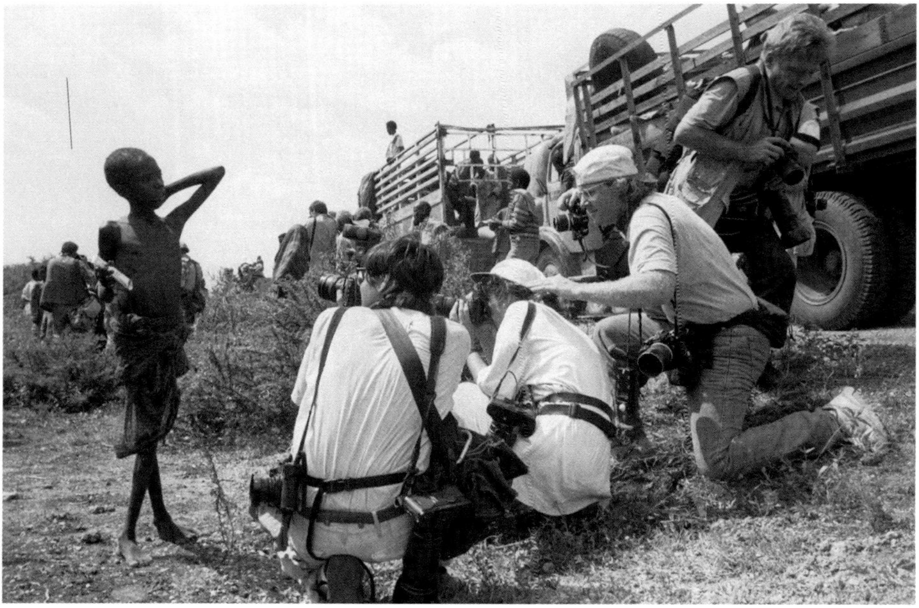

Al Tompkins of the Poynter Institute for Media Studies emphasizes the physical and mental risk of reporting from traumatic situations, noting that 'Reporters, photojournalists, engineers, soundmen and field producers often work elbow to elbow with emergency workers. Journalists' symptoms of traumatic stress are remarkably similar to those of police officers and fire-fighters who work in the immediate aftermath of tragedy, yet journalists typically receive little support after they file their stories. While public-safety workers are offered debriefings and counselling after a trauma, journalists are merely assigned another story.' Their guidance for field journalists includes the following advice.

1 Understand that your problems may become overwhelming. If this happens to you, seek counselling from a professional.

2 Understand that you may be the first to arrive at any scene. You may face dangerous situations and harsh reactions from law enforcement and the public. Stay calm and focused throughout. Be aware that a camera cannot prevent you from being injured. Do not hesitate to leave a scene if it becomes too dangerous. Any supervisor or editor should understand that a person's life is more important than a photo.

3 Treat every victim you approach at a tragedy with sensitivity, dignity and respect. Do not react harshly to anyone's response. Politely identify yourself before requesting information.

4 You will record many bloody images during a tragedy. Ask yourself whether these are important enough for historical purposes or too graphic for your readers or viewers.

5 Avoid violating someone's private grieving. That doesn't mean that you shouldn't record photos of emotion at public scenes. However, do not intrude upon someone's private property or disturb victims during their grieving process.

6 Always take care of your mind. Admit your emotions. Talk about what you witnessed to a trusted peer, friend or spouse. Write about it. Replace horrible images with positive ones. Establish a daily routine of healthful habits.

Manage your archive

Hamish Crooks Stamps of Magnum photographers, 1980 (photograph by Alex Webb)

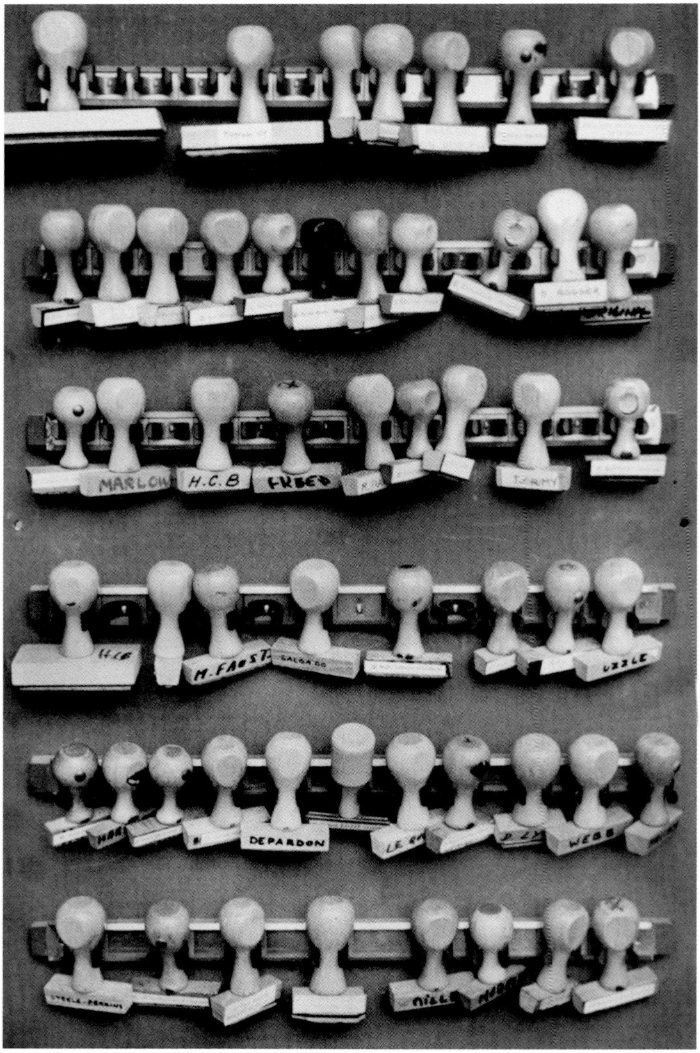

Hamish Crooks is the global licensing manager for Magnum Photos, directing its massive archives. He has this advice on how to manage your work long term.

1 **Keep your 'outs'**
Analogue photographers produced contact sheets that made re-editing and re-evaluating work easier. Digital photography instead has hard drives, cloud servers, back-ups and DVDs, but digital storage is getting cheaper – offline and online – so organize your outs after each shoot and back up.

2 **Think of your legacy from a young age and manage it**
Do not wait to do a first edit of your whole life/career when you've stopped shooting due to age. If you die before this is done, then someone else will edit it for you. And probably wrongly.

3 **Metadata management**
Find numbering, captioning, EXIF, keyword/coding and other metadata protocols that work for you and stick to them. The IPTC standards are a good start. With metadata templates, you can pre-populate most pictures before they're even shot.

4 **Rank your pictures**
Again, on contact sheets, chinagraph marks denoted the photographer/editor's ranking of their pictures. For digital photographers, add your own ranking to your images using your photo software and embed the ranking into your metadata.

Index

Index

Picture credits

The publishers would like to thank the museums, artists, archives and photographers for their kind permission to reproduce the works featured in this book. Every effort has been made to trace all copyright owners, but if any have been inadvertently overlooked, the publishers would be please to make the necessary arrangements at the first opportunity.

page 12 © Brassai Estate – RMN-Grand Palais; page 13 © Tom Hunter; page 14 © Bruce Gilden/Magnum Photos; page 15 © Marc Riboud / Fonds Marc Riboud au MNAAG/Magnum Photos; page 16 Bill Brandt/ Picture Post/Hulton Archive/Getty Images; page 18 © Estate of Harry Callahan; courtesy of Pace/ MacGill Gallery, New York; page 19 © Lee Friedlander, courtesy Fraenkel Gallery, San Francisco; page 20 Alfred Eisenstaedt/The LIFE Picture Collection via Getty Images; page 21 © Anton Corbijn; page 22 Ansel Adams/National Archives/The LIFE Picture Collection via Getty Images; page 23 © Robert Capa © International Center of Photography/Magnum Photos; page 24 Charles Sheeler/Conde Nast via Getty Images; page 25 © David LaChapelle; page 26 Tony Ray-Jones/SSPL/Getty Images; page 28 Walker Evans/The J. Paul Getty Museum; page 29 © David Hockney Collection J. Paul Getty Museum, Los Angeles; page 30 © Rineke Dijkstra, courtesy of Marian Goodman Gallery; page 33 Alexander Rodchenko/adoc-photos/Corbis via Getty Images; page 34 © Samir Al-Sharif; page 36 © Rinko Kawauchi; page 37 Bernice Abbott/New York Public Library/Public Domain; page 38 Ernst Haas/Getty Images; page 39 © Aletheia Casey; page 40 © Mary Ellen Mark; page 41 © William Albert Allard; page 43 © Lewis Baltz Trust; page 44 Yale Joel/Time & Life Pictures; page 46 © Gueorgui Pinkhassov/Magnum Photos; page 47 © Anders Petersen; page 48 Julia Margaret Cameron/SSPL/Getty Images; page 50 John Heartfield/Photo Scala, Florence/bpk, Bildagentur fuer Kunst, Kultur und Geschichte, Berlin; page 51 Berenice Abbott/Getty Images; page 52 © 2019. Digital image, The Museum of Modern Art, New York/ Scala, Florence; page 54 © Philip Jones Griffiths/ Magnum Photos; page 55 © Eric Bouvet/VII; page 56 © Constantine Manos/Magnum Photos; page 59 Joe McNally/Getty Images; page 60 © Centre Pompidou, MNAM-CCI, Dist. RMN-Grand Palais/Philippe Migeat; page 62 Sam Abell/National Geographic Creative; page 63 © Trustees of Princeton University; page 64 © The Irving Penn Foundation; page 66 © Graciela Iturbide; page 67 © Vanessa Winship; page 68 © Lara Jo Regan; page 70 © Henri Cartier-Bresson/Magnum Photos; page 71 © Simon Norfolk; page 72 William Albert Allard/National Geographic Creative; page 74 Chip Somodevilla/Getty Images; page 77 © William Klein; page 78 © The Estate of Edward Steichen/ DACS, 2019; page 80 Francis Frith/Artokoloro Quint Lox Limited/Alamy Stock Photo; page 81 Jack Mitchell/Getty Images; page 83 Jacques-Henri Lartigue/The Art Institute of Chicago/Art Resource, NY/Scala, Florence; page 84 Alfred Stieglitz/age fotostock/Alamy Stock Photo; page 86 © Alex Webb/ Magnum Photos; page 87 Walter Sanders/The LIFE Picture Collection via Getty Images; page 88 © Henri Cartier-Bresson/Magnum Photos; page 90 © Ed Kashi; page 91 © Paul Lowe; page 94 © Elliott Erwitt/Magnum Photos; page 95 © Martine Franck/ Magnum Photos; page 96 © Aletheia Casey; page 98 © Danny Lyon/Magnum Photos; page 99 © Louie Palu; page 100 © Philip-Lorca diCorcia; page 101 © Sara Terry/VII; page 102 © Roger Ballen; page 104 © Sebastião Salgado, courtesy of NB Pictures; page 105 Michael Williamson/The Washington Post via Getty Images; page 107 © Lauren Greenfield/ INSTITUTE; page 108 © Giles Duley; page 110 Joe McNally/The LIFE Picture Collection via Getty Images; page 111 © Maggie Steber/VII; page 112 © Chris Steele-Perkins/Magnum Photos; page 114 © Lara Jo Regan page 116 © Gemma Marmalade; page 118

© Susan Meiselas/Magnum Photos; page 119 © Paul Caponigro; page 120 © Mark Power/Magnum Photos; page 121 © Chloe Dewe Mathews; page 122 © Léonie Hampton; page 123 © Eve Arnold/Magnum Photos; page 124 © Tina Barney; page 126 Roz Kelly/ Michael Ochs Archives/Getty Images; page 127 © Jocelyn Bain Hogg/VII; page 128 © Tod Papageorge; page 129 © Edmond Terakopian; page 130 © Swart Ghosh; page 132 © Daniel Meadows; page 133 © Dorothy Bohm; page 134 © Tomas Van Houtryve/VII; page 136 © Alec Soth/Magnum Photos; page 138 © Bruce Davidson/Magnum Photos; page 140 © Donald Weber; page 142 Christopher Simon Sykes/ Hulton Archive/Getty Images; page 143 © Collection Martin Parr/Magnum Photos; page 144 © Trustees of Princeton University; page 145 © Laura Pannack; page 146 © Nolan Ryan Trowe; page 148 © Maggie Steber/VII; page 150 The Museum of Modern Art, New York/Scala, Florence; page 151 © Larry Fink; page 152 © Alec Soth/Magnum Photos; page 153 Pictorial Press Ltd/Alamy Stock Photo; page 155 Nik Wheeler/ Corbis via Getty Images; page 156 Alfred Eisenstaedt/ The LIFE Picture Collection via Getty Images; pages 158–9 © Elliott Erwitt/Magnum Photos; page 160 Yousuf Karsh, Camera Press, London; page 161 © Robin Maddock; page 162 © Lisa Bernard; page 164 © Bruce Davidson/Magnum Photos; page 166 © Line Ørnes Søndergaard/VII; page 170 © Taha Ahmad/VII; page 174 © Damir Šagolj; page 178 Bert Hardy/Picture Post/Getty Images; page 181 © Ilvy Njiokiktjien/VII; page 183 © Shahidul Alam; page 184 © Tom Broadbent; page 186 David Kleyn/Alamy Stock Photo; page 190 © Neil Turner; page 192 © Juno Calypso; 194 Henning Kaiser/DDP/AFP via Getty Images; page 197 © Eric Bouvet/VII; page 198 © Maggie Steber/VII; page 200 Dirck Halstead/Getty Images; page 201 © Brian Griffin; page 202 © David Hurn/Magnum Photos; page 203 © Elliott Erwitt/ Magnum Photos page 204 © Ed Kashi/VII; page 207 Michael Stroud/Express/Hulton Archive/Getty Images; page 208 © Graeme Oxby; page 211 Manfred Rutz/Getty Images; page 212 © Diána Markosian; page 215 © Martin Parr/Magnum Photos; page 216 In Pictures Ltd/Corbis via Getty Images; page 218 W. Eugene Smith/The LIFE Picture Collection via Getty Images; page 221 Hulton Archive/Getty Images; page 223 © Ed Kashi/VII; page 226 © Natasha Caruana; page 230 © Paul Lowe/Panos Pictures; page 232 © Alex Webb/Magnum Photos

Brimming with creative inspiration, how-to projects and useful information to enrich your everyday life, Quarto Knows is a favourite destination for those pursuing their interests and passions. Visit our site and dig deeper with our books into your area of interest: Quarto Creates, Quarto Cooks, Quarto Homes, Quarto Lives, Quarto Drives, Quarto Explores, Quarto Gifts, or Quarto Kids.

First published in 2020 by
Frances Lincoln Publishing,
an imprint of The Quarto Group.
The Old Brewery, 6 Blundell Street
London, N7 9BH,
United Kingdom
T (0)20 7700 6700
www.QuartoKnows.com

A catalogue record for this book is available from the British Library.

ISBN 978-0-7112-4258-6

10 9 8 7 6 5 4 3 2 1

Designed by Glenn Howard
Printed in China

MIX
Paper from responsible sources
FSC® C016973
FSC www.fsc.org